7-06

Picture Writing

Anastasia Suen

WRITER'S DIGEST BOOKS
CINCINNATI, OHIO
www.writersdigest.com

Visit our Web site at www.writersdigest.com for information on more resources for writers.

To receive a free weekly e-mail newsletter delivering tips and updates about writing and about Writer's Digest products, register directly at our Web site at http://newsletters.fwpublications.com.

08   07   06   05   04   6   5   4   3   2

Library of Congress Cataloging-in-Publication Data

Suen, Anastasia
   Picture writing: a new approach to writing for kids and teens / Anastasia Suen.
      p.   cm.
   Includes index.
   ISBN 1-58297-072-6 (alk. paper)
      1. Children's literature—Authorship. 2. Young adult literature—Authorship. I. Title.

PN147.5 .S84   2003
808.06′8—dc21   2002028249
                                                                              CIP

Edited by Kelly Nickell, Michelle Howry, Kim Agricola, Jack Heffron, and Donya Dickerson
Designed by Sandy Kent
Cover by Joanna Detz
Production coordinated by Michelle Ruberg

In Memory of Kimberly Colen Koenigsberg, 1957-2001

Cecil Stringfellow

Although she wrote her first book at age eleven, it was not until the day after her fortieth birthday that Anastasia Suen sold her first book. Today, she is the author of more than fifty books for children: board books, picture books, easy readers, and photo-essays for middle graders. She writes poetry, fiction and non-fiction for trade publishers (bookstore books), as well as school and library publishers.

Anastasia Suen's first book, *Man on the Moon*, was an American Booksellers Pick of the List, on the Florida and Arizona reading lists, and an American Library Association's Space Day choice. *Window Music* was a New York Times Best Illustrated Book, a Time Magazine Best Book of the Year, a Book-of-the-Month Club selection, and a Chicago Public Library's Best of the Best. *Baby Born* was a Smithsonian Notable Book, a Reach Out and Read selection, and a Children's Book Council Children's Books Mean Business selection. *Toddler Two* was American Booksellers Pick of the List. *Air Show* was selected as a Bank Street College of Education's Best Children's Book of the Year.

As a literature consultant for Sadlier-Oxford, Suen selected poetry for reading and mathematics textbooks. She served on the Reading Advisory Board for Rosen Publishing Group, and directed Seminars in Children's Literature. A former assistant regional advisor for the Society of Children's Book Writers and Illustrators, she has worked at writing and illustrating conferences for more than a decade.

Suen taught writing at Southern Methodist University and co-taught children's literature at the University of North Texas. She speaks at writing conferences for students, teachers, librarians, and writers across the United States and teaches in cyberspace at www.asuen.com.

✤ | Acknowledgments

This book would not have been possible without the help of my family, Cliff, Nathan and Aimee, and the many people who have helped me with this project and the previous fifty plus: Sue Alexander, Elaine Marie Alphin, Jennifer Anglin, Kim Agricola, Laura Atkins, Audrey Baird, Catherine Balkin, Leslie Baranowski, Susan Barry, Bonny Becker, Lori Benton, Lara Rice Bergen, Lisa Bernstein, David Black, Hilary Breed, Audrey Bryant, Betty Carter, Melanie Cecka, Ana Cerro, Jeri Cipriano, Judy Chaiken, Connie Charron, Cheryl Chapman, Cherie Clodfelter, Bebra Cronholm, Andrea Cruise, Andrea Curley, Debbie Dadey, Anne Davies, Donya Dickerson, Christina Douglas, Lucy Del Priore, Louise Dribben, Kathleen Duey, Deb Eaton, Kristin Eck, Judith Ross Enderle, Tara Filaski, Jennifer Frantz, Adrienne Frye, Kristin Gilson, Eric Gislason, Nancy Gjording, Ellen Greene, Stephanie Gordon, Babs Bell Hajdusiewicz, Jenny Harris, Kate Harrison, Susan Hawk, Regina Hayes, Jack Heffron, Linnea Hendrickson, Sarah Henry, Nina Hess, Kathryn Hewitt, Susan Hodges, John Hoody, Lee Bennett Hopkins, Anne Hoppe, Lenny Hort, Erin Hovanec, Michelle Howry, Adrienne Johnston, Cindy Kane, Mimi Kayden, Patricia Kelly, Helen Ketteman, Jeanne Konlande, Elizabeth Law, Philip Lee, Craig Low, Jason Low, Myra Cohn Livingston, Sally Luoma, John Man, Louise May, Kelly Moomaw, Stephen Mooser, Kathleen Morandini, Kathy Mormile, Deborah Morris, William C. Morris, Paula Morrow, Tim Moses, Jack Nestor, Kelly Nickell, Kerri O'Donnell, Lin Oliver, Christy Ottaviano, Larissa Pfiefer, Lara Phan, Alice Pope, Susan Poskanzer, Karen Ray, Robert A. Richards, Robin Roy, Melissa Russell, Chris Schechner, Gina Shaw, Jennifer Silate, Reka Simonsen, Barbara Stein, Liz Szabla, Katherine Brown Tegen, Garen Thomas, Laura Tillotson, Beth Troop, Liz Van Doren, Scott Waldman, Robert Warren, Edie Weinberg, Andrea Wilk, Judy Wilson, Jane Yolen, and Mary Ann Zapalac. I also want thank SCBWI, the online children's lit community at CCBC, ChildLit, CW, NFforKids, the Pod, and the Pub; and my students at UNT, SMU, and in the IPB workshops. Thanks for the questions, the answers, and the inspiration!
—*Anastasia Suen*

Table of Contents

PART V

Putting It All Together

PART VI

Look Again

The Appendixes

Picture Writing is three classes in one book. It's a children's *fiction* writing class. It's a children's *nonfiction* writing class. It's a children's *poetry* writing class.

At the same time, *Picture Writing* is a book about creating pictures in your words—about writing with both sides of your brain, with logic and intuition.

How your brain prefers to work will determine how you use this book.

If you prefer to study one element at a time, read the book from start to finish. Inside the covers you have a semester's worth of reading and activities.

- Week 1—Picture Writing
- Weeks 2, 3, 4, 5, 6, 7—Seeing Fiction, Nonfiction, and Poetry
- Weeks 8, 9, 10—Fiction, Nonfiction, and Poetry Characters
- Weeks 11, 12, 13—Fiction, Nonfiction, and Poetry Settings
- Weeks 14, 15, 16—Your Fiction, Nonfiction, and Poetry Manuscript(s)
- Week 17—Other Viewpoints: How the Publishing World Sees Your Work
- Week 18—The Appendixes: Writing Habits Poll, Craft and Creativity, Children's Book Awards, Best Book Lists, Book Contract Contests, Market Resources, Children's Book Review Magazines, Preparing to Mail Your Manuscript

You may prefer to study one genre at a time. If that is the case, then read the chapters in this order:

- Week 1—Picture Writing
- Weeks 2, 3—Seeing Fiction
- Week 4—Fiction Characters
- Week 5—Fiction Settings
- Week 6—Your Fiction Manuscript
- Weeks 7, 8—Seeing Nonfiction
- Week 9—Nonfiction Characters
- Week 10—Nonfiction Settings
- Week 11—Your Nonfiction Manuscript
- Weeks 12, 13—Seeing Poetry
- Week 14—Poetry Characters
- Week 15—Poetry Settings

- Week 16—Your Poetry Manuscript
- Week 17—Other Viewpoints: How the Publishing World Sees Your Work
- Week 18—The Appendixes: Writing Habits Poll, Craft and Creativity, Children's Book Awards, Best Book Lists, Book Contract Contests, Market Resources, Children's Book Review Magazines, Preparing to Mail Your Manuscript

After you decide how you will read this book, by element or genre, take out a calendar and plan your "semester." Allow two weeks for each of the Seeing chapters. Reading five board books, picture books, or easy readers in a single day is manageable. Doing the same with middle grade and young adult books will obviously take more time.

When you finish a new manuscript, come back to *Picture Writing* for a refresher course. Reread the chapters that apply to the genre you are writing. While you allow your new manuscript to "cool down," reread the plot, character, and setting chapters in your genre. Check out the competition as you read other books like yours for the exercises in the chapters. When you reach the manuscript chapter, take your manuscript out of the deep freeze and ask the tough questions you need to answer to help you write pictures in your words. Be a picture writer!

PART I

Picture Writing

Chapter One

What Is Picture Writing?

 The first rule of intuition is that you cannot force it.
—JORDAN AYAN, *Aha!: 10 Ways to Free Your Creative Spirit
and Find Your Great Ideas*

What is Picture Writing? Picture Writing is whole-brain writing, where one side of your brain sees pictures and the other side gives the pictures

A MATTER OF WIRING

How do you learn new things? With your eyes, with your ears, or with your body? *Visual learners* need to see something in order to remember it. *Auditory learners* remember what they hear. *Kinesthetic learners* figure things out by taking a hands-on approach. It's all a matter of wiring. You have all three of these learning modes, but one is usually dominant.

Intuition works to answer questions that stump your logical brain. When the answer to your question comes, your logical brain uses one of these three modes to communicate with you. How your brain is wired will influence how you experience your intuition.

This book is about visual writing, so I emphasize the visual mode throughout every discussion on ways to write books for children and young adults. That doesn't mean that intuition only works in this mode. Depending on the specific questions stumping your brain and your learning style, you may experience intuition in many different ways. You may "hear" the words you need or "feel" the answer. At times, you may experience all three modes! Trust yourself, and the answer you need will come.

words. The intuitive side of your brain thinks in pictures. The logical side of your brain thinks in words. It's all there inside of you—intuition and logic, pictures and words. You see the picture with your mind's eye, and then you give it words. With your words, you *write* the picture. That's Picture Writing.

Picture Writing begins inside of a writer's head. You don't have to know how to draw or paint to write pictures. In order to write pictures, you need to be able to *see* pictures.

How can you see pictures? By relying on your intuition. Intuition is a gift you already possess. Your intuition gives you pictures. Intuition plays with pictures, and your logical side works by organizing and writing the words. Why write with half of your brain? Use both sides, and write the pictures you see instead.

Picture Writing is the creative process in a nutshell. A picture leads to words, and those words bring a picture to mind. Pictures and words—the two are inseparable for the picture writer. You translate the pictures you see in your mind into words on the page. You work with the words over and over until they show the reader a picture. When the reader sees pictures in your words, the creative process is complete.

The Mystery of Creativity

All inspired individuals are, in some way, prepared for the experience.
—ROBERT GRUDIN, *The Grace of Great Things: Creativity and Innovation*

The creative process is a mystery, and there are many writers who prefer to leave it that way. They don't want to know how the process works for fear they'll jinx themselves. They're afraid that if they see how creativity happens, it won't work for them anymore. Other writers feel just as strongly that knowing how the creative process works helps them master their craft. The more they know about how the process works, the better.

These opposing views are reflected in the definition of the word "mystery." Did you know that mystery has two different definitions? The first one is the most common. Mystery comes from the Greek word "mysterion," meaning secret rite. A mystery is something that is not understood, something that is kept a secret. When you are struggling with words and nothing is working, it does feel like a secret rite! If only you had the magic word, why, then you could write!

The second definition of mystery comes from a confusion in Latin.

"Mysterium," the Latin word for mystery, was confused with "ministerium," the Latin word for office or occupation. Years later, the Middle English word "mysterie" meant craft or trade. Learning a craft meant learning trade secrets. You began work in your trade as an apprentice. You worked with other craftsmen who knew more than you did. Under their tutelage, you learned your craft. You didn't expect yourself to "know it all" right away. Learning your craft was a process that took years. Picture Writing works the same way.

PICTURE IT! | *It's a Mystery*

Where do you stand in this debate? Do you see writing as a secret rite or as a craft? Is it a mystery or something you can learn? Could it be both? Grudin says, "If inspiration is indeed an abandonment and a transcendence, it is nonetheless impossible without groaning effort, without the painful winning of skill."

As you struggle to understand the mystery, you can certainly work on the skills. To help learn these skills, start a writer's journal that you use only when reading this book. Keeping a writer's journal allows you to focus on your writing. Throughout the book, especially in the Picture It! sections, you will be asked to stop and write in your writer's journal in order to explore your thoughts on paper. As you make entries, you can explore the mystery of your own creativity. Trusting your insights is a vital part of the creative experience.

Your writer's journal honors your writing process. By its very existence, the journal says that your thoughts and ideas about writing are valuable. What you think matters.

Take some time now to think on paper about the mystery of creativity and your own creative process. Write in your journal about creativity and what you want to learn about Picture Writing. Then, explore the idea of writing as a secret rite or craft. Do you feel strongly that it is one or the other? Or does writing go both ways for you? ◆

Writing With Both Sides of Your Brain

The truth is, most of us are not using our brains to capacity, not because the capability is not there or because we are dumb but because we have not been taught how.

—HENRIETTE ANNE KLAUSER, *Writing on Both Sides of the Brain*

Connecting the mysteries of creativity and the brain is the best way to understand Picture Writing. To write pictures, you need to write with both sides of your brain. A small part of the brain's mystery was revealed when psychobiologist Dr. Roger W. Sperry discovered that each side of the brain worked in a different way. He won the Nobel Prize in medicine in 1981 for his discovery of left brain/right brain functions.

Sperry found that each side of the brain has its own specialty, its own strength. The left side of the brain is the logical side and likes to move quickly. It prefers order and works step-by-step. The left brain is the rational brain working to find answers to everything. This logical side of your brain works with words.

The right brain is the opposite of the left brain in almost every way imaginable. Although the logical left brain prefers words, the right brain doesn't use words. It thinks in symbols, in pictures. The right brain doesn't work step-by-step. It sees everything at once. Where the left brain is careful and deliberate, the right brain is spontaneous. The left brain plans ahead, but the right brain is receptive. It acts on what is happening now.

One part of the brain is not better than the other. The left half of your brain and the right half of your brain are simply that—halves of your brain. Sometimes you need your left brain to rush forward to find the answer. Sometimes you need your right brain to ask: Is this the right question? What else is happening that I cannot see? Do I need to read between the lines? Put the two sides together, and you have the tools you need to write pictures.

The Hare and the Tortoise

> Some mysteries can only be penetrated with a relaxed, unquesting mental attitude.
>
> —GUY CLAXTON, *Hare Brain, Tortoise Mind*

Are you a hare or a tortoise? In his book, Dr. Guy Claxton explains the dichotomy between the left and the right brain with the picture from this well-known Aesop's fable. The Hare Brain is the left brain, the logical brain, the brain that is always in a hurry. The Tortoise Mind is the right brain, the intuitive brain, the one that takes its time. "The mind," says Claxton, "works at different speeds."

Claxton argues that although our society values the speedy left brain more highly, the slower right brain also has its place. Running around chasing answers isn't always the way to figure things out.

The left brain can't solve every problem you encounter. It doesn't seek wisdom because it doesn't like ambiguity. It abhors paradoxes. The left brain doesn't want to see the big picture or read between the lines. It wants a clear answer right now, but life doesn't always work that way. Sometimes you need to wait for the answer to come.

TWO MINDS ARE BETTER THAN ONE

The Hare Brain (Your Left Brain)	**The Tortoise Mind** (Your Right Brain)
sense of urgency	not in a hurry
seeks answers	examines questions
takes things at face value	looks beyond what can be seen
values explanation	values observation
works step-by-step	sees the whole at once
prefers clarity	comfortable with ambiguity
generalizes	individualizes
controlled and deliberate	spontaneous
mechanical	organic
proactive	receptive
reasons	intuits
works	plays
literal and explicit	metaphor and imagery
words	***pictures***

You need both sides of your brain to write pictures. The left brain is literal; the right brain uses imagery. The tortoise sees the pictures. The hare writes them down. When you write pictures, you are a tortoise *and* a hare.

PICTURE IT! | *Fast and Slow*

How do you feel about being a tortoise *and* a hare? Do you prefer one or the other? Do you think it will take too long to write your book if you have to wait for the tortoise, or do you wish the hare would stop rushing you?

Capture your thoughts about your Hare Brain and Tortoise Mind in your writer's journal. Remember, hare, there are no "right" answers. The tortoise wants to know your *individual* answer.

If the hare wants to rush you, set the timer for five minutes, so you won't watch the clock. Write and explore . . . and if the words keep coming after the timer dings, keep writing! ✦

The Creative Process in Five Steps

> Doing nothing is indeed doing something very important.
> —DAVID KUNDTZ, *Stopping: How to Be Still When You Have to Keep Going*

Creativity experts agree on four steps of the creative process: preparation, incubation, illumination, and translation into action. It's the fifth step, however, that many of them have missed . . . frustration. "Frustration arises at the point when the rational, analytical mind, searching laboriously for a solution, reaches the limit of its abilities," say Daniel Goleman, Paul Kaufman, and Michael Ray in *The Creative Spirit.*

As cranky as this step makes you, it is essential to the creative process. Why? Because when you reach frustration, the project comes to a standstill. When logic doesn't work anymore, you have to rely on your intuition.

Only when logic stops explaining, can intuition see. Only when your left brain stops talking, can your right brain show you pictures. You can't write pictures until you see them!

Frustration comes very early in the creative process. In fact, as you can see from this chart, frustration is the second step.

THE FIVE STEPS IN THE CREATIVE PROCESS
Step 1   Preparation—You get a new idea and gather information about it.
Step 2   Frustration—Your project gets stuck.
Step 3   Incubation—Your subconscious works on the project.
Step 4   Illumination—The A-Ha! moment of insight.
Step 5   Translation Into Action—You take your insight and put it to work.

The creative process begins with logic. You collect data, prepare, outline, and organize. You speed until you hit the wall. If the creative process worked without frustration, your left brain would do everything by itself. You wouldn't have to stop and wait for the right brain. That hare would just keep running. But that's not what happened in Aesop's fable. The hare ran so fast, he had to stop and take a rest. Only then did you see the tortoise. Only when your left brain stops working on a project does your right brain have a chance to see pictures.

If you look at the big picture, like the tortoise does, you will see that intuition is the center of the creative process. It is the heart. Frustration is your clue that your project has entered a new phase. Stop hitting your head against the wall. Embrace the change.

"Creativity and change are two sides of the same coin," says James L. Adams in *The Care and Feeding of Ideas: A Guide to Encouraging Creativity.* "Creativity and change both imply new directions." When you hit the wall with a writing project, when frustration mounts, this is your clue to change. Stop working. Let go. The hare has done all he can. Let him fall asleep. Allow the tortoise to mull things over.

You can't force yourself to see pictures. If you want to see the tortoise and his pictures, you have to wait for him. Waiting is part of the creative process. Stillness is the center of a creative life.

PICTURE IT! | *Stillness*

Do you have any quiet in your life? Do you make time for your tortoise mind? Or is your hare running around, talking nonstop? If you want to use both sides of your brain, you have to make time for both of them. In your writer's journal, explore ways to find more time for quiet in your life. Silence, a hot bath, meditation, yoga, a long walk in the woods . . . think about ways to make time for your tortoise mind. Who knows what pictures it will show you? ✦

The Creative Seasons

> We think that making an effort is the opposite of being at ease. The paradoxical truth is that effort and ease are not in opposition—they complement each other.
> —CHIN-NING CHU, *Do Less, Achieve More*

The four seasons of the year give us a living picture of the creative process. For many gardeners, fall is planting season, so begin there. Whether you are planting seeds or bulbs, bushes or trees, you must prepare your soil first. This is the first stage of creativity: *preparation*. Get things organized. Plan ahead. Use your left brain.

Writers read and research in the preparation stage. They outline and begin first drafts. They write and write, until . . .

. . . the frost comes. That's *frustration*, the second step in the creative process. The gardener has to stop planting and move indoors. Things are quiet in the garden. It looks as if nothing is happening. Your writing ideas get cold when the frost comes. You freeze up. Nothing seems to work. The words just won't come.

For years, whenever I hit the frustration stage, it seemed to be proof positive that I had a bad idea. In nature, frost doesn't mean the gardener made a mistake. Frost means the gardener has to stop working outside. It's a natural stage, not a judgment. It took me a long time to recognize that frustration didn't mean I was doing something wrong. It simply meant that my project had gone to the next stage. I could let go without being "wrong." In fact, letting go of the left brain at this point was exactly the "right" thing to do. Once it froze up, my project was telling me that it needed to enter the right brain.

Winter comes after the fall. That's step three of the creative process: *incubation*. During the winter, plants rest. Seeds that have been planted sleep underground. For a writer, after the frost comes, book ideas appear to sleep. Nothing visible is happening. In reality, your subconscious mind is on the job even though it looks like it's asleep. During incubation, your project has entered the right brain stage.

Intuition works like a dream. In dreams, unrelated ideas and images come together to make something new. In a dream, someone you knew in grade school can talk to someone at an office party, even though in real life they have never met. Different parts of the country can appear in a dream as if they were side by side.

During incubation, your intuition makes connections. You are "getting in tune with a larger source that connects *all* information," says Patricia Einstein in *Intuition—The Path to Inner Wisdom*. Your intuition puts ideas together in a way that your logical mind would never try.

Then one day, spring comes. Step four in the creative process is *illumination*. An idea comes to you. You "see the light."

Just as you don't always know the exact day when spring will return, you are never quite sure when illumination will "turn on the light." Just like spring, it surprises you. There it is one day, a crocus or a daffodil. The day before, there were no signs of spring at all.

There you are, doing something else, not working on the project at all, when it comes to you—the answer you need. You see the light. A picture pops into your brain. Everything you need is right there in the picture. Your right brain has given you a gift; it has shown you the way.

Once again, the seasons change. Step five in the creative process is *translation into action*. Spring moves into summer, and everything grows. The world is awake now. Your left brain heats up.

After you see the pictures, your left brain translates them into words. Words pour out of you. They come so quickly you have to scramble to capture them on paper. Words grow quickly in summer's heat.

When the growing stops, it's harvest time. You gather your crops and start again. You till the soil and plant new seeds. The cycle begins all over again.

THE CREATIVE SEASONS
Step 1 Preparation—Fall Planting—The left brain organizes words and ideas.

Step 2 Frustration—Frost—The left brain freezes up, so the right brain takes charge.

Step 3 Incubation—Winter's Sleep—The right brain "sleeps" on the problem.

Step 4 Illumination—Spring's Awakening—The right brain pops up with a picture answer.

Step 5 Translation Into Action—Summer's Growth—The left brain translates the picture into words.

Farmer's Almanac

The act of creation is a long series of acts, with multiple and cascading preparations, frustrations, incubations, illuminations, and translations into action.

—DANIEL GOLEMAN, PAUL KAUFMAN, AND MICHAEL RAY, *The Creative Spirit*

I wish I could tell you that one pass though the creative writing cycle would write your book, but I can't. In truth, one pass through the seasons may only give you four lines of dialogue or tell you where to place that comma in your poem. On the other hand, you may write fifteen pages in a single day of summer's heat and wake up the next morning and do it again. Your seasons may last for minutes, days, weeks, or years.

Predicting the seasons is an inexact science. In one cycle, you may have a mild winter and move from new idea to writing in a matter of minutes. A long, hot summer with lots of rain may find you writing without stopping for days. Or, a book may remain frozen in your filing cabinet for years! The one experience you need to live through to make a book work hasn't occurred yet, and so the book waits.

The hare, your left brain, wants things to happen quickly. The tortoise, your right brain, knows that seasons come and go and come back again.

PICTURE IT! | *How Does Your Garden Grow?*

From the outside, it may appear that a creative project begins with a visit from your intuition, but insiders know the truth. "Intuition works best when you remember that 'tuition' is part of it," says award-winning Jane Yolen. "You need to have paid ahead of time (i.e., done your prep work) so as to prepare the ground for intuition."

Answers come to those who ask questions. And not just *any* question will do. If you want a specific answer, you need to ask a specific question. Ah, here's the rub, you only find out which question to ask . . . by doing your homework.

If you want to grow pumpkins, you need to plant pumpkin seeds. Not only that, you need to find out how pumpkins grow. How far down do you plant the seeds? How far apart do you plant them? What time of the year is best for planting pumpkins? How much water do the seeds need? Do you pinch the seedlings? If so, when? It might seem easier to just plunk those seeds into the ground, but if you do, the seeds may not grow.

Your intuition works the same way. If you want intuitive answers, you must prepare. You must ask questions that can be answered. In *Practical Intuition*, Laura Day says that good questions are "specific and unambiguous," "simple rather than compound," and "directly relevant."

When you rely on your intuition for creative answers, you will find that specific questions are the ones that are answered. "How can I tighten this scene?"

and "What will this character do next?" are questions your intuition can answer. "What is the next trend?" is too ambiguous.

The more you write and read in your genre, the more you will know which questions need asking. If you don't know what the questions are, how can you find any answers? Once you have a good question, you can find an answer. Winter doesn't have to be the longest (or only!) season in your creative garden. You can enjoy them all.

How does your writing garden grow? Do you prepare the soil before you plant? What kind of questions are you asking? Are you reading books in your genre to help you see which questions to ask? Do you see the frost as an obstacle or as a transition? How long are your winters? How do you feel about the other seasons? Do you have a favorite? Write about your creative garden in your writer's journal. ✦

Caterpillar, Cocoon, Butterfly

The "Look/ Don't Look/ Look" Technique is fertile ground for hunches.
—JOHN EMMERLING, *It Only Takes One*

A brainstorming tool from advertising leads to the next analogy for the mystery of creativity. John Emmerling's first advertising boss, Hanley Norins, was known as "the King of the Thirty-Foot Pad." At the start of a new project, Norins would hang a thirty-foot strip of paper on the walls around the office. As ideas bounced back and forth at the first staff meeting, Hanley wrote every idea on the wall pad. After the meeting, the paper stayed up. Staff members would come in and out, add new ideas, or fine-tune others. Emmerling calls this process "Look/ Don't Look/ Look."

First, look at the problem and attack it head on. (The staff brainstormed for new ideas and wrote everything down.) Then, don't look. Let the project sleep. (The meeting ended and the staff went on to other tasks.) After a while, look at it again. (Members of the staff would come back, look at the pad, and write new ideas on it.) Out of all this looking and not looking, a new ad campaign was born.

A creature from nature exemplifes the "Look/ Don't Look/ Look" campaign and the creative process in action. The caterpillar, who starts life looking like a worm, somehow emerges as a butterfly. After hatching from a tiny egg, a caterpillar becomes an eating machine. He increases his size several times over by eating! If you have caterpillars in your garden, you'll know. Your leaves will be eaten away. Caterpillars eat without stopping. Once a caterpillar has eaten his fill, he weaves a blanket around himself, and goes to sleep. Inside his chrysalis, his cocoon, he sleeps. Nothing appears to be happening, but inside is the most wonderful magic. As a caterpillar sleeps, he becomes a butterfly.

When the time is right, the chrysalis opens and a butterfly emerges. It takes a few moments for the wings to dry, but when they do, flight! The butterfly takes to wing.

When you write with pictures, you go through the same transformation. Preparation is the first stage of your creative process, too. You feed yourself words, instead of leaves, by doing research, reading, and preparatory writing. You read and write until you can read no more, until you can write no more.

The middle stage is one of silence. No looking happens here at all. Intuition works inside your head, without words. During incubation, what you know turns into something new. Before and after do not look alike. The link that connects the first idea and the new vision is the silence, the sleep, the waiting.

After you wait through the silence, pictures come to you. Your right brain gives you a picture, and your left brain translates that picture into words. Look again! When your wings dry, when the picture is given words, then you can fly. Now you are a picture writer.

PICTURE IT! | *Stages*

The steps you take to become an accomplished writer are like the stages in the caterpillar-cocoon-butterfly process. When you first begin, you are a caterpillar. You swallow everything you can find about writing for children. You ask a million questions. You read and write and study. You are an apprentice learning your craft.

In the second stage, you enter the cocoon. You push out the world and mull things over. You let go of what others say. As you read and write and study your craft, you figure out what works for you. With introspection, you find your genre, your voice, your vision. Now the answers to your questions come from inside of you, not someone else.

If you can make it through the difficult stage of introspection, your reward is wings. You become a butterfly. In the third stage, you have mastered your craft. You know what you like. You know what will work for you. You have the tools you need at your fingertips. When you want to create, it happens. You can fly.

Where are you in your creative journey? Are you learning a new skill and starting out as a caterpillar all over again? Or are you mulling things over, making decisions? Have you seen your wings? Write your thoughts down in your writer's journal. ✦

Read Like the Caterpillar Eats

> Reading maketh a full man; conference a ready man; and writing an exact man.
>
> —FRANCIS BACON

When you begin a new project, read like the caterpillar eats. Fill yourself with words. Some writers say that reading contaminates their writing. It might, if you read while you are writing. Reading at the beginning of a project is a completely different matter. How can you write without words? In order to begin writing, you must fill yourself with words, and you do that by reading.

Read the books you want to write. If you want to write young adult novels, read them. If you want to write poetry, read it. Each type of book has its own taste, its own flavor. The only way you can experience that taste is by eating. Nibble slowly or swallow the books whole. Read.

As you read, watch the pictures unfold before your eyes. See how other writers write pictures, even in books that don't have any art inside. Only when you have read hundreds and hundreds of books can you absorb the voice, learn the form, and write pictures.

Read like the caterpillar eats. Read until you just can't think anymore. Then, let your project sleep. Wrap a cocoon around yourself and shut out the world. Give yourself time to think, to mull things over. Your right brain will change your thoughts, ideas, and experiences into something new. When the time is right, the pictures will come. Your cocoon will open, and the pictures will turn into words.

You can't skip any steps. A caterpillar cannot turn himself into a butterfly without eating his fill, without a cocoon. If you skip a step, you miss the transformation. Without the eating and the waiting, there is no magic. Without the reading and the silent growing, you're just a caterpillar trying to fly!

PICTURE IT! | *Reading Log*

Remember the summer reading programs at the public library? You carefully wrote down the name of every book you read. Your goal was to read as many books as possible. Day after day, you immersed yourself in books.

Relive your childhood and start a reading log. In *Children's Writer's and Illustrator's Market*, Harcourt Editorial Director Allyn Johnston says, "I'm always speaking at writing conferences and telling people to read books. I'm shocked at how few people do."

You need to read in order to stay in touch with the market. New books come out two to four times a year. If you're not reading, you can spend months writing a great book, only to send it to a publisher who has a book just like it. Of course, she'll reject it! Surround yourself with books. Eat, sleep, and dream books so you can discover what makes them work. Read deeply to train your eye.

Read to discover what you like. Every book is sold because someone liked it— someone in editorial, in marketing, in sales, and in retail. Books jump through a lot of hoops to make it to the shelf, but that doesn't mean that you have to like all of them. Reading will help you find the kind of books you want to write.

As you read this book, the exercises will ask you to read five children's or young adult books to demonstrate the concept in each section. Whatever the topic, you can find examples in children's and young adult books.

For this Picture It! exercise, select a genre that you'd like to write, and read five books from that genre. Just as you did in summer reading long ago, log the titles you read in a notebook, on a calendar page, or in your writer's journal. Rate each book with a plus (Yes, I saw the pictures in the words) or a minus (No, I didn't see the pictures in the words). Write about your experience in your writer's journal. ✦

Although I have used many picture analogies in this chapter to explain the creative process, as you can see in the chart on page 16, they are simply different ways to say the same thing. You begin by doing your homework and getting

READ—THINK—WRITE							
read	caterpillar	look	fall frost	preparation frustration	hare	left brain begins work left brain stops
think	cocoon	don't look spring	winter	incubation illumination	tortoise	right brain begins work right brain gives results
write	butterfly	look	summer	translation	hare	left brain translates right brain

your ideas together. You read and research and begin to write until you hit a wall. Although it seems as if your project has stopped at this point, it has not. The frost and the frustration stages are simply a transition from one way of thinking to another. The left brain stops working so that the right brain may proceed. When the right brain has the answer, it appears, in a flash, as a picture. Another transition takes place. Now the left brain is in charge again. The pictures need to be translated into words.

When the translation is complete, the process starts all over again. The left brain gathers new information, and inevitably, another question arises, one that the left brain cannot answer. The right brain steps in and begins to work. The process repeats itself over and over again.

Two heads are better than one, the old saying goes. Well, both of those heads, those ways of thinking, are inside of you right now. The left brain and the right brain are two ways of knowing that exist inside you, whether you use them or not! Why not use what you already have?

Now you know the "secret" of creativity. You need to use both sides of your brain when you create. You need both sides of your brain to write. After the words run dry, and they will, allow the wordless part of your brain to play. When you have the gift of the pictures, translate those pictures into words, and write them down.

By understanding the mystery of the creative process, you can move from outsider to craftsman. You can be a picture writer. You may not like the frustration, but now you know that it is only a step. If you wait and stay open to the wordless moment, you will have wings. You will be a butterfly.

PART II

Plot

Chapter Two

Seeing Fiction

 We read five words on the first page of a really good novel and we begin to forget that we are reading printed words on a page; we begin to see images. . . . We slip into a dream.

—JOHN GARDNER, *On Becoming a Novelist*

We'll start learning the nuts and bolts of Picture Writing by examining the fundamentals of fiction. Fiction is a story you make up. All of the characters are pretend or make-believe. At the same time, fiction tells a truth. It tells the truth of the human heart.

Fiction allows readers to move beyond their limitations. A boy can see the world as a girl does, and vice versa. With fiction, readers can look at the world through the eyes of mice or rabbits or hobbits. New worlds that never were, and never will be, can now be explored.

When you write fiction, you think about yourself and your world. When you read fiction, you learn more about yourself. All of fiction is about the human condition. And in this chapter, we'll discuss how to write fiction for children of all reading levels that explores the human condition.

Board Books

The board book is a book for infants and toddlers made of heavy cardboard covered with plastic. Infants and toddlers put everything in their mouths, even books. The plastic coating on the pages protects the art and the words printed on the paper. The stiff cardboard makes it easier for chubby fingers to turn the pages. These books are designed with their readers in mind.

Manuscripts for board books are very short, typing out to half a page or slightly more. The books themselves are no bigger than your hand. Open a board book and the story starts. Each time you turn the page to a new *spread*, there is both text and art. A board book may have as few as five or as many as twelve double spreads. Infants and toddlers have a very short attention span, so the story moves very rapidly.

PAGE NAMES
Publishing Terminology

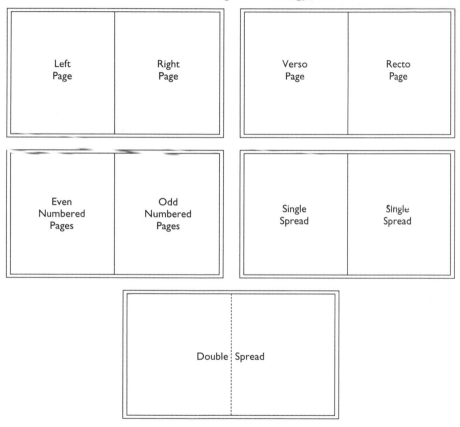

Family situations with infant and toddler heroes are the mainstay of board book fiction. Infants and toddlers know the world close to home, so that is the world in their books. Understanding the mindset of this age is essential. *Max's Birthday*, by Rosemary Wells, is a board book written for infants and toddlers. In five double spreads, you see what happens when Max opens his birthday present. The book begins:

> Happy birthday, Max, said Max's
> sister, Ruby.

In a single sentence, in seven words, you meet the two main characters, Ruby and Max, and find out the setting. It is Max's birthday. The illustration shows the wind-up lobster that Ruby has given Max for his birthday. On the facing page, Max shouts "No!" He doesn't want the lobster. This is the story problem. On the first double spread, in two sentences, you have everything you need to start a story.

Just like fiction for older readers, the problems in a board book get progressively worse in each of the three acts. In a board book, an entire act may take place on a spread, on just two facing pages. The essence of a plot for fiction—exposition; problems one, two, and three; climax; decision and resolution—appear in five to twelve spreads in a board book. The payoff is immediate. Infants and toddlers have a very short attention span.

Telling a complete story in five to twelve spreads is a challenge. Read the author names on these books and you will see that most creators are author-illustrators. So much of the story for this age is in the illustrations. If you are a writer who is not an illustrator, your chances of breaking into this market are very small. Focus on the picture book market instead.

PICTURE IT! | *Storyboarding in Miniature*

Go to the library or the bookstore and find five fiction board books. Read them through once, write the titles in your reading log, then open your writer's journal. On a fresh page, make a board book storyboard. (Add more page squares if your book is longer.)

Inside each page square, write a sentence that describes what you see on that page—in the words and in the illustrations. Do the same for each of the five board books.

Now look a little deeper. Reread the first book. Does the first double spread serve as the exposition, introducing the main character, the big story problem, and the setting? If it does, write an E for exposition.

Turn to the next double spread. Does this spread have a small story problem that comes out of the bigger one introduced on the first page? If it does, write a #1 for the first small story problem.

BOARD BOOK STORYBOARD

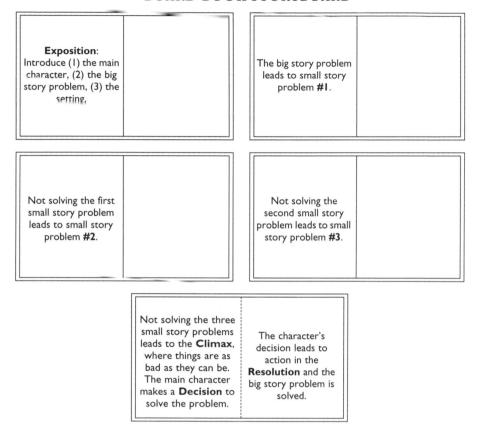

Turn the page and look for a new story problem. Can you find a second small story problem that results from the actions on the previous spread? When you see it, write a #2 for the second small story problem.

As you turn the page again, you should see a third story problem that is even worse than the previous two. If so, write a #3 on the square for this spread.

On the last, or next to last spread, are things as bad as they can get? In other words, has the story reached its climax? Has the big story problem on the first page led to a series of problems that the character hasn't solved? Write a C where you see the story climax.

Now look carefully. Does the main character make a decision to solve the story problem? Write a D where the character makes a decision.

Does the character act on his decision? Is the big story problem from the exposition page solved? Are all the loose ends tied up? If so, write an R for resolution.

You may find that your board book has more than five double spreads. The story structure should remain the same, no matter how long the story. With more spreads, you simply see more details. Write the letters and number the story problems wherever you see them.

After you finish, write about your experience in your writer's journal. Did you expect to see all of the fiction elements in a book for infants and toddlers? Did any of the books have elements missing? Now that you know what was missing, did you feel the loss of these elements? How can storyboarding help you in your own writing? ✦

Picture Books

> The slush piles at the publishing houses contain more picture books (ten to one, it seems) than any other kind.
> —OLGA LITOWINSKY, *Writing and Publishing Books for Children in the 1990s: The Inside Story from the Editor's Desk*

A picture book is the next step up from a board book. Picture books have thirty-two paper pages inside a hard cardboard or soft paperback cover. The traditional age range for picture books was four to eight, but as the market grows, publishers are reaching both down and up in age. Today picture books are written for young readers—children ages two to eight—and for older readers—middle school and high school students.

The age of the character in your story usually determines the age of the reader. Main characters in young picture books are often eight years old, the top of the traditional picture book age. Young picture books with adults as the main character focus on the childlike features of that adult. In *Mr. Gumpy's Motor Car*, by John Burningham, Mr. Gumpy's animals ask for a ride in his car, and off they go! Fantasy rules the day.

The story problem also determines the age of a picture book. Second graders could care less about potty training, a big topic for two year olds. Two year olds, on the other hand, don't worry yet about spelling tests. To ring true, the conflict in your story must match the age of your main character.

Picture books about topics such as history and war are for older readers.

The picture book retelling of Guiseppe Verdi's opera *Aida* ends with the main characters sealed in a tomb to die. Middle school and high school teachers use these older picture books in their social studies and literature classes. Libraries shelve them in the fiction section, not on the picture book shelves.

If you're not sure which problems match which age, read picture books and parenting books. Books about important milestones, such as losing a tooth or the first day of school, are the mainstay of the picture book world. In an interview for the Society of Children's Book Writers and Illustrators (SCBWI), Clarion Books Senior Editor Michele Coppola says about picture books, "I'm looking for a fresh approach to an idea that's been done before." Although these topics have been written about again and again, to the children experiencing them for the first time, they are completely new.

The Picture Book Myth

Picture books have pictures, so whenever I talk about my picture books, people assume that I found the artist for my book and told her what to draw. I call this the "picture book myth."

The truth is, when you send in your words, the publisher selects the artist and provides art direction. After you sell your words, it's not just *your* book anymore. In *Children's Writer's and Illustrator's Market*, author-illustrator Janie Bynum asks, "So, whose book is it anyway?" It's your book *and* the editor's book *and* the art director's book *and* the illustrator's book, too. "It's everybody's," says Bynum. The writer is in charge of the words and the illustrator is in charge of the pictures. You don't tell the illustrator what to draw and the illustrator doesn't tell you what to write.

Confusion over the pictures is the reason I named this book *Picture Writing*. Writing notes to the artist telling her what to draw is not visual writing. For picture books, for any book, you must write the pictures *in your words*. The images that the editor sees are in your text. The artist knows what to draw by reading the words in your story.

Look at a classic picture book, and see how it's done. *No Roses for Harry*, a picture book by Gene Zion, opens this way:

> Harry was a white dog with black spots.
> On his birthday, he got a present from Grandma.
> It was a woolen sweater with roses on it.

Harry didn't like it the moment he saw it.
He didn't like the roses.

You see pictures in the key elements of fiction on this very first page. Here in the exposition, in the introduction to the story, you see the *main character*: "Harry was a white dog with black spots"; the *setting*: "On his birthday"; and the *story problem*: "Harry . . . didn't like the roses."

Description shows the reader a picture. The reader knows exactly what the dog looks like: "Harry was a white dog with black spots." You can see the birthday present, too. "It was a woolen sweater with roses on it."

Every picture moves the story forward. The story starts with action as the birthday present arrives and moves quickly to reaction: "Harry didn't like it the moment he saw it."

The story also shows what every editor wants to see: heart. Any kid who has ever received a present he didn't like can identify with Harry. That's the hook that pulls the reader in, the emotion. The reader wants to know what Harry will do. In order to find out, you have to turn the page.

The artist draws the description and the action in your words. That's how you "direct" an illustrator, by writing pictures in your words. To fill a picture book, you need fifteen action pictures. Picture book manuscripts type out to five or six pages double-spaced. Picture books for two and three year olds may be shorter, but they must have fifteen different "scenes" in them.

PICTURE IT! | *A Storyboard*

Now it's time for you to storyboard a picture book. Go to the library or the bookstore and find five picture books with strong characters. (Save the alphabet and number books for the next chapter.) Read each book and write the titles in your reading log. Then draw a blank storyboard for one book in your writer's journal.

Remember to draw a diagonal line through the first and the last page. These pages are the end papers, the colored paper pages that hold the book together. Although some publishers decorate these pages, the writer is not usually allowed to plan text for them.

Unlike board books, which begin as soon as you open them, picture books have publishing "business" at the beginning and sometimes at the end. As you

PICTURE BOOK STORYBOARD

Endpaper.	The book begins here with a half-title page.

	Full title page.

Copyright / dedication page.	Exposition: Introduce (1) the main character, (2) the big story problem, (3) the setting.

	The big story problem leads to small story problem #1.

First try to solve the small story problem.	

	Second try to solve the small story problem.

Third try to solve the small story problem.	

	Not solving the first small story problem leads to small story problem #2.

First try to solve the small story problem.	

	Second try to solve the small story problem.

PICTURE BOOK STORYBOARD, *continued*

Third try to solve the small story problem.	Not solving the second small story problem leads to small story problem **#3**.
First try to solve the small story problem.	Second try to solve the small story problem.
Third try to solve the small story problem.	Not solving the three small story problems leads to the **Climax**, where things are as bad as they can be. The main character makes a **Decision** to solve the problem.

The character's decision leads to action in the **Resolution** and the big story problem is solved.

Endpaper.

write a sentence or a phrase inside each square to describe what you see, you may need to add a description of the page function as well.

Page 1 faces the first end paper. This front page is almost always the *half-title page*. If this is so, write "½ title" on this page square of your storyboard.

Pages 2 and 3 are often *full title pages*. If this is true for the book you have, write "full title" across the page squares. (If not, keep reading.)

Picture books often place the *dedication* on page 4. Write "dedication" here or on pages 2 and 3 If it appears there.

Now it's time for the story to begin. Some books cut right to the chase and begin their story on pages 2 and 3. Others spread across pages 4 and 5. Still others start just on page 5. Wherever it starts, write an E for Exposition where your story introduces the main character, the setting, and the main story problem. Picture books from earlier days took all of pages 4, 5, 6, 7, and 8 to introduce the reader to the character, setting, and main story problem. Newer stories tend to get right to the point and fit all of the exposition onto page 5.

Problems in the main plot are often manifested in three ways as the story progresses. This tradition of three dates back to the classics. Write a #1 when you see the first small story problem. The small story problem is a *new* problem that arises because of the main problem introduced in the exposition. With a short exposition, the first small story problem appears around pages 6 and 7. The main character would then have three page turns to try and solve this problem. That means that pages 8 and 9 are one try, pages 10 and 11 are another try, and pages 12 and 13 are the third try.

Of course, if the character solved his problem this early, the story would end before page 32! So, the problem is *not* solved. Instead, it gets worse. Turn the page for small story problem number two. With the classic threes, this would mean pages 14 and 15 introduce story problem number two. Wherever you find it in the book you are storyboarding, write a #2 on the square for that page. Classic threes also give the character another three tries. That would be pages 16 and 17 for the first try, pages 18 and 19 for the second try, and pages 20 and 21 for the third try.

It's still too early for the book to end, so the character does *not* solve the second problem either. Instead, the situation gets worse. Small story problem number three is next. Write a #3 on the page squares where the third problem arises. It may be pages 22 and 23. That would leave pages 24 and 25 for the first try, pages 26 and 27 for the second try, and pages 28 and 29 for the third try.

After three sets of three, it's time for the book to end. The character has still not solved any of the worsening problems. Things get as bad as they can get on the very next page, and the character is forced to make a decision. Write a D for Decision wherever you see one.

Now things begin happening rapidly. Once the character decides to solve the problem, he takes action and solves it, often on the very same page. Decision and resolution often occur together around pages 30 and 31. Write an R for Resolution wherever you find the action that solves the big problem of the entire story.

On the very last page, page 32, all of the loose ends from the story are tied up. The story winds down. The resolution is now complete. The reader closes the book with an Ah!

As you storyboard other books, you will begin to see variations on the theme. Some stories are not set up in classic threes. The stories simply don't work that way. On the other hand, the classic threes may show you why a certain story didn't feel right to you. The pacing of the book may be off, with the story problems too close together in one place and too far away in another. Or it may be that the story's power is lost when someone else solves the story problem. After thirty pages of rooting for the main character, it can be quite deflating to see someone else save the day. Far better to have that second person act as a mentor and give the advice the main character needs to solve the story problem on her own.

Write in your writer's journal about your storyboarding experience. Did you see the bones of the book when you storyboarded it? Did the story have heart? Did it fit the classic threes? Did you find another storyboarding pattern? If so, what was it? Can you use the classic threes or any other patterns you discovered in your own writing? ✦

Easy Readers

> Easy readers are usually packed with action that propels the plot forward and keeps the reader interested.
>
> —TRACEY E. DILS, *You Can Write Children's Books*

Just as the picture book market has grown over the years, reaching both up and down in age, so too has the easy reader. In the past, easy readers were forty or forty-eight or sixty-four pages. Intended as reading practice for first- and second-grade readers, easy readers were more difficult than thirty-two-page picture books, but simpler than two hundred-page novels. There weren't many steps in between. You learned to read with Dick and Jane and then you jumped up to Dr. Seuss. After easy readers, you made the huge leap to *Charlotte's Web*.

Today, there are books for every stage of reading. Educators label these stages:

emergent, early, transitional, and fluent. Each grade roughly corresponds with a grade level. The first three stages are covered in the easy reader category.

As you can see, quite a lot of change happens in a short time. At the same time, each child grows at her own pace. A few years ago, the major publishing houses realized that parents were looking for more guidance as to the reading levels of easy reader books. On the back and the inside covers of almost every easy reader produced now is a parent's guide. The publishers also grouped the readers into levels. Some publishers label their books: Level 1, Level 2, and Level 3. Other publishers have four levels. The characteristics of each level are clearly printed on the cover. You can use these guidelines to help you write your own easy reader.

LEARNING TO READ		
emergent readers	recognize letters, know a few words by sight	kindergarten
early readers	read 200 + sight words	first grade
transitional readers	use phonics and page clues to read new words	second grade
fluent readers	read independently	third grade

Emergent Readers

Emergent easy readers are often categorized as Level 1 easy readers. Level 1 books are very simple. With just a few words per page, these emergent easy readers are a cross between board books and poetry. Like board books, much of the story is told in the pictures. Like poetry, the writing has lots of repetition. Using the same word over and over helps a child learn that word.

At the very beginning, children are able to read so few words independently, the story must also be told in the illustrations. If you are using only a handful of words on each page, you must write pictures! You must write words that can be illustrated. If the words and the art are not an exact match, it confuses the children. Concrete and visible are the bywords of the emergent reader.

Pop Pop Pop, an emergent easy reader by David Martin, opens with this line:

Monkey sees a red balloon.

This is the only sentence on the first right-hand page. What the text says is exactly what the illustration shows. The art shows a monkey and a red balloon, nothing more. This helps the reader see what the words say.

The simplest emergent easy readers have eight or sixteen pages. The next step-up is twenty-four pages. After that, thirty-two pages is the norm. The page counts are all multiples of eight.

Early Readers

Level 2 early easy readers have more words, but still rely heavily on illustration. You must write a story that can be easily illustrated. The sentences in Level 2 books are simple, but longer, so they are broken into phrases on the page. Here is the first page of *Fraidy Cats*, a Level 2 easy reader by Stephen Krensky:

> One dark night
> when the wind blew hard,
> the Fraidy Cats got ready for bed.
> Scamper checked in the closet.
> Nothing was here.
> Sorry checked under the beds.
> Nothing there, either.

The first sentence gives readers the *setting*: "One dark night, when the wind blew hard, the Fraidy Cats got ready for bed." Readers know that the cats are at home in their own room on a dark and windy night. Then readers meet the *characters* one by one: "Scamper checked in the closet," and "Sorry checked under the beds." Readers see them in *action*, so that not a word is wasted. Each action brings a reaction. First, "Scamper checked in the closet. Nothing was here." Then, "Sorry checked under the beds. Nothing there, either." Plot, character, and setting are visual and on the move.

In Level 1 emergent easy readers, the text for each page is often just a phrase or a single sentence typed on one line. The lines do not wrap in the Level 1 stage. In Level 2 early easy readers, however, longer sentences do wrap two or more times down the page. Sentences broken into phrases are the norm for Level 2 books.

In *Fraidy Cats*, the long first sentence is broken into three phrases. If readers were reading this story aloud, they could pause after each break and still understand the story. This is intentional. It is difficult for beginning readers to read long sentences, yet you want to help them learn how to do so. Breaking longer sentences into phrases teaches children how to read longer sentences bit by bit.

If breaking your story into phrases does not come naturally to you, type your story the regular way. The publisher decides how each sentence is wrapped when the book is designed, whether you type it in phrases or not. Your job is to write a good story. Just remember to start a new line each time a new character begins speaking and to use clear tag lines, such as Joe said, Sally said, etc. You want beginning readers to know exactly who is saying what.

Transitional Readers With Chapter Stories

Level 3 and Level 4 books are the highest levels of easy readers. In these easy readers, stories are often written in chapters. Easy readers with chapters are for children in the *transitional* reading stage.

Fox at School, a Level 3 easy reader written by Edward Marshall, is divided into three chapters. Each chapter is a separate story. One way to introduce new readers to longer books is by collecting short stories together in one volume. The stories in these easy readers are about the same character, but the story in each chapter can stand alone. In the first chapter story, "Fox on Stage," Fox performs in a school play. The second chapter story, "Fox Escapes," is about a fire drill. In the final chapter story, "Fox in Charge," the teacher leaves Fox in charge of the class. Each chapter story relates to the title of the book, *Fox at School.* At the same time, each chapter story is separate and complete.

The first chapter story, "Fox on Stage," begins:

> Fox wanted a part
> in the class play.

This opening sentence shows the reader the *main character* (Fox), *the setting* (the classroom), the main *story problem*, and the *heart* or the emotional connection (Fox wants to be in a play). In eight words, you have it all! The words are simple and thus "easy to read," but all of the story elements are there. The reader is drawn in right away.

Transitional Readers With True Chapters

The next step up in reading difficulty occurs when the chapters are part of the same story. This is the top of the easy reader range. Some publishers label these easy readers with number levels, such as Level 3 or Level 4. Other publishers call them *chapter books*. Intended for second- and third-grade readers, easy reader chapter books have a cast of characters with a story that reaches beyond a single chapter. Although each chapter has a small story problem to solve, the entire book has one big story problem.

Three Smart Pals by Joanne Rocklin is a Level 4 easy reader. This forty-eight-page book has four chapters: "Fresh Fish for Sale," "Fair Is Fair," "Hal's Race," and "A Terrific Show." The book opens:

> Al, Sal, and Hal were three pals.
> They were very smart.
>
> One day they watched Mr. Bing
> open his new fish store.
> Mr. Bing placed the fish in the window.
> He swept the walk. He climbed a ladder
> to nail up a sign.

Right from the start, readers know there are three main characters in this story: "Al, Sal, and Hal were three pals." Readers learn more about them in the next line: "They were very smart." Here is the story problem for the book. Like the folktale *The Three Sillies*, these "three smart pals" solve their problems in an unconventional way.

Each chapter has its own problem, and one problem leads to another. In the first chapter, "they watched Mr. Bing open his new fish store." The three smart pals "help" Mr. Bing with his sign by talking him into painting out all of the words. The next chapter shows the pals on a picnic. The pals have a race in the third chapter and come home in the fourth chapter to find that Mr. Bing hasn't sold any fish. The pals "help" him . . . again!

This book keeps its promise. On the first page, it said that the pals were smart and Mr. Bing wanted to sell fish. In the last chapter, it all comes true. Still fully illustrated, the chapters in an easy reader chapter book are linked to each other to tell a longer story. Step by step, the readers are growing.

I Can Read!

The simplest easy readers tell a story on a mere eight pages. As children learn more words, their books grow from eight to sixty-four pages. The shorter easy readers have a single story. Longer readers have a collection of stories or chapters like a novel.

So how long will your manuscript be? It depends on the type of easy reader you are writing. Emergent easy readers can be as short as a board book manuscript, filling only one or one and a half double-spaced manuscript pages. Thirty-two-page early easy readers, like picture books, cover five or six double-spaced manuscript pages. Easy readers for transitional readers are ten to fifteen double-spaced pages.

PICTURE IT! | *Pictures in the Words*

The sentences in an easy reader may be short, but the action is non-stop! Every line moves the story forward. Children learning to read may struggle with the words, but if the story has an exciting plot and lots of action, it will be worth the struggle.

Find five chapter story easy readers (each chapter acts like a short story) and read them. Write the titles in your reading log, then create a storyboard for a single chapter in your writer's journal (see page 34).

Although the art in an easy reader supports the text, every word picture is not shown in the illustrations. In each page square, write a short phrase for *each action shown in the words* on that page. Circle the action phrase that was illustrated in the art.

Did each page have one action picture? Did it have more? Were you surprised by the emphasis on the action? What did you think about the pacing of the chapter? Did the dialogue work to reveal both action and character? How can you use this in your own writing? Summarize your findings in your writer's journal. ✦

Chapter Books

> Plots for these stories are not complicated; there is a small cast of characters, and all of the action takes place within a short time span.
> —BARBARA SEULING, *How to Write a Children's Book and Get It Published*

Chapter books didn't exist as a category until recently. Written for second and third graders, this category is another move to target more readers by creating

CHAPTER STORY STORYBOARD

Exposition: Introduce (1) the main character, (2) the big story problem, (3) the setting.	

The big story problem leads to small story problem #1.	First try to solve the small story problem.

Second try to solve the small story problem.	Third try to solve the small story problem.

Not solving the first small story problem leads to small story problem #2.	First try to solve the small story problem.

Second try to solve the small story problem.	Third try to solve the small story problem.

Not solving the second small story problem leads to small story problem #3.	First try to solve the small story problem.

Second try to solve the small story problem.	Third try to solve the small story problem.

Not solving the three small story problems leads to the **Climax**, where things are as bad as they can be.	The main character makes a **Decision** to solve the problem.

The character's decision leads to action in the **Resolution**, and the big story problem is solved.	

more reading levels. Writers and publishers use different names for these books: "transitional readers," "early chapter books," "chapter books," or "young middle grade." Children call them "chapter books," so that's the name this book will use.

Easy readers with chapters are the highest level of easy reader. The chapter books here aren't easy readers, but they are still books for transitional readers. So how can you tell the difference? Put two books side by side.

Here is the first page from *Frog and Toad All Year* by Arnold Lobel:

Frog knocked on Toad's door.
"Toad, wake up," he cried.
"Come out and see
how wonderful the winter is!"
"I will not," said Toad.
"I am in my warm bed."

Now take a look at the first page from *Knights of the Kitchen Table,* a chapter book by Jon Scieszka:

> "Halt, vile knaves. Prepare to die."
> "Is he talking to us?" asked Fred.
> I looked around the small clearing. A dirt path went from one end to the other. Fred, Sam, and I stood at one end. A large guy on a black horse stood at the other. He was dressed from head to toe in black armor like you see in those books about knights and castles.

Notice the size of the type. Book designers give easy readers a larger font size. The rule of thumb is, the younger the reader, the larger the font. Board books, picture books, and easy readers have large type with a lot of white space.

Chapter books still have lots of white space, called *leading*, between the words, but they have less leading than easy readers. The fonts used in chapter books also greatly decrease in size. As children grow, they are able to distinguish words in smaller font sizes.

How the text looks has also changed. Easy readers are typed in phrases, so children can read a sentence in small bites. This allows them to check for meaning. Chapter book readers no longer need this assistance. The sentences in chapter books wrap at the end of the page. Where the sentence wraps is a matter of space, not comprehension.

SELECTING A FONT

Selecting a font is part of the design process. The book designer matches the font to the style of the art in the book. Do not send in your manuscript with large or artistic fonts. Size 10 and size 12 fonts are the industry standard. Editors also prefer plain fonts such as Courier or Times New Roman. Artists may send in art with stylized fonts, but the manuscript itself must be plain and simple. Don't forget to double-space!

The art also changes as you move from easy reader to chapter book. The first page of *Frog and Toad* is illustrated in full color, like all easy readers. The first page of *Knights of the Kitchen Table* has no art at all. Most chapter books have only a handful of black-and-white drawings, called *spot art*, in each chapter.

The writing also changes. For board books, picture books, and easy readers, you don't describe details the art can show unless they are essential to the plot. It makes the story too long. Just give a bare-bones description and keep the action moving. The details that show Frog, Toad, the house, and winter are all illustrated in the art.

In a chapter book, all of the setting, character description, and action is in the words: "A large guy on a black horse stood at the other. He was dressed from head to toe in black armor like you see in those books about knights and castles." The children reading these books no longer rely on artwork to check for meaning.

Not only are the fonts and the art smaller, the chapter books themselves are smaller. Easy readers are almost always 6″ × 9″. Chapter books average 5″ × 7½″. (There is no standard size for board books or picture books. A single publishing house often has several different sites for both picture books and board books.)

Although chapter books are smaller in size, they have more words on the page. As readers grow older, they want more story. Spin your chapter book around a simple problem in an elementary schoolchild's life, and let the reader see what happens. Divide your story into short chapters, with forty to sixty double-spaced manuscript pages in all.

PICTURE IT! | *Chapter by Chapter, Step-by-Step*

Once you enter the world of chapter books, the storyboarding process changes. Read five chapter books and record the titles in your writer's journal. Select your favorite book and storyboard it in your writer's journal. Draw a large square for each chapter as you see on page 38.

Although lots of action happens in each chapter, the plot takes a single step forward here. Each chapter has one central action, which can be summarized in a single sentence. What is that action? What is that step?

Reread the first chapter and look again. What was the most important thing that happened to the main character in this chapter? What problem did that character face and solve? Write it in the chapter square on your storyboard.

Chapter books are written in episodes so that just as one problem is solved, another problem arises. To find out what happens next, you have to read the next chapter. The second problem is solved in the second chapter, but a third problem arises at the end, which will be solved in the third chapter. And so it goes, problem, action, decision, resolution, and then a new problem. The action rises and falls and then rises again, all in a single chapter. As you read, write the main action for each chapter on your storyboard.

Did the book you storyboarded follow the episodic pattern? What was the overarching problem—the one the main character wanted to solve? Did the problems in each chapter come out of the main character's big problem? Did one small problem lead to the next? Did the main character make a decision and solve her problem? Did the book tie up all the loose ends in the last chapter? Record your discoveries in your writer's journal. ✦

Middle Grade

What attracts me to any genre is good storytelling.

—STEPHEN ROXBURGH, PRESIDENT AND PUBLISHER, FRONT STREET BOOKS, FROM AN INTERVIEW IN *Children's Writer*

CHAPTER BOOK STORYBOARD

CHAPTER 1

ACT 1: **Exposition**: Introduce (1) the main character, (2) the big story problem, (3) the setting. The big story problem leads to small story problem **#1**. The character makes his first attempt to solve the small story problem.

CHAPTER 2

The character makes his second attempt to solve the small story problem.

CHAPTER 3

The character makes his third attempt to solve the small story problem.

CHAPTER 4

ACT 2: Not solving the first small story problem leads to small story problem **#2**. The character makes his first attempt to solve the small story problem.

CHAPTER 5

The character makes his second attempt to solve the small story problem.

CHAPTER 6

The character makes his third attempt to solve the small story problem.

CHAPTER 7

ACT 3: Not solving the second small story problem leads to small story problem **#3**. The character makes his first attempt to solve the small story problem.

CHAPTER 8

The character makes his second attempt to solve the small story problem.

CHAPTER 9

The character makes his third attempt to solve the small story problem.

CHAPTER 10

Not solving the three small story problems leads to the **Climax**, where things are as bad as they can be. The main character makes a **Decision** to solve the problem. The character's decision leads to action in the **Resolution**, and the big story problem is solved.

Genre

Middle graders read fluently and no longer need help with the words. Now that the children can understand another person's point of view, you are free to explore many worlds. Fiction worlds are divided into genres.

You can mix and match the genres to fit your story. Think about the time that's best for your story (contemporary, historical, or futuristic) and the world it needs (reality or fantasy.) What your characters want will determine the type of story you write. Do they need to solve a crime (mystery) or are they just trying to stay alive (adventure)? Are they playing a game (sports), exploring the universe (science fiction), or just being funny (humor)? Are they having a nightmare (horror and suspense) or falling in love (romance)? There are so many possibilities!

TRADE OR MASS MARKET?

Two different types of publishers buy fiction: trade and mass market. Due to mergers, trade and mass market publishers work as imprints in large conglomerates. Under the same roof, the imprints operate quite differently.

Trade publishers focus on the bookstore, and the school and library market. They publish hardcover books as single stand-alone titles. If a trade title sells well, it is reprinted in paperback. A follow-up trade book with the same characters is called a *sequel*. Sequels come out a year or more after the original book. Trade books win literary awards like the Newbery and Caldecott medals. Trade publishers are looking for timeless classics. Original hardcovers cost fifteen dollars or more, so adults purchase trade books for children.

Mass market publishers focus on retail markets, from bookstores to discount stores. Mass market publishes original paperbacks as stand-alone titles or in series. In a mass market series, new titles with the same characters come out month after month. A series may stretch over four or eight books or last for several years. Popular culture drives the mass market publisher. These books reflect what is happening in the world right now. Paperbacks are inexpensive, so children and young adults buy mass market books for themselves.

Subplots

In stories for younger readers, such as picture books, only the main character's story is seen. Young children are still egocentric. Their entire world revolves around what they themselves see and want. Their own story is the only story. When younger children read fiction, they identify with the main character. They *become* that character. One plot at a time is all that younger readers can understand.

Once children grow old enough to understand that other people see the world differently than they do, the world in their books can change. The older child (usually third grade and up) still identifies with the main character when reading a novel. At the same time, the middle grader is able to understand that other characters see the world differently than the main character. The reader can follow more than one story at a time.

With more pages in the book itself, you have room for more characters. Characters who are not the main character have their own stories to tell. The stories for these other characters are called subplots, and they start to appear in middle-grade novels. For example, Harriet is the main character in *Harriet the Spy* by Louise Fitzhugh. Harriet's nurse, Ole Golly, has her own subplot, her own story. Ole Golly dates a man during her subplot, and after taking Harriet along on a date, is fired. Dealing with the fact that Ole Golly was dating was difficult for Harriet. After Ole Golly is fired, things get even worse for Harriet. Ole Golly's subplot is her own story, and at the same time it is directly connected to Harriet's story.

The main character still dominates the plot of a middle-grade novel. Subplots that directly affect the main character are called *hinging subplots*. What happens in a hinging subplot changes the story for the main character. Harriet's life changed after Ole Golly was fired.

Although the hinging subplot affects the main character, it still needs to be the secondary character's story. Ole Golly was the one with the boyfriend, not Harriet. When Ole Golly leaves to marry Mr. George Waldenstein, the story of their romance has a beginning, a middle, and an end. A subplot is a complete story in itself.

Too many subplots confuse readers. If eight or ten characters try to tell their stories in one middle-grade novel, readers have difficulty keeping track of who is who. Keeping track of the main character and two or three other stories is enough for a third or fourth grader. Novels for ten to twelve year olds have more subplots *if* the story needs them. Middle-grade novels fill 100 to 150 typed double-spaced pages. The longer your novel and the older the reader, the more room you have for subplots.

PICTURE IT! | *To See What They Could See*

When you open a book, you open the door to another world. The beauty of genre writing is that you can enter so many different worlds. For this Picture It! section, don't read five books. Instead, go to the library or the bookstore and *read the first page* of as many middle-grade novels as you can. Pull a book off the shelf and open it. Can you tell by reading the very first page which genre it is? If so, record the title and genre in your writer's journal. Then pull out another book at random and read the first page. Is the genre obvious? Only record the title if the answer is yes. Repeat until you can't open any more books!

Now find a quiet place to write in your writer's journal. Which novels "called" you? Were they all the same genre or different ones? Did you find yourself pulled into certain books, unable to stop reading? Why did these books speak to you? Which genres were they? Are you writing in those genres now? Would you like to write in those genres? (Write the names of the middle-grade books you did read from beginning to end in your reading log.) ✦

Young Adult

"Young" YA literature is generally read by those in grades five through seven (ages ten through thirteen). "Older" YA is typically read by those in grades eight and nine (ages thirteen through fifteen).
—SHERRY GARLAND, *Writing for Young Adults*

Young adult literature is a step up from middle grade. Here the reading level is not the major difference. It is the content that has matured. Now, topics like sex, peer pressure, and drugs can be found. In fact, that is how editors tell the difference between a middle-grade novel and a young adult novel—by the content.

Not only is the content more adult now that the readers are older, novelists feel free to experiment. Novels may be written as a collection of first person poems. These poems are considered a novel because together they tell a story from a single character's point of view.

Monster, by Walter Dean Myers, is written in screenplay format, complete with camera directions. Sixteen-year-old Steve tells the story of his courtroom trial for murder.

FADE IN: INTERIOR; Early morning in CELL
BLOCK D, MANHATTAN DETENTION CENTER.
Camera goes slowly down grim, gray corridor.
There are sounds of inmates yelling from cell to
cell; much of it is obscene. Most of the voices
are clearly Black or Hispanic. Camera stops and
slowly turns toward a cell.

INTERIOR: CELL. Sixteen-year-old STEVE HARMON
is sitting on the edge of a metal cot, head in
hands. He is thin, brown skinned. On the cot next
to him are the suit and tie he is to wear to court
for the start of his trial.

CUT TO: ERNIE, another prisoner, sitting on john,
pants down.

CUT TO: SUNSET, another prisoner, pulling on
T-shirt.

CUT TO: STEVE pulling blanket over his head as
screen goes dark.

VOICE-OVER (VO)

Ain't no use putting the blanket over
your head, man. You can't cut this out;
this is reality. This is the real deal.

The pictures here aren't pretty. One prisoner is "sitting on (the) john, pants down." Another is getting dressed, "pulling on a T-shirt." The cell block corridor is "grim" and "gray." "There are sounds of inmates yelling from cell to cell; much of it is obscene." The details pull you in so you are there with Steve, even if you don't want to be. The voice-over gets to the heart of the matter: "Ain't no use putting the blanket over your head, man. You can't cut this out; this is reality."

"Novel" Formats

Novels written in verse or as a screenplay are just two variations of the novel. Novelists also borrow from other written forms, such as diaries and letters. Variations on the novel begin in the middle grades. These variations flourish in the young adult novel.

Catherine, Called Birdy, a young adult novel by Karen Cushman, is the diary of a girl who lives in 1290, making it historical fiction, too. *Snail Mail No More*, by Paula Danziger and Ann M. Martin, is a middle-grade epistolary novel made up of e-mail letters between two teens, Elizabeth and Tara*Starr.

Snail Mail No More is also an example of multiple narrators. As they e-mail back and forth, Elizabeth and Tara*Starr take turns being the narrator. In *The Pigman*, a young adult novel by Paul Zindel, the two main characters, John and Lorraine, alternate chapters. With each narrator change, the reader sees the world from inside a different character.

With older readers, you have more freedom to experiment. You might wish to try one of these "novel" formats for yourself. Just keep one thing in mind. Each of these formats begins with a character that the kids can care about and ends with that character growing or changing in some way. How long should your story be? Most young adult novels are two hundred pages typed and double-spaced.

PICTURE IT! | . . . And Action!

Borrow from another format to help train your eye. The screenplay format is a visual format. Camera directions show the setting, the actors, and the action. The dialogue is set apart. It's all there for the eye to see, written in short phrases.

STEVE

You can't throw. (Picks up rock and throws
it. We see it sail past the post and hit a YOUNG
WOMAN. The TOUGH GUY she is walking with
turns and sees the three young boys.)

Rewrite this excerpt from Walter Dean Myers's *Monster* into prose. Then go to the library or the bookstore and reverse the process. Find a young adult book that is written in prose. Take a scene from the book and rewrite it in screenplay format. Turn the prose into directions and dialogue. You are the director. Write what you see.

If you usually write, or want to write, for another age group, practice with a book from that reading level or your own manuscript. Write down what the characters see, what they say, and how they move. Now you can really see the bones of a story.

If you put your screenplay excerpt back into prose, would you write it differently? Write about your thoughts in your writing journal. As always, record any books that you read in your reading log. ◆

What Do Editors Want to See?

A story has to have some kind of emotional reach, a heart factor.
—KATHERINE BROWN TEGEN, EDITORIAL DIRECTOR, HARPERCOLLINS, FROM AN
INTERVIEW FOR *SCBWI*

Regardless of the reading level, what do editors want to see in a fiction manuscript? That's a million-dollar question, and here's a one-word answer: heart. When it comes to fiction, editors want to see heart.

What makes readers turn the page is an emotional connection to the characters in the story. Readers aren't reading fiction for facts or information. Children and young adults turn the pages of a fiction book because they want to find out what happened to the character. They care. They have an emotional connection. That's heart.

In *Children's Writers and Illustrator's Market*, Harcourt Editorial Director Allyn Johnston says, "The books that cause readers to have an emotional reaction are the hardest books to write, and they are the rarest, but they are the ones that last."

However you tell your story, whichever genre or age you choose, the closer you are to the heart of a character, the stronger your story will be. What your readers want to see is the same thing an editor wants to see . . . a story that makes them care. It's the characters that make readers care in fiction. Characters are the heart of the story and we'll discuss characters in chapters five, six, and seven.

The structure of your story is the plot, the bones of a book. But an empty skeleton isn't a story. Until you flesh it out and give it muscle, the story isn't ready. The heart is a powerful muscle. When you write fiction, remember the heart. Without heart, a story isn't truly alive.

Chapter Three

Seeing Nonfiction

 The essentials of writing nonfiction for any audience continue to be factual accuracy, an individual voice, and lively, engaging prose.

—JOHN SELFRIDGE, PUBLISHER, FROM AN INTERVIEW IN *Children's Writer*

Today's nonfiction books for children often look like magazines, with bold headings and full-color art throughout. Nonfiction introduces children to the real world, and the real world is bright and bold and loud. Vivid and visual nonfiction is what sells.

Nonfiction for children is divided into two broad areas: biographies and information books. Biographies are structured very much like fiction, as a real-life character struggles to overcome adversity. Just like fiction, biographies reach for the heart of a person and share it with readers. At the same time, all details in a biography must be true.

Information books also share the real world with readers. Ideas, however, aren't one person's story, so the bones of a nonfiction piece are put together differently. For these books, logic is the order of the day. You want one idea to flow to the next. Clarity brings readers with you on your journey of discovery.

You may remember these nonfiction structures from your "expository writing" days in school: *compare and contrast, problem and solution, cause and effect.* Expository writing seeks to explain things. That is the essence of nonfiction.

Nonfiction uses *definitions* and *examples.* It seeks to organize the world, to classify it by numbering items (*enumeration*) or by explaining a process step-by-step (*chronology*).

How do you explain the world to children who haven't experienced much of it yet? You can start with something they know and connect that to something new, using the *familiar to unfamiliar* pattern. You can also start small and work your way up to the big idea, using the *simple to complex* pattern. Or, you can flip everything on its head, start with the big idea, and work your way down to the tiny details with the *general to specific* pattern.

How do you know which structure or pattern to use? You have to think it through. What works best depends on the age of your readers and the ideas you are explaining. This is why it is important to read a wide variety of nonfiction books written for children. The more you read, the more you can see how many ways it can be done. See how other writers use these plot patterns, these nonfiction bones, and build your own book accordingly.

Board Books

Art is frequently the selling point for a basic board or concept book.
—JUDY CAREY, ASSOCIATE EDITOR, FROM AN INTERVIEW IN *Children's Writer*

Nonfiction begins with a baby's first book, the board book. You can tell if a board book is nonfiction by looking at the pages. If the words in the book are merely labels, it's a nonfiction board book. Babies are acquiring language and they want to know, "What are all these things I see?" Board book after board book seeks to answer this question.

The board book *Baby in a Buggy*, by Monica Wellington, uses this question as a part of the text. Board books begin as soon as you open them. On the left side of the first spread is the question:

> What
> does baby
> see?

On the right-hand page is the first answer:

> Sun

Turn the thick cardboard pages and you see more answers. Readers see what the baby in the buggy sees. Each page has bright colorful art and a naming word, a label for the picture. In this book, the labels are all nouns. In other naming books, the labels are all verbs.

Baby in a Buggy is a question-and-answer book. The book asks a question, then answers it. The question-and-answer book is a simple *problem and solution* plot pattern. In this book, the question is stated quite clearly. In other board books, you simply see a series of names or labels. The questions are implied. This allows adults reading the book to ask, "What is this?" as they read the book to the child. Parents use this back-and-forth dialogue as a normal part of conversation with children of this age. It helps children learn about the world around them.

As with fiction board books, it is quite unusual to see two names on the front of a board book. Labels are often the only text that nonfiction board books have, so most nonfiction board books are written by author-illustrators. Unless you have a very unusual concept, an editor is not going to pay you to write eight to ten words for someone else to illustrate.

PICTURE IT! | *Welcome to My World*

Nonfiction board books take a close-up look at the world of an infant. Find five nonfiction board books in the bookstore or the library. After you list the book titles in your reading log, make a storyboard for each one. Draw a square for each page of the book, and write the name of the object pictured there. Now ask yourself, "What does this book show readers?" *Baby in a Buggy* shows readers what the baby in the buggy could see. Does the book you storyboarded name different animals? Or is it a book of baby faces, with babies laughing, eating, crying?

Write about your discoveries in your writer's journal. Did each book have a central topic, or was it more of a stream of consciousness pattern? Were the books you read "original" board books or reprints of famous picture books? Did you want to share these books with a toddler, or did they leave you cold? Why? ✦

Picture Books
Concept Books

The first nonfiction picture books are concept books for toddlers and preschoolers. A concept book is an idea book. For toddlers and preschoolers, the concepts are very simple. Concept books show colors, numbers, letters, and other simple ideas such as shapes, sizes, opposites, and spatial relationships (i.e., over, under). Just as they did with board books, parents and children read these books to develop language. "What is this?" the parent asks, and the child names the object in the book. Children learn how to search for information in these very simple nonfiction books.

Brown Bear, Brown Bear, What Do You See?, by Bill Martin Jr., is a concept book that begins with a question:

> Brown Bear,
> Brown Bear,
> What do you see?

The answer is on the other side of the spread:

> I see a red bird
> looking at me.

This simple book works on many levels. Each spread has a different animal and each animal is a different color. The words on each spread rhyme, helping the child memorize the text like a song. The children then "read" this book by reciting the rhyme as they turn the pages, another step in learning how to read.

The *question-and-answer* pattern in this book makes it *predictable*. Children see the brown bear on this double spread and, with the answer, know what is

---

OTHER CONCEPT BOOKS

Although educators and librarians refer to books about colors and numbers as concept books, some publishers use the term for a different type of book. A concept is an idea, after all! Other concept books are about *self-concept* (self-esteem) and *social issues* such as disabilities, disease, and death. Social issue books fit into all three genres: fiction, nonfiction, and poetry. Before you begin writing, read as many books about your topic as you can find. This will help you decide which genre is best for you, let you know what works and what doesn't, as well as provide you with a list of publishers who have published books about your topic.

coming next. It will be a red bird. Preschoolers love predictable books. They like to know what is coming next.

Each spread in this concept book does five things at once. It's a color book, an animal book, a question-and-answer book, a predictable book, and a rhyming book. All this with only one sentence a page! You can see why this book has sold millions of copies. The secret to selling a concept book is to keep it simple and make every word work.

PICTURE IT! | *More Than a List*

Find five concept books in the library or the bookstore. Read five books on the same concept (such as shapes or colors) or five books by the same writer (like Bill Martin Jr.). Write the titles in your reading log, and in your writer's journal, create a picture book storyboard for one of the books. Draw a square for each page of the book, and with a phrase, write what happens there. Then look at how the book is organized.

PLOT PATTERNS FOR YOUNG NONFICTION

Question and Answer (a variation of the problem-resolution pattern)
Sequence (numbers, letters, days of the week)
A Day in the Life (begins in the morning, ends at night)
Predictable (a clue in the text tells you what happens next)
Cumulative (repeats and builds, like *The House That Jack Built*)
The Journey (travels from one place to another)
Cause and Effect (one thing leads to another)
Compare and Contrast (an elephant is big, a mouse is small)
Definition (tells what something is)

Is the book merely a random list, where the page order could be changed without affecting the outcome? Or do the pages move from one to the next in an organic or logical manner? If the book has a pattern, can you identify it? Did the book have more than one pattern or topic? Did any ideas for new approaches for these books (or your own!) come to you? Explore your thoughts in your writer's journal. ✦

Information Books

Nonfiction picture books explain the world in a way that young children can understand. In very young nonfiction, elements of fiction are used. *Boats*, by Anne Rockwell, uses facts in the text and fiction in the art:

> Boats float.

. . . says the first page of this book. This is true, but the painting on this page shows a bear wearing a sweater and a captain's hat piloting a cabin cruiser called the *Honey-B*. While the boat is accurately drawn, the bear is pure fantasy.

The facts in this simple *definition* book are true. The text defines boats by showing how and where boats work and play. The bears in the book do all the things with boats that people do, making the bears *anthropomorphic*. Information books for young children often use this mix of fantasy in the art and reality in the text.

A Safe Home for Manatees, by Priscilla Belz Jenkins, is also illustrated with paintings, but these animals look and act like real animals. The first page tells you that this is a realistic book:

> In the quiet stillness of the warm Florida lagoon, a baby
> manatee swims close to his mother. She chirps to him,
> and he chirps back.

The fictional elements in this information book are in the words, not the art. All of the information is true, but it is arranged in a narrative fashion. On this first page, the exposition page, you see the *setting*—"In the quiet stillness of the warm Florida lagoon"—and meet the *main characters*—"a baby manatee swims close to his mother." They swim and talk the way real manatees do. "She chirps to him, and he chirps back." (Action and reaction or *cause and effect*.) The title, *A Safe Home for Manatees*, gives you a hint of the story problem. Overcoming this problem (a *problem-resolution* pattern) is the crux of the book.

Starting the book with a mother and child adds another pattern, the *familiar to unfamiliar* pattern. The book begins with something that children know, a family. After establishing this common ground, children can learn about something new: habitat, endangerment, and sanctuary. Each new idea is closely linked to the mother and child, keeping the book tightly focused.

FACTION

Stories that blend fact and fiction are called *faction*. Faction moves beyond the use of narrative elements, such as setting, character, and a story problem. Using setting and a story problem doesn't change what happens in the real world. Faction, however, presents facts in a story that is clearly fiction. The characters in these stories do things that could never happen in the real world.

The Magic School Bus books, written by Joanna Cole and illustrated by Bruce Degen, are the most famous example of faction. These books have four story lines on every spread. The first story line is the fantasy story in the text where the kids and their teacher go on magical adventures with a school bus that can change into anything (even a surfboard!). The second story line is the fantasy story in the captions, where jokes abound and everyone, even inanimate objects, has their say. Each spread also has nonfiction "school reports" on yellow notebook paper. Only two or three sentences long, each report in this third story line acts as a science sound byte, explaining the concepts on the page. The fourth story line is in the nonfiction elements added to each page. Labels, maps, charts, and timelines extend the text page after page. With four story lines, these pages are jam-packed!

PICTURE IT! | *Mix and Match*

How much fiction is mixed with fact in the picture book world? It's your turn to read and find out! Visit the bookstore or the library and read five nonfiction picture books. (Remember to write the titles in your reading log.) After you read each book, go back and look for fictional elements in the text. How would you categorize each book?

A. The text is faction. The events that take place could not happen in real life.
   (Real school buses don't turn into surfboards.)

B. Only the art is fiction. Everything in the words could be illustrated realistically.
   (Boats float. The bears in the art are anthropomorphic, that is, they act like humans.)

C. The text uses narrative (with setting, character, and action) to present the facts.
   (In a Florida lagoon, a mother and baby manatee chirp to one another.) ✦

Picture Book Biographies

Biographies, real stories from the lives of real people, are introduced to children in the picture book format. Today's biographers don't invent facts or dialogue, as was done in years past. Biographers writing for children use primary resources, just like any other historian would use. They research documents written by and about the person during the individual's lifetime. They also read enough to get a feel for the time in which the person lived. If you are going to represent the life of a person to a child, you must be accurate. What you write may be the first introduction a child will have to the individual profiled in the biography.

So how do you fit an entire life into a picture book? Some biographies focus on a *single event* in the life of a famous person. Others begin with a *life-changing event* in childhood and follow that child to his adult years, when he makes a difference in the world. Still others cover *birth to death*—in thirty-two illustrated pages—by focusing on how that person came to be famous.

You Forgot Your Skirt, Amelia Bloomer!, by Shana Corey, begins this way:

> Amelia Bloomer
> was NOT a proper lady.

Amelia Bloomer was a suffragette, a woman who wanted to change the world. Here, in a single sentence, her personality is summed up: "Amelia Bloomer was NOT a proper lady." With this introduction, the reader expects someone who makes waves, and that is the story of Amelia Bloomer's life. Bloomer is famous for the article of clothing named after her, the bloomer. After introducing Bloomer, the text delivers an account of how the bloomer came to be and how it changed the world of fashion.

This picture book biography follows two patterns at once. The picture book text focuses on a single event in a famous person's life. The Author's Note on the last page is a birth to death account. Both focus on the one thing that made Amelia famous, the bloomer. Written primarily for older children and adults, the Author's Note goes into more detail about Bloomer's life and the women's movement. Just like the picture book text, the Author's Note ends with words about how the clothes we wear today were influenced by the bloomers that Amelia championed. The same life can be written about in many different ways.

Let Me Count the Ways

With so many kinds of picture books, you can see why "one size fits all" doesn't apply to page counts. Concept books for preschoolers with just one sentence a page will most certainly have a lower page count than the picture book biographies written for older readers. Two to three typed double-spaced pages are probably best for preschoolers. Six to nine typed double-spaced pages are just enough for elementary school–age readers. Picture books for older readers may fill ten pages or more. Before you submit your manuscript, find other books like yours and compare them.

PICTURE BOOKS FOR OLDER READERS

Picture book biographies are often written for readers older than the picture book age. For books that cannot be illustrated with photographs, this format is ideal. Older picture books may be longer than the traditional thirty-two pages. You may find forty or forty-eight pages in these picture books.

Wilma Unlimited: How Wilma Rudolph Became the World's Fastest Woman, by Kathleen Krull, is written for different ages, depending on who you ask. *Booklist* categorizes the reading age for this picture book biography as grades 2 to 5. *Kirkus Review* says ages 6 to 9. Amazon.com lists it for both ages 4 to 8 and ages 9 to 12. Barnes and Noble recommends ages 5 to 10.

Wilma Unlimited begins with Wilma's birth and follows her through childhood until she becomes, as promised in the subtitle, the world's fastest woman. This biography follows the *childhood to adulthood* pattern. Wilma's famous accomplishment is the climax of the book. The Author's Note on the last page tells the reader what happened after Wilma won three Olympic gold medals at age twenty. This back matter item gives the entire book a *birth to death* pattern.

The confusion over the age of the reader for this biography stems from the difference between the traditional age range for picture books (4 to 8) and the material covered in that format. If you find a picture book with many ages listed, you have found a book for older readers.

PICTURE IT! | *What's in a Number?*

So how do publishers figure out the readers' ages for picture book biographies? Let's see if you can guess which age goes with which book. For this exercise, go to the bookstore or the library, and open as many picture book biographies as you can find. Skim them quickly, and write down the book titles and the ages of the children you think will read the books. Also make a note of the age the publishers recommend. After you make a list of titles and ages, log on to the Internet, and read what the reviewers say about the age of the readers.

Type in the titles of the books you read; after you find each book, read the reviews listed there. How close were your guesses? Did the reviewers agree with you or the publishers, or did they suggest ages that were all over the place? Write about your findings and feelings on the matter in your writer's journal. List any books that you read in your reading log.

FINDING BOOK REVIEWS ON THE WEB

Check the online bookstores:
    Amazon.com
    Barnesandnoble.com
    Borders.com

Or use a search engine, and find out what educators, librarians, and children themselves think:

google.com	(This "spider" search engine finds words inside a document.)
c4.com	("Parallel" searches comb through ten search engines simultaneously.)
searchenginecolossus.com	(Search 161 countries around the world in English, French, or Spanish.)

Easy Readers
Emergent Readers

Easy readers also introduce children to the real world. Just as they do in fiction, these readers grow with the children. Emergent readers are the first step. Children at this reading level know how to read just a few words. This makes nonfiction emergent readers a challenge to write. Writing accurate information with just a few words is difficult, but how can you tell someone's life story with a handful of words? For this reason, nonfiction emergent readers are almost always information books.

Publishers often categorize emergent readers as Level 1 books. *I Am Water,* by Jean Marzollo, is a Level 1 information book easy reader. This simple *defini-tion* book shows the reader the many forms that water takes:

> I am snow for sledding.

Most of the spreads in this thirty-two-page book have a single sentence. This gives you one new idea per spread. The words on this page are quite visual. You see snow and sleds as soon as you read it! Nothing ambiguous here.

Another "learning to read" pattern comes from music and poetry. Like a song with a chorus, this book uses a "refrain" that alternates with the "verses." The verses, in this case, are the sentences with the repeating sentence pattern. Since the refrain is repeated, too, it is easy for the reader to remember. When readers know so few words, you must write pictures in the words and use as many other tools as you can find.

Early Readers

Early readers are the next step up in the easy reader category. Children at this reading level are usually in the first or second grade, and by this time, they know two hundred to five hundred words by sight. They also have the ability to sound out new words. This gives you more room to move.

Bats: Creatures of the Night, by Joyce Milton, is an information book and a Level 2 reader:

> Outside the cave,
> a screech owl
> sits high in a tree.
> Suddenly the owl swoops down!
> Just in time, the young bat
> darts out of the way.

Longer sentences broken into phrases are the sign of an early reader. Three sentences type out to six lines on this double spread. The page is also typed out as if it were double-spaced. The white space around each word, called *leading*, helps young readers see the words more clearly.

Look at all the word pictures. The first sentence shows the first *character* on the page: "a screech owl." The *setting* is also detailed. The owl is "outside the cave," where it "sits high in a tree." As soon as the reader knows where the owl is . . . *action*! "Suddenly, the owl swoops down!" This is quickly followed by *reaction* as "the young bat darts out of the way." The second character on this page gets away "just in time." From stillness to a life and death moment . . . in just twenty-seven words. The active verbs make it happen quickly: "the owl swoops" and "the young bat darts." Early readers crave action, even in their nonfiction. Every sentence in an early reader moves the story forward.

With character, setting, and action, this information book uses a narrative style. None of the bats are named, however, as they would be in a fiction story. Instead, they are described in more scientific terms, such as "spotted bats" or "big brown bats." A simple chart (a nonfiction element) shows bat sizes, from the largest bat, a "Samoan flying fox," down to the smallest, the "bumblebee bat." This *definition* book also uses the *compare and contrast* pattern as the reader learns about different types of bats.

Transitional Readers

Biographies in the easy reader category usually begin with transitional readers. The large number of words that children can read at this stage gives the writer enough words to tell a real-life story, a biography. Level 3 and Level 4 easy reader biographies are fully illustrated in color. The illustrations help the reader understand the words in the story.

Easy reader biographies are structured just like picture book biographies. Some easy readers focus on a single incident in a famous person's life. Others give an overview, from birth to death, focusing on the accomplishment that made the person famous. *Clyde Tombaugh and the Search for Planet X*, by Margaret K. Wetterer, begins by retelling a childhood experience that shaped this world-renown astronomer's life, the first time he looked through a telescope.

> Twelve-year-old Clyde waited
> while his mother and father looked
> at the night sky through the telescope.
> Although Clyde had never looked
> through a telescope before,
> he knew it would make faraway things
> look bigger and closer.

This real-life story begins when Clyde is not much older than the reader. As the pages turn, the reader follows Clyde as he grows. The problems that Clyde encounters are discussed in a narrative fashion, in a *problem-resolution* pattern. The narrative ends on a high note, when at age twenty-four, Clyde Tombaugh discovers the planet we now call Pluto. This easy reader biography keeps the promise it made in the title: *Clyde Tombaugh and the Search for Planet X.* Clyde searches for Planet X and he finds it!

The front matter and back matter extend the book beyond the twelve years chronicled in this story. The Author's Note on page 3 comes before the story, making it *front matter.* Sky watching in ancient times, the invention and use of the telescope, the subsequent discovery of the seventh and eight planets, and the reason why there might be a ninth planet are covered in this introduction. After the discovery of Planet X in the text, the Afterword on page 47 tells more about Clyde's discovery and his life's work. Page 48 has a time line of "Important Dates" in Tombaugh's life. This book has one page of front matter and two pages of back matter. The story in the biography is tightly focused. The front and back matter add another dimension.

PICTURE IT! | *Which Lens Is Best?*

Biographies for the young reader snap a word picture of someone's life and share it in just a few pages. When the Tombaugh biography was published, Clyde Tombaugh was ninety years old. Yet the story of his life fit into a forty-eight-page book! The biography itself was like a zoom lens, focusing on only twelve years. The front and back matter added the rest of Tombaugh's life and hundred of years of sky watching, with a wide-angle lens. You can tell a big story in a small amount of space by using different lenses at different times.

Look at other young biographies and see which lenses they used where. Go to the bookstore or the library and find five easy reader (or picture book) biographies. After you read all five books, fill out the questionnaire to see how the book was plotted.

YOUNG BIOGRAPHY PLOT QUESTIONNAIRE
The Story
1. Where does the narrative (the story of the person's life) begin?

A. At birth

B. In childhood

C. With adulthood

2. On what page of the narrative do you find out the person's life passion?

A. On the very first page of text

B. On the second page of text

C. After several pages of text

3. Does the story end on a high note?

A. Yes, the story ends with the person's great accomplishment.

B. No, the story ends with the person's death.

4. How many years of the person's life does the narrative cover?

The Front Matter

1. How does the front matter introduce the story in the biography?

A. It tells the reader about the person's background.

B. It tells the reader about the times in which the person lived.

C. It tells the reader about the person's field of study.

2. What types of front matter are used?

A. Author's Note

B. Preface or Introduction

C. Maps and charts

D. Other _____

3. How many pages are devoted to front matter?

The Back Matter

1. How does the back matter conclude the story in the biography?

A. It tells the reader about the rest of the person's life.

B. It gives a birth to death summary of the person's life.

C. It tells the reader more about the events of the story.

2. What types of back matter are used?

A. Author's Note

B. Epilogue

C. Maps and charts

D. Other _____

3. How many pages are devoted to back matter?

Write the titles in your reading log, then look over your answers to this questionnaire. Did the books use different camera lenses? Did they zoom in for the narrative and use a wide-angle lens for the front and back matter? Do you think you could write an easy reader biography with this zoom lens / wide-angle lens approach? Who would you like to write about? Brainstorm ten possible names. Record your thoughts in your writer's journal. ✦

Photo-Essays

Art is nothing without form.
—GUSTAVE FLAUBERT

After the picture book and the easy reader, nonfiction readers move up to the photo-essay. As fiction for this age moves into chapter books illustrated in black and white, nonfiction keeps its color. In years past, photo-essays were illustrated with black-and-white photographs, and older nonfiction books had only black-and-white line drawings, but all that has changed. As technology changed the printing process, publishers used color photographs in children's nonfiction. Children liked the new color photographs, and so did parents, teachers, and librarians. Photo-essays with full-color photographs sold so well, they became the new standard in children's nonfiction.

Young Photo-Essays

Young photo-essays look like picture books, so the two are often confused. In a young photo-essay, the photos and the words work together to tell a bigger story than either one could tell by itself, just like they do in a picture book. The difference between a young photo-essay and a picture book is the complexity of the language. Now that your readers are older, you are able to use words that younger readers may not understand.

Outside and Inside Dinosaurs, by Sandra Markle, delivers exactly what the title promises.

> Look at the X ray of a living alligator's bones and a dinosaur's *skeleton*. In the process of becoming fossils, the dinosaur's skeleton fell apart into a pile of bones. To put the skeleton together, researchers study the bony framework of similar living animals like alligators.

Fossilization is described in picture words: "the dinosaur's skeleton fell apart into a pile of bones." The cue for the photographs comes out of the text. A large color photograph of a "living alligator" fills two-thirds of this page. In the lower corner, the reader sees the X-ray photograph. On the facing page is a color photograph of "a dinosaur's *skeleton.*" This nonfiction photo-essay uses the *compare and contrast* pattern.

Young photo-essays are short and to the point. Single spreads have one or two paragraphs and photographs often fill two-thirds of the page. Double spreads pair full-page photographs with one to four paragraphs of text on the facing page.

Technical vocabulary (skeleton, fossils, researchers, framework) strengthens the young photo-essay. The sophistication of the language separates the young photo-essay from the picture book. At the same time, the terms are carefully explained. In this excerpt, skeleton is italicized the first time it is used. Italicized words are defined in the Glossary/Index sections of such nonfiction books. The glossary also has a pronunciation guide.

PICTURE IT! | *One to One*

When children learn to count, they learn that each number has a name. That's one-to-one correspondence. Young photo-essays work the same way. With one new idea per page or spread, the text and the photo that goes with it must match exactly—one to one. When the text talks about a baleen whale, that is exactly what the photo must show.

Visit the bookstore or library, and find five young photo-essays by *Seymour Simon.* Read them and write the titles in your reading log. Now look carefully at the one-to-one correspondence. Notice how the photos go hand in hand with the text on each page. Don't let the large font size fool you! These books have only one to three paragraphs per page. Words from one page don't carry over to the next. The words match the photo exactly. There is one idea per page, or per spread. One short explanation matches one large color photo, one to one.

If you wish to study young photo-essays with more text, step up to books by Caroline Arnold. Some spreads in her young photo-essays have three to five paragraphs, and ideas may flow over two or three spreads. The photos, however, still match the text directly.

What do you think about these young photo-essays? How do they compare to illustrated picture books on similar topics? If you had an open book contract for a young photo-essay, what would your topic be? Capture your thoughts in your writer's journal. ✦

Young Photo-Essay Biographies

Young photo-essay biographies have a 50:50 mix of art and text. By necessity, these biographies are about individuals who lived in the age of photography. This is why there are so many picture book biographies for older readers. You can't create a photo-essay without photos, and finding photos that match all of the events in your story can be difficult.

Norman Rockwell: Storyteller with a Brush, by Beverly Gherman, with its ten short chapters, is a step up from a picture book biography. Each chapter is four to six pages long. Black-and-white photographs of Rockwell and full-color reproductions of his art fill half of each chapter. Rockwell himself began to use photographs in his work in the 1930s. Here is a sample paragraph from the book:

> Once the photographs were developed, he spread them out all over the floor to chose the ones he liked best. Then he made a few small pencil sketches to organize his material. At last he was ready to do a full-sized charcoal drawing. He liked to vary the size from time to time, but he never did a cover so large that it wouldn't fit in a taxicab or a car for its trip to the *Post*'s office in Philadelphia. Sometimes he made the painting as small as the actual cover would be (eleven by eleven inches), but most of the time he painted large oils and let the art director reduce them to fit the magazine.

The details here make this passage come alive. The reader sees what Rockwell is doing step-by-step. (The steps are typed in capital letters.) "ONCE the photographs were developed, he spread them out all over the floor" Why? "To chose the ones he liked best." "THEN he made a few small pencil sketches" Why? "To organize his material." "AT LAST he was ready to do a full-sized charcoal drawing." One action leads to the next.

Norman Rockwell was famous for his illustrations, which are the focus of

FINDING PHOTOS

When you write a photo-essay, you may be asked to find your own photos. "I was responsible for all the photos for *Clara Schumann: Piano Virtuoso*," says author Susanna Reich.

Trade publishers consider finding the photographs a part of creating the book. In *Children's Writer*, Dutton Publisher Stephanie Owens Lurie says, "With all of our recent photo-essay acquisitions, the authors were either photographers or arranged for the photos." Unlike picture books, where the writer splits the royalty with the artist, if you find your own photographs, all of the royalty is yours.

If you are required to find photographs, it will be specified in your contract. Some publishers set aside a photo allowance, which pays for the permission fees and covers the printing costs for the photographs you submit.

If your contract does not have a separate photo allowance, the money for the permissions and copies comes out of your advance. This puts the burden on you to spend wisely. There is no standard permissions fee. The photographer decides what the photo will cost.

School and library publishers often have contracts that ask you to write *art specs* instead of finding your own photographs. Author Tanya Stone has "published almost thirty nonfiction books for kids that had photographs. For the vast majority of those, I compiled a photo 'wish list' that the art department or the photo research person then uses to gather photos from a variety of sources."

Writing art specs is quite common for nonfiction series books, as the look of the series is already established. The art department finds all of the photographs and pays the permission and copy costs. Before you write the book, the publisher tells you how many photographs you will need. In the manuscript, you describe or *specify* the type of photographs you would like to see.

If the art department is finding the photos, they may send you copies. Stone "selected the 25 to 30 photos from the 500 or so images the publisher" sent. For my two nonfiction series, the publisher sent some photos before I began writing. They found others after the manuscripts were edited.

this *birth to death* biography. After his birth is mentioned, readers meet "a pale, skinny eight-year-old" who "began sketching the characters" while his father read Dickens at night. (This is a good age to zero in on because the intended readers are also eight years old.)

This photo-essay jumps right into the story without any front matter. In the back matter, the *Important Dates* time line page begins with Rockwell's birth and ends with his death and the death of his wife. Two pages of *Notes* list background information and source material in chronological order, by chapter and page. The *Selected Bibliography* gives a full citation for selected sources listed in the Notes. The *Illustration Credits* fill two pages and are listed chronologically by their order in the book. Photographers are named; magazine covers are dated; and the method, size, and location of Rockwell's paintings are noted.

PAGE COUNTS

Young photo-essay manuscripts are longer than picture book manuscripts, averaging about ten to twenty typed double-spaced pages. Fiction manuscripts for this age fill forty to sixty manuscript pages, but the art is not a factor in the writing of these books. Young photo-essays are coffee table books for the younger set. A picture is worth a thousand words, so when you have both in a photo-essay, you can write less and say more.

PICTURE IT! | *Picture Book or Photo-Essay?*

If you want to write a biography for younger readers, how do you decide which format to use? Should you write a picture book or a photo-essay? Select a famous person and take the Picture Book or Photo-Essay quiz.

PICTURE BOOK OR PHOTO-ESSAY QUIZ

1. Was this person born in the age of photography?
   No? Write a picture book for older readers instead and let an illustrator paint the scenes.
   Yes? Go to question two.
2. Are photographs of this person "static poses" or "action shots"?
   Static poses work better in books where the text tells most of the story.

Action shots work best for younger readers, who rely on the pictures to tell much of the story.

3. Do the photographs match your story?

No? Write a picture book for older readers using the photos you found as reference materials.

Yes? You're getting closer! Go to question four.

4. Are there enough pictures to tell the entire story?

No? Investigate other sources and try again.

Yes? Start writing those permission letters! (You need permission to use someone else's photos.) ✦

Middle Grade
"Sound Byte" Information Books

Some middle-grade information photo-essays can also be called "sound byte" books. Instead of traditional chapters, these information photo-essays change topic with each page turn. Each double spread has its own heading and acts as its own chapter. The "story" in the book builds from spread to spread.

The topic on each double spread in *Emergency!*, by Joy Masoff, could fill a book of its own; yet in this information photo-essay, each topic is covered in two pages. Topics include "12 Things Every ER Needs," "Under the Knife," and "Milestones in Medicine." Tight writing is the name of the game. Photos fill up half of each spread. Photo captions take up space, and so do the sidebars and boxes on each spread. You must get to the point, and quickly, in a sound byte book.

> IN THE BLINK OF AN EYE . . .
>
> An accident has just happened. A midfield collision during a ball game has left one player motionless on the field. A crowd gathers, unable to do anything but worry. The coach kneels at the side of a player, trying, with trembling fingers, to feel the soft rhythm of a PULSE, a sign that the heart is still moving blood through the body. The injured player needs help, but everyone feels helpless. What can they do? Where can they even begin?

After a doctor introduces the field of emergency medicine, this book begins with an accident and follows the process from the 911 call to hospitalization. Unlike a fiction story, which would name both the player and the coach (and talk about their emotions), this information book uses narrative only to set the scene. The player and the coach are not the focus of the book. Rather, it is the emergency medical system that is the main "character" of this book.

The pictures in the words are clear. The paragraph begins with setting: "An accident has just happened." More specifics follow: "A midfield collision during a ball game has left one player motionless on the field." This unfortunate action causes a reaction: "A crowd gathers, unable to do anything but worry." The camera zooms in: "The coach kneels at the side of a player, trying, with trembling fingers, to feel the soft rhythm of a PULSE."

The coach's reaction to the accident leads the reader to a science concept. The science word is typed in capital letters and is followed by a definition: "PULSE, a sign that the heart is still moving blood through the body." The narration continues with the very next line: "The injured player needs help, but everyone feels helpless." A problem needs resolving. The writer asks the reader: "What can they do? Where can they even begin?" Now the reader is hooked. You have to keep reading to find out what happens next.

PICTURE IT! | *How-To*

How-to books give instructions step-by-step. You have to decide, which step is first? Do you start with the big picture and move down to the tiny details in a *general to specific* pattern? Or do you start small and easy and work your way up to difficult and complicated with the *simple to complex* pattern? Which pattern works best depends on your topic.

Arts and crafts books often start with a big idea and then give specific examples. *Make Sculptures!*, by Kim Solga, opens with "A Note to Grown-Ups" and a double spread for the table of contents. The next double spread, "Be a Good Artist," talks about "Work Habits" (left) and "Art Terms" (right). After a brief definition of sculpture on the Art Terms page, this book gets to work. Each double spread after that is a new sculpture project with a list of "Materials Needed" and numbered step-by-step instructions. The materials, the instructions, and the finished sculptures are all illustrated with photographs. This arts and crafts book introduces many different types of sculpture as it moves from general to specific.

Ice Skating Basics, by Aaron Foeste, is a sports instruction chapter book. The table of contents shows how the book is organized.

1   Ice Skates of All Types
2   Fitting, Purchasing, and Caring for Skates
3   Getting Started: What You'll Need
4   The Adult Beginner
5   The Basics
6   Teaching a Child to Skate
7   Moving On: Intermediate Skating
8   Skating Backward
9   Awesome Forward Crossovers
10 Amazing Backward Crossovers
11 Power Skating and Skating Tips

This book begins with a simple idea: "Ice Skates of All Types." "Fitting, Purchasing, and Caring for Skates" is next, followed by "What You'll Need" (mittens, wrist guards, pads). Once you're out on the ice, it's time to learn how to skate. The skating moves photographed and explained step-by-step in this book become more complicated as the pages turn. From "The Basics" you move on to "Intermediate Skating," then "Skating Backward" and "Forward Crossovers," followed by "Backward Crossovers." The book ends with "Power Skating." For the overall structure of this book, simple to complex works best.

Go to the bookstore or the library and read five simple how-to books. After you write the titles in your reading log, take a closer look at each book's table of contents. The chapter or section titles will usually tell you how the book is organized. Does the book begin with a general introduction and then give specific examples? Or does it start with a simple idea and then grow more complex? Do you think the topic determined which approach worked best? Why or why not? Did you find any books that might have been organized a different way? Outline your findings in your writer's journal. ✦

Collective Biographies

A collective biography tells the life stories of several individuals in a single book. A common thread runs through the book. The lives of the individuals in the book are connected in some way, whether by the time period, life situation, or their life's work. The children in *Voices from the Fields: Children of Migrant Farmworkers Tell Their Stories,* by S. Beth Atkin, all share a common situation in life. In *Around the World in a Hundred Years: From Henry the Navigator to Magellan,* by Jean Fritz, the "characters" are all famous explorers who changed the way Europeans looked at the world. Telling many stories in one place helps readers see the big picture, whether it is a situation in life or a change in history.

In the Line of Fire: Presidents' Lives at Stake, by Judith St. George, looks at presidential assassination attempts. The events in this collective biography are told in chronological order. The assassination stories (Lincoln, Garfield, McKinley, and Kennedy) are organized in chronological order, as are the survivor stories, from Andrew Jackson in 1835 to Ronald Reagan in 1981. The events themselves are also told chronologically.

> The doctors agreed that immediate surgery was necessary to save the president's life. Nancy Reagan insisted on seeing her husband first. Ronald Reagan had always depended on jokes and stories to get a point across or to lighten up a difficult situation. Trying to reassure his wife, he quipped, "Honey, I forgot to duck."
>
> Republican President Reagan even managed a joke in the operating room. "I hope you people are all Republicans," he said to the doctors.
>
> "Today, we're all Republicans, Mr. President," replied the surgeon, who happened to be a liberal Democrat.
>
> During his thirteen-day hospital stay, Reagan learned that the gunman had been overpowered moments after the shooting.

A personality trait is mentioned: "Ronald Reagan had always depended on jokes and stories to get a point across or to lighten up a difficult situation." In the next line, the writer uses Picture Writing to show the trait in action: "Trying to reassure his wife, he quipped, 'Honey, I forgot to duck.'" Immediately afterward, another illustration in words: "Republican President Reagan even managed a joke in the operating room. 'I hope you people are all Republicans,' he said to the doctors."

Biographies use narrative to move readers through the scene. Action: "The

PAGE COUNTS

For middle-grade nonfiction, page counts may vary from 60 to 100 typed double-spaced manuscript pages. Although this is less than the 100 to 150 pages typically sold for a middle-grade novel, once again, the visual elements come into play, extending the text in ways that words alone cannot. When you add the text for the boxes and sidebars, your page count may be higher.

Most nonfiction books for middle graders are sold at the book proposal stage; so rather than writing the book and sending it, you send a proposal to an editor instead. Although you need to have a page count in mind when you send a proposal, once you have sold the book and begin writing it, your editor will work with you on the exact page count.

doctors agreed that immediate surgery was necessary to save the president's life." Reaction: "Nancy Reagan insisted on seeing her husband first." Action: "Nancy Reagan sees her husband." Reaction: "Trying to reassure his wife, he quipped, 'Honey, I forgot to duck.'"

Immediately after mentioning the surgery, the story moves to recovery: "During his thirteen-day hospital stay . . ." Every sentence moves the story forward. There are enough details to inform readers, but not so many that the story bogs down in minutiae.

Collective biographies tell many stories in a single volume. Readers who want to find out more about the individuals or life situations chronicled in these collections can look for other books about these topics.

From Middle Grade to Young Adult

All topics are open game in YA literature.
—SHERRY GARLAND, *Writing for Young Adults*

Fewer Photo Ops

As readers grow into middle grade, photographs begin to disappear from their books. The ratio of photographs to text moves from 50:50 to 25:75. Some of the space used for photographs is replaced with charts and graphs, maps and diagrams. These nonfiction elements illustrate the ideas in the words, but they are not photographs. As children grow, not every idea in their books can be illustrated with a photograph.

The only photo in *Private and Personal: Questions and Answers for Girls Only* is on the cover. Written by Carol Weston, the columnist for *Girl's Life* magazine, this book is a collection of letters.

> Dear Carol,
>
> I think my best friend is trying to steal my boyfriend. She tells me he cheats on me and she calls him a lot. I don't want to lose my best friend or boyfriend.
>
> Fallen in Love

> Dear Fallen,
>
> Your friend isn't being very friendly. Assuming your boyfriend cares about you, can he think of anyone who might like to go out with her (so she can leave you two alone)? Tell your friend that it bothers you that she calls your guy so much and that you'd appreciate it if she backed off a little.

There are actions in the words, but you don't need a photograph to see them. In fact, there are no illustrations of any kind in this book. It doesn't need maps, charts, or diagrams to show readers what is happening. The teen writes, "She tells me he cheats on me and she calls him a lot." The pictures in the words are clear.

Young Adult Biographies

Biographies for young adults deal with the entire person, warts and all. Teenagers are well aware of adult imperfections. This is the age when they rebel against adult authority. Reading about the entire life of someone famous allows readers to see the choices that individuals can make and what the effects these choices have, both good and bad.

Young adult photo-essay biographies use the 25:75 approach. One-quarter of the book is illustrated and three-quarters of the book is text. Now that readers are older, most of these books take a *birth to death* approach to biography. Young adult biographies look not only at a person's life, but also at that person's place in the world. The writer shares specific details to help readers understand the customs of another time. In the end, readers want to know why this person was famous. How did this person change the world?

After talking about how Plains Indians gained honor by risking their lives, *Sitting Bull and His World*, by Albert Marrin, shows the reader Sitting Bull's first coup. (Sitting Bull's childhood nickname was translated as "Slow" or "Thoughtful One" because as an infant he examined his food slowly and carefully before he ate it.)

> An experienced warrior would have flung himself to one side of his horse to avoid the arrow. Not Slow. He came like whirlwind, leaning forward with an outstretched coup stick. Before the Crow could shoot, he whacked him across the arm, spoiling his aim. The arrow flew off harmlessly. *"On-hey!"* the boy shouted at the top of his voice. "I, Slow, have conquered him!" The others arrived seconds later. They killed the Crow and went on to kill a few more of his companions. Next morning they started back. 16

Here you see detail from Sitting Bull's world interwoven with his own life experience. First the world: "An experienced warrior would have flung himself to one side of his horse to avoid the arrow." Then Sitting Bull's experience: "He came like whirlwind, leaning forward with an outstretched coup stick." The action in the pictures moves quickly. The mention of seconds alerts the reader to how quickly things are happening. Then, in the next two sentences, time slows down, and day turns to night and back to day: "Next morning they started back. 16"

The number 16 refers readers to the notes at the back of the book. Organized by chapter, these notes refer to the author's reference source. The page number in the reference source is also cited. For ease of use, the note numbers start with one for each chapter. Original source material is critical when a book delves so deeply into a person's life. The back matter also includes an extensive list of additional books to read and an index. Scholarship is especially important in biographies.

 PICTURE IT! | *Counting YA*

How long is a young adult nonfiction book? It depends! Look at the young adult nonfiction books at the bookstore or library. Some books have about one hundred pages, and others have over three hundred! Open as many young adult nonfiction books as you can, and write down the page count, the publisher, and the topic.

Did you see any trends? Were the thin books published as part of a series, while the thicker ones were mostly individual titles? Did the thin books look as if they were written for school reports? Were the thick books about personal topics, like sex and dating? Did you find the same publishers over and over? Or did you find that there weren't any trends? Record your findings in your writer's journal. Write the titles of any books you read in your reading log. ✦

What Do Editors Want to See?

Learn to structure and organize your work well.

—LIONEL BENDER, EDITORIAL DIRECTOR FROM AN INTERVIEW IN *Children's Writer*

When it comes to nonfiction, editors want to see logic. For a nonfiction book to work, it needs to be well organized. Simply gathering lots of information is not enough. To share information with your readers, you must organize your thoughts.

Writing a book is like building a house. If you have a blueprint, then you know how to build the book. Having a blueprint helps you decide what to place where so everything makes sense. Logic dictates where the pipes and wires go so that when you need them, the lights turn on and the water flows. The reader doesn't need to know how you built the house; they just want to live there and enjoy it. They don't see the blueprint; they see the results.

Chapter Four

Seeing Poetry

 I wish our clever young poets would remember my homely definitions of prose and poetry; that is, prose,—words in their best order; poetry,—the best words in their best order.
—SAMUEL TAYLOR COLERIDGE

Poetry looks at the world with a zoom lens. It moves up close and snaps a picture, or it captures a moment in time. Poetry looks at the world around us, taking events both real and imagined and bringing them into sharper focus.

Every word in a poem has to work triple time. Each word must fit into the pattern of spoken music that is poetry. Each word must show a picture and capture the image the poet has in her mind. Each word must move the reader deeper into the story of the poem.

Poetry written for children and young adults today matches their developmental stages. Knowing the stages of *poetry appreciation* can help you find the best place for your writing. One size doesn't fit all. If your poetry doesn't match the age it was written for, the editor will not buy it. Editors buy what sells in the marketplace.

The first stage of poetry appreciation is *word play*. Infants and toddlers learn how to speak by playing with words. Poetry with word play is enjoyed for years. The word play just gets more sophisticated as the children grow.

After children learn to speak, they learn about story. *Narrative poetry* is the second stage of poetry appreciation. In a picture book, a single narrative poem tells a story. Narrative poems also grow with the reader.

Lyrical poetry shares the thoughts and feelings of another person. Although lyrical poetry is the type most commonly written, children do not appreciate it until they are able to see another person's point of view. This usually begins after the age of seven.

Board Books

> The step from Mother Goose to other forms of poetry is a small one.
> —LEE BENNETT HOPKINS, *Pass the Poetry, Please!*

Almost all of the poetry you see in board books is Mother Goose nursery rhymes. Parents grew up with Mother Goose and want to share these nursery rhymes with their children. Even the name "nursery rhyme" tells you these rhymes are for children in the nursery. Illustrators show their interpretation of these old favorites.

As with fiction and nonfiction board books, poetry board books are primarily a format for illustrators. Nursery rhymes are copyright free, so the price is right! The publisher is only paying one person, the illustrator. Parents are familiar with these rhymes, so the books have a guaranteed audience.

Use the best of nursery rhymes to inspire your writing for the very young. Although editors may not buy board book text from writers, they will buy

ONE VOICE OR MANY?

Where is the best place for you to start? A *picture book poem* is a single poem that tells a story. A *poetry collection* is a group of poems on a single theme written by one poet. A *poetry anthology* reprints poems from many poets.

Begin with yourself. Send your work to a publisher. Don't wait to be "discovered" by an anthologist. As popular as anthologies are with teachers and parents, your chances of being published in an anthology are very slim. Not only must you be aware that an anthologist is gathering poems, your poems must also fit into the anthologist's vision for the collection.

As a literature consultant, I have collected hundreds of poems for textbook publishers. For some programs I collected four times as many poems as were needed, simply to give the curriculum planners a choice. Needless to say, three-quarters of these poems were rejected, and these were published poems!

If you want your work to appear in an anthology, write your own collection first. Skip the hoping and wishing, and start writing!

picture books for the very young. Picture books about new babies and toddler life abound. Use the three R's of writing poetry—rhythm, rhyme, and repetition—and write for these little ones in another format.

PICTURE IT! | *The Stretch Test*

Children learn to speak by playing with language. Recite a poem to an infant or toddler and watch him move to the rhythm of the words. Word play is the first stage of poetry appreciation, and it begins in the nursery, before a child can speak!

As mentioned previously, the young prefer rhyme, so any poetry you find for the nursery, rhymes. Little ones don't always understand the meaning of the words, but the music appeals to them. The music of rhyme reaches all the way into preschool.

Find five Mother Goose rhymes to experiment with rhyme. Give them the stretch test. Read each rhyme aloud and ask yourself, does this still work? When you read it aloud, do you have to *stretch* certain lines to make them fit the rhythm? If so, find another. Mother Goose rhymes are handed down to us from English tradition and the pronunciations have changed over the years. Changing the way you say a word changes the rhythm of the piece.

Mother Goose has a following because of tradition. You don't have this "in" with editors. If you find yourself stretching your own poetry when you read it aloud, rewrite until your poetry rhymes prefectly. After you write the titles of the poetry books you read in your reading log, stretch yourself in your writer's journal. Do you find nursery rhymes appealing? How could you update them? What kind of rhymes do you want to write? ◆

Picture Book Poems

Poetry can also tell a story. Poetry that tells a story is called *narrative* poetry. This poetic form matches the second stage of poetry appreciation. As children grow, they come to love poetry that tells a story.

A picture book poem follows two sets of rules. First, it must be true to poetic form and capture the essence of an experience. Secondly, a narrative poem must also tell a story. This means following the rules of fiction. Your story must build, having a beginning, middle, and end. The pictures in your scenes must change, so you need fifteen different scenes for a picture book poem.

"Hoops," by Robert Burleigh, begins this way:

Hoops.
The game.
Feel it.

From very first line—"Hoops."—you know this is a poem about basketball. The second line has just two words—"The game."—but they also tell you more about the story in the poem. This poem is going to be about a basketball game. More than one person will be playing. How will readers experience the game in this narrative poem? It's in the next line—"Feel it."

With five simple words, the story begins. Readers can see the setting, a basketball game. The characters are the players, and the action will be the game itself. This poem concentrates on the way it feels to play basketball. Readers see the game with a zoom lens, up close.

The feelings are shown with action. As the pages turn, one team makes a basket, and then the other team tries to score. The game is the story. After the second team makes a basket, the book ends. The reader has experienced both defense and offense. The poem ends on a high note, with the ball sliding through the hoop.

This poem had more than fifteen different scenes. If you have a poem with lots of action, remember that when you count single spreads, you have twenty-eight pages to fill. The poem in this book began on page 3, so the poem itself covered thirty pages. Five of those pages were illustrated as double spreads.

Will you be able to direct the artist to break your poem into different pages? The answer is in your poem. If you have enough action in your story, the page breaks will be clear. Fifteen is the minimum number of spreads you need to plan. If you plan for fifteen different spreads, each verse will have two pages of art, or a double spread. This "one idea per spread" plan works quite well with preschoolers.

Older children want more story, so write more action for the older readers. A mix of double and single spreads works quite well. The action moves quickly with lots of single spreads and slows for drama with the double spreads. Fiction writers also use this mix of fast and slow as a storytelling device. If the big moments happen too quickly, readers don't realize they are important. Slowing down gives the characters in the story (and readers) time to think. When writing narrative poetry, use both narrative tools and poetry tools.

Picture book poetry manuscripts follow the fiction page length guidelines, so two to three pages are best for preschool, and five to six pages are more appropriate for elementary school–age readers. When submitting a picture book poetry manuscript, follow both the picture book format and the poetry format. Type the manuscript body with double-spacing between the lines of your poem and triple-spacing between stanzas.

PICTURE IT! | *Poetry on the Move*

Writing a poem that tells a story can be tricky. Some poems just don't have enough action. Go to the bookstore or the library and find five picture book poems. Look in the poetry section or in the picture books section. If you want to write poetry that rhymes, type "stories in rhyme" into the bookstore or library computer. If you prefer poems that don't rhyme, search under "juvenile poetry." Read all five books and write the titles in your reading log.

Now storyboard the poems for action. (For guidance, see the picture book storyboard on page 25.) Draw a little square for each page of the first book, and *write the action* you see on the page in each square. Then storyboard the other four books. Look over all five books, and answer these questions in your writer's journal. Was there enough action to keep the reader interested? Or did the story drag? Were things added to the story just to make it rhyme? Could this story be better told without rhyme? Or did the rhyme add another dimension to the story? ✦

Easy Reader Poetry

> I never understood why people thought that easy-to-read material for children had to be clunky and dull.
>
> —LILIAN MOORE, FROM AN INTERVIEW IN *Pass the Poetry, Please!*

Poems for easy readers are written or selected because of their simple vocabulary. Not only do the poems have to be interesting to children at this age, they also have to include words that easy readers can pronounce. Children at this age still enjoy word play, so the poems can be fun and silly.

Here are two lines from *Soap Soup and Other Verses*, by Karla Kuskin.

> Tick goes the clock.
> The clock goes tock.

There are only five words here: tick, tock, goes, the, clock. These words are very simple and easy to read. At the same time, repetition and word play make the two lines poetry. First you hear the sound: "Tick goes the clock." Flip it over and you start with the clock: "The clock goes tock." Put the two together, and now it rhymes.

The picture is the same for both lines. You see a clock. Word play is about *sound*. The sound changes, and the words make music. Forward and backward, the sentences flip over. It's fun to play with the words!

Line length is also a consideration in easy reader poetry. In our sample, each line is only four words long. In fiction and nonfiction easy readers, long sentences are broken into phrases. The same is true for easy reader poetry. Count the characters (including the spaces between the word and the punctuation) in a line. You will see that easy reader poetry lines are thirty-six characters maximum. Most lines, like those in Kuskin's book, are only twenty characters each. The poems themselves are also short. A sixteen-line poem is considered long.

An easy reader collection has a story line running through it, so that the collection as a whole has a beginning, middle, and an end. This can be done poem by poem, or the poems can be clustered into chapters. In each chapter the poems carry a small story line, and together the chapters build to tell a larger story. With forty to sixty-four pages to fill, easy reader poetry collections have twenty or more poems.

The market for easy reader poetry is extremely small. Currently, only anthologists and well-known poets have published books of poetry for the easy reader. Rather than limit your word choice and line length for this market, use all the words you need, and find a home for your poetry in other markets.

Poetry for the Chapter Book Age

After the easy reader comes the chapter book. Fiction for this age has moved to the books with small type and black-and-white drawings inside. For the most part, poetry books for this age follow the same trend. While the anthologies for this age look like oversized picture books, poetry collections resemble fiction chapter books.

Poetry anthologies for second and third graders include hundreds of poems. Collections for this age are more manageable. Just as the chapter books are slim, so too are the poetry collections. A chapter book collection has twenty to thirty poems. The poems themselves are usually short, rarely extending beyond thirty lines.

A collection may be divided into small chapters or may simply flow from one poem to the next. Just like fiction chapter books, some collections have black-and-white line art on every page, while others have art every few pages.

PICTURE IT! | *Get Dramatic!*

Although the poems in a collection share a theme, they don't have to share the same voice. The narrative voice tells a story. The lyrical voice talks about the poet's feelings. In *Poem-Making: Ways to Begin Writing Poetry*, Myra Cohn Livingston says that with the *dramatic voice*, you "put on the face or body of someone or something else."

The dramatic voice also talks to things that cannot answer. I used this voice to begin *Man on the Moon*, a nonfiction picture book poem about the Apollo 11 mission.

> Moon,
> do you remember
> your first visitors?
>
> It was 1969 . . .
> Astronauts Collins, Aldrin and Armstrong
> suited up.
>
> Each had flown in space,
> but no one had *ever* touched the moon.
> No one.

Only the first stanza is written in the dramatic voice, but I used it to pose a question, which the story in the rest of the book answered. If the moon had answered my question, then another dramatic voice would result: the dramatic voice of dialogue, or conversation.

The names for these dramatic voices come from Greek drama. The first two forms of dramatic voice are monologues. Only one person is speaking. Taking on the voice of another person is called *persona*. (Greek players wore masks, so this form is also called a *mask*.) When a Greek player turned away from the audience to address someone or something not present, that was called an *apostrophe*.

The third dramatic voice is a dialogue. In a *conversation* poem, more than one person speaks. The words of the conversation are the poem. You can help readers keep the voices straight by using italics for one speaker, by typing the words on opposing sides of the page, or by using separate stanzas.

Try it yourself! Write your own dramatic poem. Talk to someone who can't answer. Become something that doesn't have a voice. Create an imaginary conversation. Brainstorm a list of objects found in a classroom, on the playground, and in a child's room. Select one and listen to what it has to say. Write about your experience in your writer's journal. ✦

Middle-Grade Poetry Collections

Poetry for middle graders covers all three stages of poetry appreciation. Middle-grade readers still enjoy word play. And now, they have more words to play with. Middle graders also enjoy story, so narrative poetry appeals to them. The third stage of poetry appreciation begins in the middle grades. As children grow, they see how other people think and feel. Poetry that shares a person's thoughts or feelings is called *lyrical poetry*.

Lyrical poems often begin with "I." Other first person words such as "me," "my," "we," "us," and "our" also help you to identify a lyrical poem. When a poet shares his thoughts and feelings, he often puts himself into the poem.

The name for this form also comes to us from the Greeks. In earlier times, poetry was sung. A stringed instrument called a lyre was played when poetry was sung, so the words were called *lyrics*.

The Mighty Eye

I shrink in my skin
When Mr. Culp
Gives me the mighty eye.

This lyric poem from *If You're Not Here, Please Raise Your Hand: Poems About School*, by Kalli Dakos, shows the reader how the poet felt. The poem begins with "I," a sign that a lyric poem is coming. A physical description shows how the poet feels. "I shrink in my skin." Showing a picture is much more effective than saying, "I was upset."

When and why the child was upset appear in the next two lines: "When Mr. Culp/ Gives me the mighty eye." What child hasn't felt that "mighty eye" staring at them? "Me, too!" says the reader, as he is pulled into the poem. He keeps reading to find out what happens next.

Word choice also makes the writing vivid. The first line could have read, "I shrink in my *chair.*" This is a visual image, something you can see. The choice of the word "skin" is more effective because it's closer to the experience. You don't have to be in a chair to shrink in your skin. You can be anywhere. The word "skin" makes the reader concentrate on the feeling, not the place.

Middle-grade poetry collections vary greatly in length. *Neighborhood Odes,* by Gary Soto, had only 21 poems, but each ode was two to three pages long. *Falling Up,* by Shel Silverstein, on the other hand, had 147 poems, many of which were four to eight lines long. How long the poem is depends on what the poet has to say. The same can be said for the collection.

PICTURE IT! | *Me, Myself, and I!*

Lyric poetry is the most natural form of poetry because the poet simply shares what's on her mind. Even if it doesn't begin with "I," if the poem talks about what the poet thinks or feels, chances are that poem is lyrical. Go to the bookstore or library with a pad of sticky notes. Find five middle-grade poetry collections and, as you read, place a sticky note on each poem that shares the poet's thoughts or experiences. After recording the names of the poetry collections in your reading log, go back and count how many sticky notes you placed in each book. Then count how many poems were in the book so you can calculate the percentage of the collection that was lyrical. Was it 23 percent, 78 percent? Record your findings in your writer's journal. ✦

Young Adult Poetry

Young adult poetry deals with the nitty gritty of teenage life. Although the words might not be more difficult than those in middle-grade poetry, the topics are definitely young adult: dating, sex, pregnancy, drugs, crime. Poetry for young adults can be found in collections, anthologies, and novels written in verse.

Young adult poetry equals teenage angst. Lyric poems, filled with emotion, dominate this age group.

Wait Till When

How many times
did you fall in love
this week

This poem from *Behind the Wheel: Poems About Driving*, by Janet S. Wong, is written in second person. Using the "you" voice, it asks a question about teenage life. Teens continue to read to find out the answer.

YA poetry collections have fewer poems than YA poetry anthologies. Young adult collections by individual poets have from thirty to fifty poems. YA poetry anthologies have from one to two hundred poems.

Different anthologists collect poetry for the teenage audience. Reading these anthologies gives you a feel for the wide range of emotion and mature subject matter found in YA poetry. As with younger anthologies, YA anthologists are either scholars or famous poets. Anthologies created by museums for both younger and older readers combine art and poetry in photo-essay style.

Is It a Novel or a Poem?

Blank verse and *free verse novels* are another form of poetry found in the YA category. You can find these poetry/novels in the poetry section and in the fiction section of the library. A search for "teen poetry" at Amazon.com will show you titles of novels in verse.

Poets and novelists use this form in two ways, by either writing from a single viewpoint or from multiple viewpoints. Books categorized as "novels" have a single narrator, with poems written in a journal or diary style. On the other hand, books categorized as "poetry" use multiple narrators to tell their story. Regardless of the way they are told or where they are shelved, these poetry/novels are narrative poetry.

In *The Taking of Room 114: A Hostage Drama in Poems*, Mel Glenn recounts the high school years of the seniors in Room 114. Their teacher has taken the class hostage. Each person in the room remembers his life, his years in high school.

Holly Lester: Senior

Never go out with a musician;
They're all losers.
All each one thinks about
Is his own instrument,
Or his own ego.

The angst of high school life is combined with the terror of a hostage situation in this collection of narrative poems. The details woven into these poems make them so true to life, you must turn the page to find out what happens next.

PICTURE IT! | *Young at Heart*

Young adult poetry is about the teenage experience, about growing up and finding your identity. Go to the bookstore or the library and find five YA poetry books. Read until a poem pulls you back into your own teenage years. Close your eyes and feel the pain and the joy of those tumultuous years. Then open your eyes and write. Brainstorm a list of feelings, places, and events. The years have passed, but the experiences are still yours. Step back in time, and write a poem from the fifteen-year-old you. After you finish, write about your time-traveling experience in your writer's journal. ✦

What Do Editors Want to See?

What do editors want to see in a poetry collection? Unity. Each poem should stand on its own and, at the same time, add something to the collection as a whole. To sell a collection, there must be a reason your poems are gathered. The fact that you wrote them is not enough. The strength of each poem is not enough. When the poems in a collection are read together, randomness is not an option.

A poetry collection is like a symphony orchestra. The orchestra is made up of many different instruments. Each player is the master of his instrument. Each instrument has a different voice. Yet when the instruments in the orchestra play together, they sing as one voice.

Do the voices in your poems sing together? Do they harmonize or clash? Does your collection, your orchestra, sound like one voice?

All voices in the orchestra are perfectly tuned. Each poem sings its own song to perfection, and at the same time, it sings with the other poems in the collection. The orchestra sings as one. That's what the editor wants in a poetry collection—an entire orchestra singing as one voice.

PART III

Character

Chapter Five

Fiction Characters

 In great fiction, the dream engages us heart and soul; we not only respond to imaginary things—sights, sounds and smells—as though they were real, we respond to fictional problems as if they were real.

—JOHN GARDNER, *The Art of Fiction*

Fiction tells the truth in a way that nonfiction can't. While nonfiction is about truths you discover outside yourself, fictional stories are about truths you discover inside yourself. The reader discovers these truths by living vicariously through the characters of a story.

Everything in a story is make-believe, and at the same time, everything is true. It is the emotions that are true in fiction. Despite the costumes, the make-up, and the stage settings, deep down, readers recognize themselves in the characters they encounter in a story.

But what does your character want? You must know this before you begin. What the main character wants determines what that character says and does. Action and dialogue come from the core of the story, the character's heart.

Meet the Character

When readers open a book, they meet the main character on the very first page. They want to know the answer to two key questions: Who is this character? What does he or she want?

In *Counterfeit Son*, by Elaine Marie Alphin, the reader meets the main character in the Prologue.

He couldn't remember exactly when he had discovered the

file cabinet in the corner of the small cellar storage room. Pop always locked him in the cellar while it happened. He hated the cellar—he hated the blows and the cries from upstairs, muffled only slightly by the locked door and the flooring, and he hated the smell. Pop kept spreading quicklime and fresh earth over the dirt floor, but the smell never went away completely. You could hardly smell anything upstairs, but when he was shut down in the cellar the thick, sickly sweet odor got inside his nose and he couldn't get rid of it. If he breathed through his mouth, he tasted it—a heavy taste like a rabbit a dog had torn apart and left half-buried in rotting leaves.

The first word in this paragraph, "He," shows you that the point of view (POV) is third person. Over and over again, the main character is referred to as he. Using the word he or she places readers outside the head of the main character and allows them to observe everyone. The third person point of view is the most commonly used POV in fiction.

If this novel were written in first person, the character would say "I" instead. This would make the first sentence read as follows: "*I* couldn't remember exactly when *I* had discovered the file cabinet in the corner of the small cellar storage room." The first person POV places readers inside the main character's head. It also limits readers to seeing only what the main character sees and makes the emotional attachment to the main character very strong.

The third person voice, the he or she voice, is the most commonly used because that is how readers naturally experience most stories. They really are on the outside looking in. Readers' distance from the story affects the point of view you choose, but don't let it dominate how you show the story. Readers want to know as much about that character as possible and that means you must write pictures to create a vivid, well-rounded character.

Look at the pictures in this third person excerpt. The first word in the paragraph is "He" so the reader knows that the main character is a boy. The boy is in a "small cellar storage room," thinking about "the file cabinet."

Why is the boy in the cellar in the first place? As the boy tries to "remember exactly when he had discovered the file cabinet," he recalls that his "Pop always locked him in the cellar while it happened." Naturally, readers want to know what happened. This is what keeps readers turning the pages.

This excerpt uses the general to specific pattern, beginning by focusing on the filing cabinet, and then showing where it is located, followed by why the boy was near the file cabinet in the cellar in the first place. Experiencing the cellar comes next, with specific details about first the sound and then the smell of the cellar. In the final sentence of this paragraph, he even tastes "the thick, sickly sweet odor."

Four senses are used in this paragraph, letting readers sense exactly what the character is sensing. Readers see the cellar and the filing cabinet and the dirt floor. They hear the beatings, and smell and taste the odors that come afterward. Although the use of third person POV means readers are not inside the boy's head, sensory details draw readers deeply into the scene, making it real.

When you use senses to develop your characters, you're showing readers what the characters are experiencing by taking them inside the characters. If the characters would notice a sight or sound or touch or taste or smell, add it. Draw readers into the story by using words that allow them to use their senses, too, because readers already know how to experience the world with senses. Move from the familiar (the readers senses) to the unfamiliar (the new world of the story).

PICTURE IT! | *POV Check*

One size doesn't fit all when it comes to point of view. *Counterfeit Son* uses the third person POV, the he or she or sometimes they voice. In other stories, another POV may work better. First, we'll explore each different point of view. Then, try each on for size in your own story.

Second person POV is the "you" voice. The author gives readers directions. The "Choose Your Own Adventure" ® books ask readers to make a choice.

Return of the Ninja, by Jay Leibold, gives readers many choices as the story progresses. How the story flows depends on readers' choices. In some cases, "you" rescue a character or outsmart the ninja. With different choices, "you" are captured by ninjas or hit by a taxi. One strand of the story reads like this . . .

> "You must go," the *shugenja* tells you. "You can find Sakai's hut by yourself."
> "No," you say. "I will stay and help you."
> "You have helped us enough," he says. "You must look for your friend."

At the bottom of the page is a choice:

If you try to find Sakai, turn to page 22.
If you stay with the shugenja, *turn to page 48.*

First person POV is the "I" or "we" voice. Here the narrator tells his or her own story. *Dovey Coe*, by Francis O'Roark Dowell, opens this way . . .

> My name is Dovey Coe, and I reckon it don't matter much
> if you like me or not.

The point of view you select is up to you. Knowing which POV other books use can help you make your decision. Go to the bookstore or library, and do a POV check. Open *fifty* books in the age range you prefer (picture books, easy readers, chapter books, middle grade, or young adult) and check the POV. Make a POV Survey chart in your writer's journal and fill it out as you go.

Don't read the books from beginning to end. Just open each book and check the POV. You're taking a census, creating a survey. Start at one end of the shelf, and open books until you reach the other end. If you haven't opened fifty books yet, keep going!

Write about your survey in your writer's journal. Which POV did you find the most? Which POV do you prefer? Would you like to try a new POV in your next book or change the POV in the book you are currently working on? ✦

Inside the Character

What the character says and does in a story shows readers what that character wants. What the character says and does is the *external* plot. What the character wants is called the *internal* plot. The external plot shows readers the internal plot. The two go hand in hand.

In *The First Day*, the opening chapter of the easy reader *Oliver Pig at School*, by Jean Van Leeuwen, Oliver gets ready for school.

> There were pancakes for breakfast.
> They were Oliver's favorite.
> But it was hard to sit still to eat.

Oliver took three bites.

"Is it time for the school bus yet?" he asked.

"Almost," said Father.

Even Oliver's breakfast shows specific details about his character, helping readers see what he does (external plot) and what he wants (internal plot). The reader sees "Oliver's favorite" breakfast and finds out that "Oliver took three bites." These show the external plot. Why? Oliver wants to know, "Is it time for the school bus yet?" Oliver's words and actions show the reader that Oliver is anxious about the first day of school, which is the internal plot.

Concrete details show readers a clear picture. Oliver had "pancakes for breakfast." He only "took three bites." The more specific you are, the easier it is for readers to see the character.

The action moves quickly in this easy reader. Oliver eats and asks about the bus. There is no dillydallying. Action is what the children who read these books want, so that is what you should write. Action shows readers a picture.

With dialogue and action, you can show readers what the main character wants, or the internal plot. With dialogue and action, you can also show readers what the main character does, or the external plot. The internal plot and the external plot work together to reveal character, even if readers only know five hundred words!

PICTURE IT! | *Hand in Hand*

Dialogue and action work hand in hand to reveal the internal and external plot. For this exercise, read five fiction books in a genre or reading level you would like to write. After you completely read the books, write the titles in your reading log. Then randomly select a page in each book, and prepare it for note taking. Copy a paragraph from that page (or the entire page) on your computer or in your writer's journal. With a highlighter or a colored pen, highlight all dialogue in the selection. Then highlight the action phrases with a different color.

Did you highlight the entire selection? Or are there blank spots, phrases where the character neither talks nor moves? Do those blank spots show readers a picture? Or do you hear the author telling you something? Write S for show and T for tell near the blank spots.

Decide if each line reveals the internal or external plot, or both? If the line shows what the character did, write E for external next to that line. If the line shows how the character felt, write I for internal next to that line. (If it shows both, then give it an E and an I.)

After you finish, look at the entire page. Did the selection do more showing or telling? Did you feel that the telling could have been rewritten? Or did the author use the telling as summary to move the book along? Did every phrase move the plot forward? Or are there sections you would rewrite? Did any phrases work double-duty, showing both internal and external plot? Write your thoughts in your writer's journal. ✦

Round and Flat Characters

Not all characters are created equally. Your main character needs to be round. The main character is the star of the show and, as such, needs to be fully developed.

Flat characters are important to the story because they show readers another aspect of the round character. When the main character interacts with a flat character, readers learn more about the main character, thus making him more round.

You can see a round and a flat character in this scene from *The Amah*, by Laurence Yep:

> "Just around the corner," I said.
>
> The cabby roared off and around the corner, screeching to a halt.
>
> Now that we were out of sight, I counted out all my money and gave it to him. "There's fifty cents for you too. Sorry."
>
> "Great. I'm halfway to a cup of coffee," he said sarcastically.
>
> I wish I could have told him how long I had worked to earn that much, but I just got out of the taxi. He raced away as if he couldn't wait to escape girls with pretensions of being rich.

The girl in the cab in this first person story is Amy Chin, the main character. Her words and deeds tell us a lot about her character. Amy, the star of the book, is a round character. This scene reveals more about Amy than it does the cabby.

Although you see the cabby in action as he "roared off and around the corner, screeching to a halt," you never learn the cabby's real name. The cabby is a flat character. He speaks his two lines with sarcasm: "Great. I'm halfway to a cup of coffee." Then, "He raced away," speeding out of Amy's life and out of the book.

It is through Amy's eyes that you see a motive in the cabby's speed. She thinks that the cabby "raced away as if he couldn't wait to escape girls with pretensions of being rich." The cabby didn't say this, Amy did. The cabby is a flat character, but he is there to move the story forward for Amy.

You create round characters by imitating real life. Real people have strengths and weaknesses. If your main character is always perfect, that makes him flat, not round. Perfection is predictable. Who wants to read page after page about a person who never makes a mistake? Boring!

Round characters have good days and bad days, just like you and just like all your young readers. They do things right, and they do things wrong. The secret is, readers never know quite what will happen next.

What readers want is to get to know the character better. Your task is to show readers more and more of the character's personality in action and in dialogue.

PICTURE IT! | *Center of the Solar System*

When it comes to a book, only one character can be the center of the solar system. The main character is the sun, the brightest star. Everything else in the solar system revolves around that sun. Everything else basks in the sun's light.

Read five fiction books for this exercise, and watch for the role of the flat characters in the story. Do the flat characters have names or titles? Do they spin around the main character? Do they shine only in the reflected light of the main character? Do their words and actions help the reader to see the main character in a new way? Do their actions move the plot forward? Or do they (gasp!) try to steal the light away from the main character? Write about the roles of these flat characters in your writer's journal. (Remember to write the book titles in your reading log.) ✦

Triangles

Time and again, conflict between characters comes in threes. A character triangle is a natural for conflict. Two against one: We see it again and again in our books, in our movies, in our newspapers. He said. She said. Somebody else said. What happens next? Readers must turn the page to find out!

In *The Adventures of Captain Underpants*, by Dav Pilkey, you can see the triangle quite clearly.

> "George Beard and Harold Hutchins, please report to Principal Krupp's office at once."
>
> "Uh-oh!" said Harold. "I don't like the sound of *that*!"
>
> "Don't worry," said George. "They can't prove anything!"

George and Harold are best friends. Even though they play pranks on everyone in the school, they are the heroes of the story, the protagonists. Mr. Krupp, the principal, is the antagonist. Two against one keeps the action moving.

Giving your main character a best friend allows readers to learn more about that character without you "telling" the story. Your readers learn more about your character the same way they learn about people in the everyday world, through dialogue and action. It feels natural because it is familiar.

In works for younger children there is usually only one triangle. Because the story is told through their characters, the characters in the star's triangle need to be fully developed. They need to be round.

A TRIANGLE IS THREE:

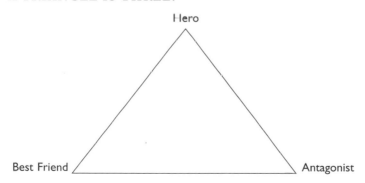

THREE MAKES SIX

The three characters in a triangle have six relationships.

Hero ➜ Best Friend
Hero ➜ Antagonist
Best Friend ➜ Hero
Best Friend ➜ Antagonist
Antagonist ➜ Hero
Antagonist ➜ Best Friend

In novels with subplots, flat characters may form their own triangles. Although flat characters are developed to a lesser degree, they can still have relationships that move the story forward for the main character. No matter who is in the triangle, the focus of the story should be the main character.

PICTURE IT! | *Three's a Crowd*

Picture books tend to have a single triangle. You see all three characters introduced in one short letter at the beginning of *World Famous Muriel and the Magic Mystery*, by Sue Alexander:

> Dear World Famous Muriel,
>
> The Great Hokus Pokus will put on his Magic Show at my theater today. He is going to practice some new magic tricks this morning. Please come and watch.
>
> Your friend,
> Professor M.C. Ballyhoo

While the Great Hokus Pokus practices his tricks, he disappears. The professor asks Muriel to find him, and so she does. Although you see other people in the pictures (and lots of rabbits), they have no lines. Only the three main characters, the three parts of the triangle, speak. The story stays focused on the main characters.

Middle-grade and YA novels, on the other hand, have hundreds of pages to explore triangles. The nuances of these relationship triangles make the books interesting. The more characters you have in a book, the more triangles you can explore! Each triangle comes back somehow to the main character and his or her journey of discovery.

How many triangles will you need in your next work of fiction? Read five works of fiction written for the age level you prefer (picture book, easy reader, chapter book, middle grade, or YA) and find out. Write the book titles in your reading log and make a list of the cast of characters for each book in your writer's journal. Create a relationship chart (see page 93) so you can see how many relationships the book had.

How many triangles did you find? Was the star in a triangle of round characters? How many triangles involved the main character? Did you see any triangles made entirely of flat characters? Were you surprised at the number of triangles you discovered? Write about these triangles in your writer's journal. ✦

Show, Don't Tell

Action and dialogue show the reader your character in a way that telling never can. Telling gets to the point more quickly, so it may seem more efficient. But telling comes from the outside, not the inside. Telling talks *about* the character. Showing lets readers see the character in action. When readers see their own picture, it makes the story part of the readers' experience. Readers are *in* the story too.

In *American Diaries: Amelina Carrett: Bayou Grand Coeur, Louisiana, 1863*, by Kathleen Duey, the details draw readers in.

> "Is Nonc Alain gone now?" Perrine asked.
>
> Amelina nodded and gave her usual answer. "Down to Vermilionville," he said. "Supposed to be back soon."
>
> Perrine smiled, tucking a strand of long dark hair back beneath her bonnet. "I would be afraid in a house all by myself."
>
> Amelina shrugged. "I am used to it, I suppose." She took in a breath, wanting to tell Perrine about the marchand, to ask if he had stopped here, too. But before she could say anything more, Perrine shuddered theatrically.
>
> "I would be afraid. I don't think I could stand waking up in an empty house. But you manage, don't you?" She bent to pick up her baskets, shaking her head and smiling as though they were talking about whether or not Amelina liked crawfish bellies, or about how she preferred peppers in her rice.

But it wasn't a thing like that, Amelina thought, her cheeks flushing. She hated it. It wasn't as if she wanted to wake up in a silent house every morning. Or that she liked being alone a lot of the time. Amelina felt her eyes flooding, but Perrine didn't notice. She was gathering stray tufts of cotton from the dock planks.

The details in this excerpt not only ground the book in the Louisiana bayou of 1863, they also show readers how far apart the two cousins are. While Perrine idly chats about not wanting to be alone, her cousin struggles with this issue, which is the heart of the story. Dialogue, action, and specific detail allow readers to draw their own conclusions about Amelina and Perrine. Telling isn't necessary. By showing the details through Picture Writing rather than direct statements, this story pulls readers in.

Weave the action and the dialogue in your story around your character's biggest concern. Who your character is and what he wants *is* the story.

The difference between showing and telling is the difference between scene and summary. Scene shows a picture you can see. Summary uses the author's words to tell you something about the story. There is a time and a place for both.

Summary feeds the reader information quickly. With summary, the author speaks as an omniscient narrator, explaining the character's background from high above. Summary isn't story. Summary is background information. Summary is the author talking *about* the story.

Scene, on the other hand, should make up the majority of your story. The details that show what the character says and does are the story, not explanations from on high.

"Amelina talked to her cousin at the docks" is a summary. The scene above shows a picture. With the give and take of dialogue, readers see how each of the characters thinks. As the characters move, they reveal more about themselves. The pictures in the words show readers your characters.

Bring your characters to life by showing specific details. Add physical details. ("Perrine smiled, tucking a strand of long dark hair back beneath her bonnet.") Add emotional details. ("Amelina felt her eyes flooding.") Add action details. ("Perrine didn't notice. She was gathering stray tufts of cotton from the dock planks.") Show readers your characters by using specifics, by using Picture Writing to create vivid characters and scenes.

PICTURE IT! | *Talk the Talk*

As previously mentioned, dialogue is an effective way to reveal character. With specific details, the character in your story becomes a real person to your reader. Writing dialogue, however, isn't just a matter of putting sentences into a character's mouth. Real people don't always think or speak in complete sentences. But the ums and ahs that fill the gaps in real conversation aren't interesting to read either. So what works?

A combination of sentences and phrases capture the thoughts of a teenager in this excerpt from *Speak*, by Laurie Halse Anderson.

> I must talk to Rachel. I can't do it in algebra, and the Beast waits for her outside English. But we have study hall at the same time. Bingo. I find her squinting at a book with small type in the library. She's too vain for glasses. I instruct my heart not to bolt down the hall, and sit next to her. No nuclear bombs detonate. A good start.

How children think and speak changes as they grow older, which is reflected in the books written for each age. Does what you're writing match the age of your readers? Read five fiction books for the age level you prefer (picture book, easy reader, chapter book, middle grade, or YA), and write the titles in your reading log.

In the world of these books, how do the kids think and speak? In your writer's journal, record five different examples of dialogue or character thoughts from each book. Did the characters use complete sentences? Did they speak in phrases? Did they use a mix of both? Did you see any slang? Did the words seem dated or too old for the speaker? Did it feel as if an adult were speaking, not a child?

How did the writer mix action with dialogue? Did the actions blend with the conversation, or did you find them distracting? Write your thoughts about "talking the talk" in your writer's journal. ✦

The Heart of a Story

Create characters who intrigue and fascinate you. If you're not interested in them as people, your reader isn't likely to be.

—SCOTT EDELSTEIN, *The Writer's Book of Checklists*

The character's emotions are the heart of the story. Keeping readers close to the character's emotions makes the story come alive. When children read fiction, they read so they can live vicariously, so they can live another person's life. They don't read to learn a lesson. Show them the pictures of a story instead.

Allow your readers to get to know your character the way they would a friend, bit by bit. In real life, you don't have someone telling you large chunks of background information. You know real people by what they say and what they do.

Step inside your character, and tell his story from the inside. Even if you don't use first person point of view, you need to know what your character is thinking and feeling so you can share that information with readers. Write the pictures you see when you look through the eyes of your character. Character *is* story.

Chapter Six

Nonfiction Characters

Primary research takes you to artifacts straight from the character's time—letters, diaries, photographs, oral histories, newspapers, magazines, literature and so forth.

—PEG ROSS, EDITOR, PLEASANT COMPANY, FROM AN INTERVIEW IN *Children's Writer*

A character is a character, no matter what the genre is. With action and dialogue, readers learn more about your character. The details you show that make your characters come alive.

At the same time, writing about nonfiction characters is not the same as writing about fictional ones. As a nonfiction writer, you must accurately portray what really happened in your character's life. You can't make things up!

Research is the foundation of every character portrayal you find in nonfiction, even if your nonfiction character is a giraffe. If your writing is not based on research, you're writing fiction, not nonfiction.

How a nonfiction character grows in the book depends on the type of nonfiction. In a biography, the character has grown and changed emotionally, like a fictional character would. In an information book, however, the character learns new information. Changes of the heart are not the primary emphasis in an information book. Knowledge is. How you bring characters to life in your nonfiction writing depends on your goals.

Meet the Character

Young nonfiction often uses characters to introduce topics to readers. In the information book *I Call It Sky*, by Will C. Howell, the first person narrator is a child. The topic of the book is the air. Here is the opening page:

Every morning,
when the sunlight jumps through
my window,
I burst out the door.
I am surrounded by air.
It nips at my nose
and tosses my hair.
It is inside me when I breathe,
and it is outside me
everywhere.

This information book uses the narrator's senses to show readers the topic. Picture book readers see the world from a "me" perspective, so the first person point of view here is just right.

As this child moves, readers experience what the character experiences. The details are specific and concrete. Each experience is sensory and active.

This excerpt starts with a familiar experience, waking up in the morning. The pictures in each line describe something readers have also experienced. Use of this familiar to unfamiliar pattern allows readers to say, "I've done that too!" This is what editors want when they ask for narrative for young readers. The character in a young nonfiction information book is there for readers. As readers experience what the narrator experiences, readers learn more about the topic, which in this case is air. The facts are presented through a child's eyes.

Observation is an approach to science writing that young readers understand. They can observe the air, but they are not ready for chemical analysis of the air. They are not ready to talk about pollution. This is a *definition* book. It shows the reader what air is.

Characters in information books do not experience a change of heart. Instead, they learn something new. The growth and change that occur in a nonfiction picture book are related to the information. If the character has problems to solve, they are intellectual problems, not emotional ones.

Does that mean there is no emotion in nonfiction? Of course not! Characters in fiction books learn new information as they work to solve their problems. Characters in nonfiction books can experience life fully too. "I burst out the door," is a moment filled with emotion. Allow your passion about the subject to show in your character's words and actions. Write about the whole character, not just their brain.

PICTURE IT! | *Speaking for the Star*

Sometimes nonfiction books use animals or even objects as characters. Since their characters can't speak, certain problems arise. How will you share the information you find? Who will speak for the star of your book? One choice you have is to give the star a voice, even though it cannot speak in real life. This is the case in *I Am Water*, by Jean Marzollo.

> I am snow for sledding.

The water speaks for itself in this example. It's like a persona poem. The writer speaks for the water, which cannot speak for itself.

In *I Call It Sky*, the child narrator speaks.

> I am surrounded by air.
> It nips at my nose
> and tosses my hair.

As the narrator describes his experience, readers see the air move. They learn more about the air, the true star of this book.

Is It Dark? Is It Light?, by Mary D. Lankford, uses the question-and-answer pattern. Throughout the book, two children use opposites to describe the moon.

> Is it square? No, it's round.

The moon doesn't speak, the children do. The children act as characters in this book, but the moon is the "big cheese." All of the words the children speak describe the moon. Readers don't learn anything about the speaking characters. This book uses the third person point of view to talk about the moon, the topic of the book.

For this exercise, visit the bookstore or the library and look for five young nonfiction books. As you read each book, look for the star—the main subject of the book. Notice who speaks and who doesn't. Does the star speak for itself?

Does a human narrator speak about the star? Which point of view is used: first, second, or third? Record your findings in your writer's journal. (Don't forget to write the titles of the books you read in your reading log.) ✦

Inside the Character

When you write about characters in a biography, you need to show the character both inside and out. Just as in fiction, you must show readers why your character did what he or she did.

As you research, your character's motives will become clear. What she said and did will reveal her inner desires. The what, the how, and the when will lead you to the why.

When writing your manuscript, show your readers what motivates your character. Start your story with the why. The picture book biography, *Snowflake Bentley*, by Jacqueline Briggs Martin, shows what the character wanted on the first page:

> there lived a boy who loved snow
> more than anything else in the world

As the pages turn, this boy's love for snow shows clearly in his actions.

> While other children built forts
> and pelted snowballs at roosting crows,
> Willie was catching single snowflakes.
> Day after stormy day he studied the icy crystals.

The first page introduces the character to readers. It also makes a promise. After reading the first page, readers know that this book will be about a boy who loves snow. Keeping this promise means that the book will show readers "a boy who loved snow more than anything else in the world."

In a biography, as in fiction, the internal and the external are linked. What the character wants leads to what he does. What the character says is not added to these third person excerpts. Here, Willie's actions do the talking.

When the children play in the snow, readers see a compare and contrast example. Willie's actions are compared to the actions of the "other children."

When it snows, what did they do? The "other children built forts," says the text. They also "pelted snowballs at roosting crows." For these children, snow means play.

Willie didn't play with the snow. He caught it. Then "he studied the icy crystals." His mother had given him a microscope, so, "Day after stormy day he studied the icy crystals." Willie wanted to see each crystal up close.

The compare and contrast model works even better because of the visual nature of the text. Each line is an action picture. The reader doesn't listen to children talking about snow. Instead, action moves the story forward.

PICTURE IT! | *Promises, Promises*

On the first page, a book makes a promise to its readers. It introduces the main character both inside and out. Right from the start, who the character is and what he wants is linked to what he does. Whether your main character can speak or not doesn't make a difference. When you open the curtain, what readers see first is what they expect to see throughout.

If you begin a book by writing about a giraffe's birth, readers expect to see that giraffe grow up. If you really want to talk about the giraffe's habitat, make that clear at the very beginning. Mention the habitat from the start. Otherwise, it feels as if you have changed topics midstream.

Go to the bookstore or the library, and find five nonfiction books for the age group you write. You may wish to select five books on a topic you would like to write about so you can use this exercise as research for your own project.

Open each book, and read the first page or chapter. Then turn to the back and read the last page or chapter. Did the book keep its promise? Did the words written in the beginning come true in the end?

Take it a step further, and copy the promises in your writer's journal. After you list each title, copy the lines from the first page or chapter that make the promise. Directly under this promise, copy the words from the last page or chapter that keep the promise.

Did the books you examined keep their promise? Or did they fall short? Did you find out what the character wanted from the very beginning? Did the character achieve his goal? Did the topic change in the middle of the book? Record your thoughts under each entry. If you decide to read the middle of the books also, remember to write the titles in your reading log. ✦

Round and Flat Characters

Only one character can be the star of the show, especially in biographies for younger readers. In a picture book biography, there simply isn't enough space to share the limelight. In *Seeker of Knowledge: The Man Who Deciphered Egyptian Hieroglyphs* by James Rumford, the spotlight is on Jean-Francois Champollion.

> Then, on a September morning in 1822, Jean-Francois found a small package on his doorstep—from a friend in Egypt! In it were the names of pharaohs copied from a temple wall. Each name was a jigsaw puzzle of letters and pictures. Jean-Francois studied the names and saw the link! The pictures were sounds, too. Not single letters, but syllables, even whole words!

After years of study, Jean-Francois Champollion unlocked the mystery of hieroglyphics. "A friend in Egypt" provided the key that helped Jean-Francois open the door, yet this friend's name is not even mentioned. All of the focus here is on the star, Jean-Francois. The "friend in Egypt" is a flat character, known only by a title and his country of residence.

If you were writing this biography, you would have discovered this friend's name and life story in your research. Yet like this author, you would probably not have added it here so as not to confuse your young reader. The focus here is on Jean-Francois, not the friend who provided the key.

The older the readers, the more details you can add about the secondary characters. In a biography for older readers, the "friend in Egypt" would probably be mentioned by name. In a middle-grade or YA biography, you could even add a subplot about how the "friend in Egypt" came to find "the names of the pharaohs" and copy them down. But in the end, Jean-Francois would still be the star. It is his biography, after all.

PICTURE IT! | *The Tip of the Iceberg*

Once you've completed your research, how do you decide what to leave in and what to leave out? Most of what ends up in a book is only the tip of the iceberg. You need to know everything about your subject so you can write the book, but your readers don't need to know everything to understand what is going on.

For this exercise, select a famous person, and find three biographies about that individual written for different ages. Find a picture book biography, a short chapter book biography, and a biography written for the young adult. (If you want to write for young adults, you may wish to compare these books with adult biographies.)

Read each book from beginning to end, then compare and contrast the information shared at each level. Create a storyboard for each book on a separate sheet of paper. When you finish, place the storyboards side by side so you can compare them.

How much time in each person's life did the book cover? Was it birth to death? Was it childhood to adulthood? Was it a single incident in the person's life?

How much detail did each book cover? Did you see events in the books for older readers that were not mentioned in the younger biographies? Do you think these events could or should be added to the younger biographies?

Is the main character fully developed in these biographies, regardless of the readers' ages? Did the secondary characters have more speaking parts in the biographies for older readers? What other differences did you notice?

Compare and contrast these biographies in your writer's journal. (Don't forget to record the book titles in your reading log.) ✦

Triangles

In nonfiction, three sides of a triangle join to show readers a character: action, dialogue, and research. Action and dialogue show readers pictures of the character. The third side of the triangle, research, gives you both the dialogue and the action you need.

Quotes from actual sources act as dialogue in nonfiction. You intersperse action with quotes to create a scene. This technique can be used in any nonfiction book. Dialogue and action aren't limited to biography. Here is one example from *The Way Things Never Were: The Truth About the "Good Old Days,"* by Norman H. Finkelstein.

Many children of those blacklisted individuals could not escape the fear and anxiety of their parents. Casey Murrow,

son of the famous news broadcaster Edward R. Murrow, revealed that his father often helped blacklisted writers and journalists. "There were a lot of threats," Casey later said, "against
them [his parents] and against me. I never knew what was
going on at the time. They worked so hard to keep things
normal." Once during the McCarthy era, Murrow told his
wife, "We must never allow Casey to be unattended." For a
long time thereafter, Casey was escorted daily by his mother
or a maid to and from school. One of Ed's colleagues recalled,
"Ed always felt there were times during the McCarthy era when
his phone was bugged." 2

The first sentence sets the scene. "Many children of those blacklisted individuals could not escape the fear and anxiety of their parents." This topic sentence
is followed by specific examples of "the fear and anxiety" shown in the life of
"Casey Murrow, son of the famous news broadcaster Edward R. Murrow."

As is the case with most journalistic reporting, this paragraph uses the general
to specific pattern. The topic sentence contains the general idea. The sentences
that follow show readers the specific details.

The focus is on Casey's life, so Casey and his father are both quoted directly.
The final quote is attributed to "one of Ed's colleagues." The colleague isn't
named here, but a source is quoted with the use of the number 2 at the end of
the paragraph. The colleague is a flat character as is the maid who walked Casey
to school.

Without research and careful quote selection, this paragraph would look
quite different. It is possible to tell the information here rather than show it,
but why do that? Quoting the actual sources gives the paragraph credibility and
brings it alive.

PICTURE IT! | *Quote Me*

Nonfiction shows conflict with dialogue and action just like fiction
does. What it looks like on the page is quite different, however. Nonfiction re-creates the drama by interviewing the witnesses and sharing that information with the readers. In his book *Creative Nonfiction: Researching and Crafting Stories of Real Life*, Philip Gerard says, "You can't just pour your interview

notes onto the page. You have to choose carefully from everything your subject said and present his or her words in a dramatic context."

For this Picture It! exercise, find five nonfiction books that use quotations in the narrative. Select a paragraph with quotations from each book, and prepare it for note taking. Make a copy of the page or write the paragraph in your writer's journal or on your computer. Highlight each quotation in the paragraph and count the number of quotations.

Now rewrite each paragraph *without* any quotations. After you finish, compare the two versions, quoted and unquoted. Did the plain paragraph seem as alive as the quoted one? Or did it feel like hearsay? He said, she said, who said? Did your hands feel tied while writing the plain version? Did you need more words to say the same thing? Quote yourself, and write about your experience in your writer's journal. ✦

Show, Don't Tell

It's the details that show your character to readers. The details in *Margaret Bourke-White: Her Pictures Were Her Life*, by Susan Goldman Rubin, bring the character to life.

> When Margaret was about four, the family moved from the Bronx where she was born to the town of Bound Brook, New Jersey. In the daytime, Margaret began running away to explore. Finally Minnie started dressing her in a bright red sweater with a sign sewed on the back: "My name is Margaret Bourke White. I live at 210 North Mountain Avenue. Please bring me home."

As mentioned earlier, to find the details that make your character come alive, you must do your research. The deeper you dig, the closer you come to finding the details you need to write pictures. If you only read the research material that everyone else reads, how will your book be different? When you take that extra step to go back to primary sources, you will find that gem, that detail that will help your writing come alive.

A check of several sources on the life of Margaret Bourke-White didn't reveal any of the details in the paragraph above. Yet when you look at the pictures in the words, these details reveal her character. It is clear that Margaret was an adventurer from the get-go. "When Margaret was about four," she "began running away to explore."

Knowing the little things, like the details about the "bright red sweater with a sign sewed on the back," not only create a vivid picture, they show expertise. The reader can trust a writer who has done her homework.

Where can you find these sources? The answer depends on your character. In the back matter of the young adult biography *Margaret Bourke-White: Her Pictures Were Her Life*, the bibliography lists seven different categories. The first section, Books, is divided into four different categories: Books about Margaret Bourke-White, Books by Margaret Bourke-White, Books about Photography, and Books about History. The bibliography continues with Videos, Other Sources, and Interviews. The video was an Edward R. Murrow interview of Margaret in her home in 1955. The Other Sources include the *Margaret Bourke-White Papers and Memorabilia* as well as a speech given by a staff member at *Life* magazine. The author also conducted seven interviews with individuals who knew and worked with Margaret.

If you want to find the details that show your readers pictures, you need to dig. With the public library and the Internet, you can find resources from around the world. At the public library, begin with the *Guide to Reference Books*. University libraries are another excellent resource. Some libraries, including the Library of Congress, have information available on their Web sites.

The bibliographies of other books on your subject are an excellent resource. If a title sounds intriguing and it is not available in your local library, try to borrow it through ILL, the Inter-Library Loan system. If you know the title and the author, you can fill out a request form and the ILL system will search the databases of all participating libraries, including universities. No matter how you find your sources, just make sure you do your research thoroughly.

PICTURE IT! | *Finding the Details*

Just checking the encyclopedia is not enough. Today, even picture books list resource information. The picture book biography *Seeker of Knowledge: The Man Who Deciphered the Egyptian Hieroglyphs* has a bibliography under the hieroglyphics box on page 31. Book sources listed date back to 1906.

Where can you find the details you need to show, not tell? Go to the bookstore or the library and analyze the bibliographies from five children's and young adult biographies. Make a chart in your writer's journal so you can see what kind of sources these biographers are using.

PRIMARY SOURCES CHART
Biography title
Type of resource
Books
Magazines
Photographs
Video
Other (list)

In each category, if the item listed in the bibliography was:
1. created by the source (the person you are researching), write an S
2. created by a contemporary of the source, write a C
3. created after the source's death, write a D

Be sure to write the number of sources you found for each category. Here is an example for you to follow:

Title: *Margaret Bourke-White: Her Pictures Were Her Life*, by Susan Goldman Rubin
Resources:
Books: 9 S, 4 C, 29 D
Magazines: none listed
Photographs: photos throughout bio: S, C
Video: 1 C
Other (list): personal papers: 1 S; speech: 1 C; interviews: 7 C

Write about your findings in your writer's journal. Were you surprised at the number of sources that were cited? Did the numbers seem high or low? Do you know how to find the resources listed? Do you have a university nearby? Can you use ILL, the Inter-Library Loan service? Are these resources available online? (If you read the biographies to see *how* they used these resources, list the titles in your reading log.) ✦

Sharing Real-Life Characters

There is always a hunger for detail and it's the details that make history come alive.

—MARCIA MARSHALL, EXECUTIVE EDITOR, FROM AN INTERVIEW IN *Children's Writer*

When you write nonfiction, the characters in your work are alive, and yet you are not inside their heads unless they left writings behind. It can be quite a challenge to bring a real character to life on the page. Yet it is not impossible. You don't have to make things up! With careful research and observation, you can re-create a person's life in your writing. You can bring that real-life character alive on the page.

Research will bring you quotations both from the character you are studying and from his peers. With careful selection, you can create a picture of that person's life with your words and share it with young readers. Using the tools of fiction, you can balance the dialogue of these quotes with the action that occurred when they were happening. In so doing, the motives of the character will be revealed. Readers will see both the internal and external plot.

If your character is a part of nature, you may wish to use the tools of poetry to bring your character to life. You can keep the actions true to the real-life character and be poetic at the same time. Use every tool you can find. Why not? Whoever said nonfiction had to be boring?

Chapter Seven

Poetry Characters

 If there were a recipe for poetry, these would be the ingredients: word sounds, rhythm, description, feeling, memory, rhyme and imagination.

—KARLA KUSKIN, *Dogs & Dragons, Trees & Dreams*

How you show characters in a poem is different than other forms. In a poem, you also work with rhythm and rhyme and repetition. The story mixes with the music of the words and the pictures in your head.

At the same time, the characters in a poem reveal themselves with action and dialogue, just as they do in other genres. You select a point of view, organize your ideas, and share pictures with your readers.

Meet the Character

In poetry, as in fiction and nonfiction, you need to introduce the main character as soon as possible. Poetry is economical. Not a word is wasted. In the poem "Maple Shoot in the Pumpkin Patch," by Kristine O'Connell George (from her collection *Old Elm Speaks: Tree Poems*), the reader first meets the character—the maple shoot—in the title. When the verses begin, the maple shoot starts talking . . .

> Remember me?
> I helicoptered past
> your kitchen window last fall,

The maple shoot speaks directly to readers. "Remember me?" asks the shoot.

The word "me" lets you know this poem is written in first person. The poem will be up close and personal. The maple shoot has a story to tell.

After beginning with a question, the maple shoot follows up with an answer. Did you remember the shoot? He's going to tell you when he first met you. "I helicoptered past," says the shoot. Maple seeds spin like helicopters, so the poet used that image in the verb "helicoptered." "Spun" or "flew" might also have been used here. The actions are quite similar. Yet the image in the word "helicoptered" is so much more vivid. It's also a word you don't expect to see when you talk about seeds or trees. The poet moves beyond cliché, and the result is a picture word.

That maple shoot isn't finished yet. He wants you to remember him. Where did he meet you? By "your kitchen window," says the shoot. When did it happen? Why, "last fall" is the answer. All of these specific answers, the details of the flight, appear in just five words. The pictures in the words are quite clear.

PICTURE IT! | *Behind the Mask*

"Maple Shoot in the Pumpkin Patch" is a persona or mask poem. In a mask poem, the poet pretends to be someone or something else. Things that cannot speak now have a voice, the poet's voice.

Persona poems are written in first person. When you wear a mask, you become who or what you are writing about, so you speak in his voice. Although persona poems for adults are almost always about people, mask poems for children often "personify" and bring nonhumans to life.

Go to the bookstore or library, and read poetry until you find five mask poems. Write the titles of the books you read in your reading log, then look at the mask poems again. Did you see the pronouns "I," "me," "we," or "us" in these poems? Did your mask poems have people hiding behind the mask? Or did animals or other living things—like a maple shoot—speak? Perhaps an inanimate object—like a washing machine—spoke? If you put on a mask, which one would you choose? Write about your findings in your writer's journal. ✦

Inside the Character

Characters in poetry act just like characters in fiction and nonfiction. The action you see in the story of the poem begins in the main character's mind. A character's internal motivation drives his external actions. In "A Gold Miner's Tale," by Bobbi Katz (from her collection *We, the People*), a young man joins the gold rush of 1849.

> Water and sand. That's ALL it takes.
> Swish your pan. Pick out the flakes!

This refrain is repeated several times throughout the poem. The action taken here comes from an inner motivation. Like so many who panned for gold, this young man wanted to get rich.

Although the refrain is typed as two lines, when you read it aloud, it sounds like a quatrain. The punctuation instructs readers to pause briefly, so you *hear* four lines.

> Water and sand.
> That's ALL it takes.
> Swish your pan.
> Pick out the flakes!

Typed as a quatrain, you can see the full rhyme pattern. The first and third lines both end with "an" sounds. Line one ends with "sand." Line three ends with "pan." The second and fourth lines both end with "akes" words. The second line ends with "takes." The fourth line ends with "flakes." Takes and flakes are a perfect rhyme.

So what is the action here? What motivates the character? First, the young man tells you what you need to find the gold: "Water and sand." In three short words, you see what you need. The poet is very specific.

Once he tells you what you need, the miner crows about the information. "That's ALL it takes." You can read the miner's thoughts here. All you need is water and sand. The word "all" is typed in capital letters to emphasize the point.

So what do you do with that water and sand? "Swish your pan." Now the poet brings the readers down in the river itself. The readers see the miner swishing the pan. We already know what's in the pan: "Water and sand."

What's next? What do you do after you swish your the pan with the water and the sand? "Pick out the flakes!" Flakes of gold will just appear in your pan, or that's what the miner thinks. All these vivid details are excellent examples of Picture Writing. And character is revealed in the details.

In this refrain, in fourteen musical words, the miner sings about how easy it is to get rich. With four short phrases, the poet paints readers a picture of what the miner is doing and why. The words the miner speaks show readers what the miner is thinking. The actions in the words are clear and specific. Seeing a character inside and out with such clarity is Picture Writing.

PICTURE IT! | *Mind Reading*

Can you read your characters' minds? In this exercise, you're going to look for poems that show both plots—internal and external. In "A Gold Miner's Tale," the poet revealed the character's thoughts through his words and actions. What the miner says and does (the external plot) tell you what he thinks and what he wants (the internal plot).

As you read new poetry for this exercise, ask yourself: Does the character show his thoughts in his words *and* deeds? Does the character act on his feelings, or does he just talk?

You may find poems where the character talks about her feelings. Lyrical poetry comes from the heart and talks about exactly that—the poet's thoughts and feelings. For this exercise, however, look for more than thoughts and feelings. Look for action.

Once you find action, see if you can figure out the character's motivation. Can you see what the character thinks? Is there a link between the character's thoughts and feelings (the internal plot) and the character's actions (the external plot)? How does what the character thinks and feels get translated in deeds? What pictures did you see?

List the titles of the books you read in your reading log, and don't forget to translate your thoughts into action—write about your search in your writer's journal. ✦

Round and Flat Characters

When you have more than one character in your poem, you must decide how important each character is. In some poems, only one character is the "star." Only one character is fully developed or *round*. The other characters in the poem are one-dimensional or *flat*.

You can tell who the star is by seeing who receives the most attention in the poem. Watch for the spotlight as you read this excerpt from "At the Florist," by Deborah Chandra (from her collection *Balloons: And Other Poems*).

> A woman bends over
> Cuttings of cold roses,
> Their mouths frozen closed.

Did you see the roses in the spotlight? In the first line, "A woman bends over" them. Then, in the next line, we see "Cuttings of cold roses." First, the woman moves toward them. Then, the camera zooms in so we can see the roses themselves.

After we see the stars of the show, the camera zooms in even closer. The "Cuttings of cold roses" have "Their mouths frozen closed." The reader sees the mouths of the roses in this close-up shot.

The roses are the stars of the show, but the camera didn't start with them. This poem actually started with a line about the "chamber" at the florist where the roses were stored. The big picture came first. With each subsequent line, readers are drawn closer and closer to the stars of the poem, the roses themselves.

When you write about characters in a poem, you don't have a lot of time for character development. Unlike a novel or a biography, you don't have pages to go on and on about the characters. For children, a twenty-line poem is considered long. This means you must round out your poetry characters as quickly as possible. If a novel is a tall drink, a poem is just a sip. In that sip, you show readers the essence of a character.

You round out your character by writing pictures. The reader sees the stars of the poem, the roses, in a series of pictures. This is how you reveal character in a poem, line by line and picture by picture.

The star of the poem has the most lines and the most pictures. Flat characters are mentioned, but readers don't learn that much about them. Flat characters help move the plot along, but they don't have the spotlight on them. Here the flat character is "A woman," not a character with a name. You don't learn much about her. It's not necessary. This poem is really about the roses, which, in this case are the round characters.

Don't spend time (and lines) talking about the flat characters. Stay focused on the main character. Show the readers images of the main character. Use the flat characters to draw the readers' eye to the main character. Direct your flat characters to talk and act so that the main character is on center stage.

If your flat characters refuse to stay flat, you may have written a relationship poem. Relationship poems are covered in the next section.

TALKING ANIMALS

In children's literature, animals, plants, and other objects talk and act just like humans. In this chapter, you have read one poem written by a maple shoot and another describing roses with "Their mouths frozen." Giving roses or any other object human features is called *personification*. With personification, the writer makes something act like a person. Attributing human characteristics to nonhumans is also called *anthropomorphism*, as we discussed previously.

Despite many editors' admonitions against talking animals, anthropomorphic books are on the shelves in every bookstore and library. When asked whether he would publish books with talking animals, one publisher replied, "It depends on what they have to say."

The character itself is more important than the form it takes. Develop your characters fully so they have something to say to your readers. If your alligator is really a child in disguise, show the reader pictures of the alligator's life as a child. On the other hand, if your alligator is speaking so readers can experience the life of an alligator, show readers those real-life pictures instead. Stay true to your character.

PICTURE IT! | *The Star of the Show*

In poems about a single character, it's easy to see the star of the show. When other characters enter the poem, that's when the pecking order begins. Someone has to be the star.

For this exercise, read new poetry books until you find five poems with multiple characters. After you write the book titles in your reading log, take a closer look at the poems. Who is in the spotlight? Who has the most lines? Who has his name mentioned in the title? Most importantly, who do you remember after you finish reading? Write about these stars and your thoughts about round and flat characters in your writer's journal. ✦

Relationships

Relationships can also be the topic of a poem. In relationship poems, the characters aren't round and flat. All of the characters need to be round and their interactions create the conflict of the story.

"This Girl and This Boy," by Eve Merriam (from her collection *If Only I Could Tell You: Poems for Young Lovers and Dreamers*), is a relationship poem.

> Look at them laughing,
> their arms around each other
> like Christmas wrappings.

As you can see from this excerpt, the narrator is on the outside looking in. Although none of the characters have names yet, you can tell they are equally important. And their relationship is the focus of the poem itself.

The poem begins with action and emotion. "Look at them laughing," says the first line. The language tells you how the narrator feels. He is on the outside looking in. The reader sees two emotions at once. The couple is laughing. The narrator is not.

The narrator goes on to describe how the couple looks. They have "their arms around each other," says the next line. More detail rounds out the characters.

The third line reveals even more. The couple has "their arms around each other" in a specific way. It looks "like Christmas wrappings." The narrator shares an image with readers, one that represents the couple's relationship. "This Girl and This Boy" (the title of the poem) are wrapped up in one another.

With each line, the girl and the boy grow closer to one another. First, they are "laughing." Then they have "their arms around each another." Finally, they look "like Christmas" presents, wrapped together. With each new word picture, the poet is rounding out their characters.

As the poem continues, specific details about what the characters look like and the actions they might take rounds out all three characters. It is not until the end of the poem, in the sixteenth line, that the poet reveals the identities of "This Girl and This Boy." The narrator is looking at an old photograph of his parents.

By revealing only a few details at a time, the poet creates one word picture at a time. Too much detail overwhelms readers. You don't want to overwrite. On the other hand, without any detail, you lose the readers' attention. It's a delicate balance. Add just enough detail to create one word picture per line. Line by line, each new detail will round out your characters.

PICTURE IT! | *1, 2, 3*

As you create characters, you need to keep your readers in mind. Poetry written for children and young adults matches their developmental stages. Knowing which type of poem works for each age can help you find the best place for your writing. One size doesn't fit all.

As children grow, their interest in poetry changes. The very young are interested in word play. Infants and toddlers are still learning how to speak, so their poems tend to be less complicated character-wise. For example, the nursery rhyme "Higglety Pigglety" has three characters: the dog, the pig, and the cat.

"Higglety Pigglety"

Higglety pigglety pop
The dog has eaten the mop
The pig's in a hurry
The cat's in a flurry
Higglety pigglety pop

After the dog swallows the mop, the pig runs away and the cat acts upset. The relationship between the three characters isn't very complicated, and that's just right for the very young.

Once children move into preschool, they are ready for more story in their poetry. At the same time, they are still ego-centered. Poetry with characters for the preschool age and the primary grades tends to be more about "me and you," that is, two people in a relationship. It still relates back to "me" because that is how the young see the world.

Once children learn to see the world from another person's point of view, they are ready for the next stage of poetry. This usually begins after the age of seven, so that children in the middle grades and up are your audience. Lyrical poetry, like "This Girl and This Boy," shares the thoughts and feelings of another person. Although lyrical poetry is the type of poetry most commonly written, children are not able to appreciate it until they are able to see another person's point of view. Once this happens, the relationships in their poetry can become more complicated.

Go to the bookstore or library, and find five poetry books with characters in them. Make a character chart in your writer's journal, and fill it out as you read the poems.

CHARACTER CHART

Title of Poem / Number of Characters / Internal Plot / External Plot / Age of Intended Reader

"Higglety Pigglety" / 3 / no / yes / preschool

"This Girl and This Boy" / 3 / yes / yes / teens

Did you see any trends? Did the younger poems have more action, while the older poems had more emotion? Or did you find poems for all ages that had both internal and external plots? Did the relationships grow more complicated as the reader grew older? How will these findings affect the characters in your poetry? Turn the page in your writer's journal and write about your findings and your own poetry. ✦

Show, Don't Tell

"Show, don't tell" is an old writing adage, yet the question remains: How do you develop a character by showing, not telling? The poem "Alligator," by Maxine W. Kumin (from Jack Prelutsky's anthology *The Beauty of the Beast: Poems from the Animal Kingdom*), shows you how. The answer is in the details.

> Old bull of the waters,
> old dinosaur cousin,

You meet the alligator here in his natural habitat—"the waters." Right from the start, you see that this is one powerful beast. The word choice sets the tone. The poet addresses the alligator as "Old bull," showing the readers that this alligator is an old male. The males of many species are called bulls, and the word "bull" is associated with strength and aggression. This "Old bull" lives in "the waters" so the poet calls him "Old bull of the waters." It's an accurate description; and at the same time, the words show the readers that the alligator is an ancient and primitive beast.

The next line builds on that ancient and primitive image. Once again, the alligator is addressed as "old" and another association is made. He's not just "old," he's an "old dinosaur cousin." Alligators lived in the days of the dinosaur, so this is historically accurate. Yet the alligator outlasted the dinosaur, showing the alligator's strength.

The images in the details show readers how the poet sees the alligator. There is only one image per line. With five words, the first line shows the first image. With three words, the second line shows the reader a new picture. The specific details in each line show readers not only what the alligator looks like, but also where he comes from. The word choice shows readers the alligator's personality too. All this in eight words! This is Picture Writing!

PICTURE IT! | *My Name Is . . .*

What's in a name? Names connect readers to characters. As you read new poetry books for this exercise, look for five poems about people or animals with names in the title. (The poem above was titled "Alligator.")

Once you find five name poems, record the titles in your reading log and prepare the poems for note taking. Type them out in your computer or copy them into your writer's journal.

Using two different colored highlighters, read each poem again and mark all of the action words with one color and all of the descriptive words with the other color.

What did you see? Did the words work overtime? Did some of the action phrases also have descriptive words? Did each line also work with the other lines in the poem? Did the words in the poem show you the character or tell you about him? If you were asked to rewrite this poem, what would you change? Write about showing and telling in your writer's journal. ✦

Snapshots

Every writer finds a new entrance into the mystery.
—LU CHI

A poem with pictures in it is like a series of snapshots. Line by line, readers see the pictures you have created. Who are the characters in your poem? What do they want? What do they do? Who will speak and act? Who will remain still and silent? Only you and the characters in your poem can answer that question.

The choices you make as a writer create the pictures in your poem. How you bring out the personalities of the characters in your poetry is up to you.

If the pictures you write don't please you, look at your characters from a different angle. Try another point of view. Make another character the star; or let your character perform a solo, and take the other characters out of the poem. Show the character in a different scene so the reader can see him in a new way.

PART IV

Setting

Chapter Eight

Fiction Settings

Every story would be another story, and unrecognizable if it took up its characters and plot and happened somewhere else.
—EUDORA WELTY

Are you using the setting in your story to its best advantage? Answering the six questions that journalists ask can help you strengthen your use of setting. As you think of your story's setting, ask yourself the big six: who, what, when, where, why, and how. Setting is a place, so start with where.

Where a story takes place is the first question you need to ask. Where is your character physically? A house? A park? Another planet? The place you select helps readers see your character emotionally too.

When a story takes place is the second question. When is not only a place in history, it is also part of the plot structure. Younger readers experience time sequentially; their stories move from beginning to middle to end. Older readers can start with a crisis moment and then go back to explore what led up to that crisis.

Who is your setting? Does your setting interact with the story's characters? It may be that your setting acts as a story character. It can do this without uttering a single word. Is that what your story needs?

What do you place in your setting? How a character interacts with the physical objects in her world reveals both character traits and plot. In some stories, the props in a story are the reason for the story itself.

Why did you select your setting? Does the place where your character lives influence his speech and his actions? Are your setting, character, and plot so closely related that one influences the other?

How does the reader see the setting in your story? Which point of view are you using? Is the story told in first person (the "me and we" voice), in second person (the "you" voice), or in third person (the "he, she, and they" voice)?

The setting isn't just a backdrop for your story, it is the stage! How you decorate that stage is up to you. Ask these six questions as you make decisions about your setting. Remember, if you ask a question, your intuition works to find an answer.

Where
Setting Is a Place

Where your story takes place is the setting. When readers open the book, they see the setting through your eyes. What pictures are you writing? Where in the world are you? What do readers see as the story begins?

Notice how Pete Hautman uses Picture Writing to develop setting in the first chapter of *Hole in the Sky*.

> I stand at the edge of the world.
>
> Between me and the north rim lies twenty miles of space and a billion years of rock. I have lived here for more than half my life, but I still get this feeling in my gut. The canyon fills me with emptiness. Wind whips up the canyon walls, inflating my lungs, cool and clean, scented with juniper and pine. Below, I see layers of limestone, shale, granite. Red, green, gray, and a thousand shades of brown.

In first person point of view, sixteen-year-old Ceej shows readers his world by beginning with himself. "I stand at the edge of the world," he says. Ceej stands at the top of the canyon, so the description moves from top to bottom. If he were on the canyon floor, the order would be reversed.

The pictures in the words are quite specific. "Between me and the north rim lies twenty miles of space and a billion years of rock." Readers see the details of the canyon long before the word "canyon" is introduced.

A character experiences the setting with his senses, emotionally and physically. "I still get this feeling in my gut," says Ceej. "The canyon fills me with emptiness." The character doesn't just describe the setting; he interacts with it.

Where you set your story influences how the story is told. In New York City, "twenty miles of space and a billion years of rock" is not what Ceej would experience. The sights and sounds and smells of New York City are quite different.

What the character experiences will also be different. The isolation in Ceej's world is both physical and emotional. Moving Ceej to New York City would change the emotion of the story, the internal plot. Feeling emptiness in a major metropolitan area is different than feeling emptiness in a canyon.

The external plot of the story would also need to change if the location changed. Physical isolation is quite tricky to pull off in New York City. In a different setting, a character has to solve his internal problems in different external ways.

Geography is destiny. Change the geography of a story, and you change the character's world. In a different place, the way people speak and move changes. In another setting, the way characters think and act changes. Plot, character, and setting are inseparable.

PICTURE IT! | *First Pages*

Go to the bookstore or the library and open as many fiction books as you can in five minutes. Read the text on the first page until you find the setting. Once you find it, stop reading, and put the book in a pile on your right. If you read the entire first page and don't see any mention of setting, place the book in a pile on your left. Keep reading until your five minutes is up.

How many books did you open? Count the books on your right, then count the books on your left.

What did you notice about the books that showed the setting? Is the setting or the character mentioned first? Did you see the setting through the eyes of the character or a narrator? How long was the description? Was it a paragraph or just a few lines?

How do you feel about the books that didn't mention the setting? Did they draw you in? Did they feel as strong as the books that showed a setting? Write about your findings in your writer's journal, and if you read any books from beginning to end, write their titles in your reading log too. ✦

When
Setting Is Time

When a story takes place can be a vital part of the setting. In the prologue to *Pharaoh's Daughter: A Novel of Ancient Egypt*, by Julius Lester, a box in the page heading reads:

> Year 29 of the Reign of Ramesses the Great,
> 4th Month of Shemu, Day 28

The year, the month, and the day are all mentioned. You immediately know the setting of this book is another place and time. In historical novels, adding a "time" heading is a quick and easy way to alert readers to the setting.

When the prologue begins, how the character experiences time is the topic.

> I sit on the stone bench in the garden of the Women's Palace. I have sat here almost every morning since I came to the palace fifteen years ago. Nothing has changed in all that time. The ibises wading in the lake could have been here when Ra'kha'ef built Hor-em-akhet a thousand years ago. In Khemet nothing changes. Past, present, and future merge and eternity is always now. At least that is how it was for me.

In this first person narrative, Almah begins by telling readers where she is. "I sit on the stone bench in the garden of the Women's Palace." Specific detail shows readers a picture. Then time enters the setting. Almah has done the same thing at the same time "almost every morning" for fifteen years.

Time seems to stand still for Almah. Remembering her mornings "on the stone bench in the garden," she reflects: "Nothing has changed in all that time. The ibises wading in the lake could have been here when Ra'kha'ef built Horem-akhet a thousand years ago." For Almah, it feels as if "nothing changes," as if "eternity is always now."

In Gary Paulsen's *Soldier's Heart*, the time is also established in the heading.

> Chapter One
>   June 1861
>   He heard it all, Charley did; heard the drums and songs and slogans and knew what everybody and his rooster was crowing.
>   There was going to be a shooting war. They were having town meetings and nailing up posters all over Minnesota and the excitement was so high Charley had seen girls faint at the meetings, just faint from the noise and hullabaloo. It was better than a circus.

Change is coming to Charley's life. Change was coming "all over Minnesota." "There was going to be a shooting war."

Time is a vital part of the setting in this Civil War novel, but the reader doesn't see the clock ticking. Time passes with the action in the word pictures. Readers hear "the drums and songs and slogans." Readers see "town meetings and nailing up posters" and "girls faint." Readers also see Charley's reaction: "It was better than a circus." The only specific mention of time is in the chapter title.

In both of these historical novels, time was used in the heading to establish the setting. The time period was mentioned right away to highlight the time difference between the character's life and the reader's life. Before the narrative begins, readers find out that these events took place in the past.

PICTURE IT! | *Rewind*

Time is a factor you need to consider in your story planning. For the youngest reader, times move in a traditional manner, in sequence from beginning to middle to end. Stories for the youngest readers begin with a dramatic moment and move on from there. Flashbacks are not a part of the picture book world.

As children grow older, you can change the order of events to make your story more exciting. A chapter book or a novel may begin with a dramatic moment, then flashback to show what led up to the moment. Once the story reaches that dramatic opening moment a second time, the story moves forward into the character's future.

If the time on the very first page is considered to be "the present," then the pattern for *Pharaoh's Daughter* (and many other novels) would be present, past, present, future. (Please note: The future referred to here is not your future—as in the year 2205—but rather the *character's future* in the story.)

Go to the bookstore or library, and read five fiction chapter books or novels. After you write the titles in your reading log, make a "time zone" chart for each book in your writer's journal. Note the time period of the novel as well. If the events in the novel could take place today, simply write "Contemporary" as the time period.

TIME ZONES

Title: *Pharaoh's Daughter: A Novel of Ancient Egypt*, by Julius Lester

Time in History: Year 29 of the Reign of Ramesses the Great

Time Sequence: Present— Past—Present —Future [Flashback]

Title: *The Kite Fighters*, by Linda Sue Park
Time in History: 1473
Time Sequence: Present to Future [Sequential]

A book with multiple flashbacks moves from present to past to present several times during the course of a story. Whether you need one flashback or many depends on what the story needs.

If you want to find more elaborate patterns, try science fiction and time travel books. *Rewind*, by William Sleator, for example, begins with the funeral of Peter, the main character. In a *Groundhog's Day* twist, Peter is given the chance to go back and live his life over. It takes Peter three tries to makes the changes he needs to stay alive.

After you chart the time zones of the books you read, record your experience in your writer's journal. Did you read any sequential chapter books or novels? Or did all of your books have flashbacks? Did you read any books with multiple flashbacks? Were the books with the multiple flashbacks for middle grade or YA?

Do you think one of your novels could use a flashback pattern? If so, which dramatic moment would you use to open the book? Could you use multiple flashbacks? Or do you prefer the simplicity of the sequential time pattern? ✦

Who
Setting as Character

The setting itself can be a character in fiction. The title often hints at this. Here is the first page of *The Snowy Day*, by Ezra Jack Keats.

> One winter morning Peter woke up
> and looked out the window. Snow
> had fallen during the night. It cov-
> ered everything as far as he could see.

In the first sentence, the main character, a boy named "Peter," and the "winter morning" are introduced. The setting on this page is Peter's bedroom. "Peter woke up and looked out the window." (This story uses third person point of view.)

The "winter morning" acts as a character in this picture book. As the pages turn in this book, Peter goes out into the snow and has a "Snowy Day." Peter's experience with the snow *is* the plot of the book. As Peter interacts with this setting, the world of the snowy day becomes a character. Setting acts as a character when your main character explores or even fights with the natural world. This doesn't happen if your main character just passes by.

In the picture book, a simple exploration is the most common use of setting as character. Exploration fits perfectly with the developmental needs of this age. For the very young, every experience is new.

In books for older readers, you find the setting acting as a character in the "man vs. nature" plotlines, such as *Island of the Blue Dolphins*, by Scott O'Dell, and *Hatchet*, by Gary Paulsen. In survival stories, nature is both friend and foe. The crack of thunder, the roaring of a tornado, and the howl of a blizzard, these acts of nature speak louder than words.

PICTURE IT! | *Listening to the World*

When the setting acts as a character, it doesn't have a speaking part. You are the one with all the words. As your main character sees, hears, touches, tastes, and smells the world around him, your words bring that world alive.

Go to the bookstore or library, and read fiction books until you find three where the world of the story interacts with readers. You want to find examples where the world itself is a major part of the story.

After you find three examples where the setting acts as a character, record the books in your reading log. Then prepare a paragraph or page in each book for note taking. Copy it into your writer's journal or type it on your computer. With a highlighter or a colored pen, highlight each word or phrase that describes that world with one of the five senses. Next to each phrase, write which sense it used. Did readers see it, hear it, touch it, taste it, or smell it?

How many senses did each selection use? Did appealing to two or more senses make the selection stronger? Or was the writer trying to do too much at once? Were the sensory details significant? Did they add to your understanding of the setting as a character? Did they show readers a clearer picture? Or did the extra details just take up space? Write about your findings in your writer's journal. ◆

What

What Do You Place in Your Setting?

The props you place in your setting can reveal character and propel plot. In other words, how a character interacts with the physical objects in his world shows readers that character's personality. How a character uses that object can also move the plot forward.

The picture book *Aunt Hilarity's Bustle*, by Helen Ketteman, wouldn't be the same story without a prop. As you can see from this opening paragraph, without the "bustle" there wouldn't be any story!

> I was just a child when my Aunt Hilarity got the bug to have a bustle. That's one of those padded sit-upons that women in the olden days used to wear when they wanted to look fancy. Aunt Hilarity saw a picture of a bustle in some magazine, and nothing would do but for her to have one.

In *Aunt Hilarity's Bustle*, the entire story centers around Aunt Hilarity's desire to have a bustle. Here the prop acts as a propeller, spinning the story around itself. The prop makes the story fly. It moves the plot forward.

In the young adult suspense novel, *The Killer's Cousin*, by Nancy Werlin, the shoppers at Porter Square Star Market exchange supermarket cards. Although David, the main character, is reluctant to do this, he participates anyway. Every time he shops at the supermarket, he has a card with a different name.

> In my first night in the new apartment with my parents, I dreamed I stood in the Porter Square Star Market, in the "8 items or less" checkout line. In front of me in line stood a redheaded woman. She turned. It was Kathy.
>
> She didn't seem surprised to see me. She fumbled inside a tote bag and pulled out a supermarket card. Gravely, she offered it to me. I pulled out my own card.
>
> Silently we swapped, and I examined my new card. It said DAVID YAFFEE. I looked up and met her eyes. She held out the card I had just given her, so that I could read the name on it.
>
> It said LILY SHAUGHNESSEY.

Here in the Epilogue, the reader sees that David has been given back what he craved throughout the book, his identity. Kathy also has what she wanted all along, her sister Lily.

In *The Killer's Cousin*, the prop reveals character. The supermarket card acts as an identity card in the real world. In the world of the story, this prop symbolizes David's search for his identity.

Props can play a physical and emotional role in a story. In stories for older readers, props even act as symbols, as they do in stories for adults. In stories for younger readers, however, symbols are rarely used. The children are not mature enough to understand symbolism. Their props are simply that, props.

There must be a reason to use a prop. If you are going to focus the reader's eye on a physical object in the setting, it must be essential to the story. A prop must move the story forward in some way. If it doesn't, you are cluttering up the story with unnecessary details.

PICTURE II! | *The Prop Test*

Go to the bookstore or library, and find five fiction books with props in the titles, like *Aunt Hilarity's Bustle* or *Whirligig*, by Paul Fleischman. After you read all five books, record the titles in your reading log. Then give each book the "prop test." Can you take the prop out without leaving a hole in the story? If so, then the story really didn't need that prop.

If all of your books pass the prop test, look a little deeper. Does the prop reveal more about the character? Does the prop move the plot forward? Where in the story is the prop introduced—at the beginning, the middle, or the end? If the book is for older readers, does the prop act as a symbol? If so, what does it symbolize? Write about your test results in your writer's journal. ◆

Why
Selecting Your Setting

Your story setting is closely related to both character and plot. The setting can affect who the character is and what the character does; therefore, it is important to ask why a book takes place in its specific setting.

In the first chapter of *Dancing in the Cadillac Light*, by Kimberly Willis Holt, Jaynell sits in the broken cars at Clifton Bailey's Automobile Salvage and Parts in Moon, Texas, and pretends to drive.

> I drove everywhere, covering miles and miles, even though none of the cars actually ran. Usually I drove when I felt so full I couldn't hold my feelings inside me without popping a vein. . . .
>
> Leaning back against the seat, eyes closed, chin up, hands wrapped around the steering wheel, I moved beyond the dirt roads, away from Moon, into Marshall to rescue Grandpap from Aunt Loveda's. We'd head down to Highway 80, which stretched across Texas, and we'd be riding in a big fancy car, the kind that made people sit up and take notice, like the Dyer's Cadillac.

What the character wants is clearly portrayed in this setting. Using the first person point of view, Jaynell shows readers she wants to rescue Grandpap. Sitting in the broken cars at Clifton Bailey's, she acts out her wish. Jaynell has all the details worked out, showing readers a clear picture of her life and herself.

Each setting the character travels to shows readers a picture of your character. Starting the story with Jaynell standing in her room wishing on the moon would show readers a different Jaynell. Opening the book with her talking about Grandpap while washing dishes with her sister is still another Jaynell. Personality and place go together.

Who your character is will help you decide which setting to select. If your character is physically active, show that character on the soccer field or riding a motorcycle. If you have an extroverted character, show your character talking during lunch at school or at parties.

The plot also plays a part in selecting a setting. What the character needs to do helps determine where the character is. A character with a school problem needs to be in a school setting. A character struggling to survive in the wild must have an outdoor setting. The place, the character, and the action cannot be separated.

PICTURE IT! | *Geography Is Destiny*

Where a story is set is intertwined with the characters in that story. The setting influences how the character speaks and acts. The place where a character lives also influences not only his word choice, but also the way he moves.

The weather in a place influences speech. If it's 105° in the shade, you will speak a completely different way than if it was 17° below zero. It's hard to speak quickly when it's hot and humid. If you're freezing, you get right to the point!

Your character's body will also move differently depending on the weather. Clothing affects movement, and clothing varies depending on the weather. The character wrapped up in a parka moves differently than the one in a swimsuit.

Where you set your story influences the characters in your story. Speech and lifestyle vary from place to place. Rather than see geography as a hindrance, use it to your advantage. Allow the regional influences of your settings to come through in your character's speech and dress. Let the setting play an active part in your writing.

For this exercise, go to the bookstore or library, and look for five fiction books set in different regions. As you read each book, watch for regional speech and dress. Notice how the setting itself is mentioned. After you finish reading, write the book titles in your reading log. Then open your writer's journal and write about how the authors showed the setting in the character's speech and actions. Did the characters use any words unique to that region? Did the weather influence the way they spoke? Did the characters in cold regions have more staccato speech patterns, while the characters in warmer regions had more flowing legato speech? Were you able to see any difference in how the characters dressed? Were the characters' activities, for example, surfing or mountain climbing, influenced by the region? Did the geography play any part in the story? Do you think the writer could have added more regional touches? How will this influence your own writing? ✦

How
Setting Inside and Out

Setting isn't just a location; it's everything that makes a place come alive. The setting is both physical and emotional in a work of fiction. And as I keep emphasizing, fiction is about truths of the heart.

How your character sees the setting depends on how your character feels. The inner world and the outer world are connected. Staying home on a rainy day can be a blessing or a curse, depending on your character. One child is happily making a fort under the table with bed sheets. Another is angry to be stuck inside because his ballgame was rained out. At that moment, each of them experiences his home in very different ways. The words you use to establish the setting will change depending on the circumstance.

Remember, setting is intertwined with plot and character. These three cannot be separated. Where the character is contributes to who the character is. Don't slow your story's pace by "dumping" large clumps of setting detail. Add only what is important to your character. If it's important to the character, then it must be important to the story. Let the story be your guide.

Chapter Nine

Nonfiction Settings

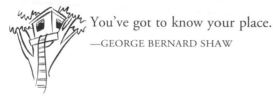 You've got to know your place.

—GEORGE BERNARD SHAW

When you write nonfiction, you share the world with your readers, the real world. When you write about setting in a nonfiction book, you have to know as much about it as you do about your topic. And of course, you must also consider the age of the reader and their developmental needs.

What you share about the world in your book depends on your topic. If you are writing a biography, you need to re-create the world your character lived in. If you are writing an information book, you need to show the world behind the information.

Age level considerations also come into play. The same topic will have different word pictures depending on the age of the reader. The settings you show in a picture book will be simpler than the settings you show in a middle-grade book. As your readers grow, your word pictures can become more complex.

Of course, regardless of the reader's age, tap the senses when you write about the setting. You experience the world with your senses. Why change what works?

Don't talk *at* your reader; use words that *show* the reader the setting. Write pictures by using active verbs and specific details. Bring your reader inside the setting. The real world is an exciting place!

Where
Setting Is a Place

Where a person lives and works directly shapes that person's life. In *Kids At Work: Lewis Hine and the Crusade Against Child Labor*, by Russell Freedman, the setting is an integral part of the story. The working conditions of child laborers caused a mild-mannered schoolteacher to risk his life photographing and documenting this setting so that change could be made.

Kids At Work: Lewis Hine and the Crusade Against Child Labor is two books in one. Not only does it tell Hine's story, making it a biography, it also tells the story of child labor and the reform movement, making it a historical nonfiction book. In this excerpt from page 2, the writer sets the scene:

> Thousands of young boys descended into dark and dangerous coal mines every day, or worked aboveground in the stifling dust of the coal breakers, picking slate from coal with torn and bleeding fingers. Small girls tended noisy machines in the spinning rooms of cotton mills, where the humid lint-filled air made breathing difficult. They were kept awake by having cold water thrown in their faces. Three-year-olds could be found in the cotton fields, twelve-year-olds on factory night shifts. Across the country, children who should have been in school or at play had to work for a living.

Sensory description fills this paragraph. Not only can you see the air, you can touch and taste it too. The boys who "worked aboveground" breathed "in the stifling dust of the coal breakers." The girls who worked "in the spinning rooms of cotton mills" see, touch, and taste "the humid lint-filled air."

In order to understand Hine, you need to see the world in which he lived. The more details you know about his world, the more alive the story becomes for the readers. The setting here isn't a single room or even a city. The setting here takes place in workplaces "Across the country." In five sentences, the writer shares this world with sensory imagery. You see, hear, touch, taste, and smell the world these children worked in. With specific and concrete images, the world of a thousand places comes alive. By the end of this paragraph, readers understand why Hine felt this world needed to change.

The scene is set with the simple to complex idea pattern. Simple scenes, snapshots of child labor, are shown one after the other. In quick succession, the author shows the reader the child labor in different settings, allowing readers to see for themselves the conditions of various work places.

If the order of the paragraph were reversed and the last sentence were stated first, then the paragraph would have used the general to specific pattern. The sentence about child labor would have been the general information. Each picture of child labor would have acted as a specific example.

Which pattern works best depends on you and the material. With the general to specific pattern you tell readers what you want them to see and then you show them pictures of it. Journalists use the general to specific pattern.

On the other hand, the simple to complex pattern, which Freedman chose to use, shows readers the pictures first and then draws a conclusion. The statement at the end sums up what you wanted readers to see. The simple to complex pattern is often used in science writing.

Notice how specific words allow readers to create a picture in their minds. The phrase "humid lint-filled air" is more specific than "hot dirty air." Readers can see the lint and feel the air sticking to their own skin. Concrete words are picture words. They exist in the real world. "Torn and bleeding fingers" is a concrete image readers can picture, creating not just an idea but a reality.

History and biography go together in this photo-essay. The book is written from a third person point of view, although some of the quotations from primary sources are written in first person. First person quotes strengthen the credibility of the writing. With just a few words, you add an "expert" to your piece, making you an expert too! If you can find the first person quotes in your research, try to add them if at all possible.

PICTURE IT! | *See It, Hear It, Touch It, Taste It, Feel It*

Sensory details bring readers into the world of a book by allowing them to experience that world for themselves. You don't need to set aside an entire paragraph to mention sensory details. It only takes a word or two to bring sensory images alive.

For this exercise, find five nonfiction books for a reading level you wish to write. Keep a stack of sticky notes beside you; each time you find a word about the setting that uses one of the five senses, put a sticky note on that word.

You may run out of sticky notes after a single chapter. Or you may read page after page without any sensory detail about the place at all. It depends on what the writer is trying to accomplish in that section.

When you finish reading the five books, record their titles in your reading log, and write about your findings in your writer's journal. Did a word here and there add to the reader's sensory experience of the places in the book? Or did the writing bog down with too much description? How can you add sensory detail into your writing? ✦

When
Setting Is Time

Tick-tick-tick! Time is often an important part of the setting in nonfiction. In an instruction book, time helps readers follow your directions. Do you stir the dough for one minute or five? Does the quarter in the game last fifteen continuous minutes or does the clock stop between plays? How long something takes is one way to look at time in nonfiction.

In the book *Sensational Trials of the Twentieth Century*, by Besty Harvey Kraft, there are several other kinds of time . . .

> The holiday season was a busy time for Bartolomeo Vanzetti, an Italian fish peddler selling eels and codfish from a cart on the streets of Plymouth, Massachusetts. He was there, the immigrant said later, early on the morning of December 24, 1919, delivering fish for the holidays. According to Vanzetti, he had been up before dawn and had gone into a neighborhood bakery shop at 7:45 that morning. His thirteen-year-old helper said he had been with Vanzetti just before eight o'clock. The exact times were important. Vanzetti said he was peddling fish, but the police disagreed. They said he was committing armed robbery.

The time of year is mentioned first. "The holiday season was a busy time for Bartolomeo Vanzetti." If the season of the year is important to your story, you should add this type of setting detail to your own writing. The actual date—December 24, 1919—is mentioned later, so that the same information is given to readers again in another way. This reinforces the time of year in the setting without repetition. Starting with the date would have made the text feel more like a document. Mentioning the holiday season and showing the main character making preparations for it show the readers a picture. Seeing the character in action is more interesting than looking at a calendar.

The time of day is also a time you may need to use in your own settings. In this story, the time of day is crucial to solving the crime since where Vanzetti was at a certain time makes him innocent or guilty. Over and over again in this story, the time of day is mentioned. Vanzetti "was there . . . early." He was "up before dawn." Specific clock times ("7:45" and "just before eight o'clock") are also part of the narrative.

Time flows in sequential order in this paragraph. This is the easiest way to share time with readers. Following the natural sequence allows readers to see the setting in a familiar way so that you may introduce something unfamiliar, the story itself.

The time in history is also a factor in this narrative. The date itself is not mentioned until after readers see a picture of the character in action. The details in the picture, with the names of the fish—"eels and codfish"—and the location—"a cart on the streets"—show readers that this event took place in the past. When the year itself is mentioned as "1919," it comes as no surprise. Today, most children will not see a "fish peddler . . . on the streets . . . delivering fish." The pictures in these words show readers what it looked like in "Plymouth, Massachusetts" in 1919.

The time pictures in this setting focus on the main character. Readers see what Bartolomeo Vanzetti was doing on the morning of "December 24, 1919." You don't need to show all of Plymouth that morning. "His thirteen-year-old helper" is mentioned because he gives readers more information about Vanzetti.

Don't try to show readers pictures of everything in the character's world. Show them the time only when it adds to story. If the story can move forward without a certain detail, leave it out. When you add too many details that require your readers to stop and look, you slow down the story. You don't want time to drag.

PICTURE IT! | *Tick-Tock!*

There are so many kinds of time to keep track of when you write. There is the time period in history, the time of year, the time of day, and the time as it occurs in your manuscript. How do you manage it all?

Go to the bookstore or library, and conduct a time management study. Read five nonfiction books in the age level you write, and notice how other authors manage their time. Do the books open with a mention of time? Do they begin with a time in history, a time of the year, or a time of the day? How does time tick by in the different books? Do the books proceed in chronological manners, so that events are shown in the order in which they occurred? Or do the books use flashbacks to move back and forth in time?

Do the books skip over any time periods? If so, did the gaps interfere with your understanding of the stories? Or did the stories flow smoothly over the gaps?

Record the book titles in your reading log, and take some time to write in your writer's journal . . . about time. ✦

Who

Setting as Character

A setting can become a character in your story. As you interact with the setting, it comes alive, as if it were a living, breathing character. See it happen in *Amazon: A Young Reader's Look at the Last Frontier*, by Peter Lourie:

> We glided slowly upstream along the banks—Bolivia on the right and Brazil on the left. Tall dark green trees and thick bushes sloped down to the surface of the water. The air was heavy as if after a rain, and the forest had the sharp odor of rotting earth and tropical flowers. Cicadas whined throughout the long, hot, muggy day. The sun was a hazy yellow ball high in the sky.

This paragraph moves from general to specific. At first, the readers see that the first-person narrator is on a boat in the Amazon. This is the big picture. Each image that follows is more specific. Readers learn the boat's location in the world of the river—"upstream"—and in the political world—"Bolivia on the right and Brazil on the left."

Sensory description follows. Pictures of the riverbank are followed by touch, smell, and sound. "The air was heavy as if after a rain (touch), and had the sharp odor of rotting earth and tropical flowers" (smell). "Cicadas whined" (sound).

As this paragraph moves from general to specific, it also moves your eye from bottom to top, bringing the Amazon to life for readers. It starts with the river, the lowest physical point, and moves up. The readers' eye moves from the boat in the river to the riverbanks. Along the banks, readers see the bushes and the trees in the forest. After experiencing the forest, after feeling the air, smelling the earth, and hearing the bugs, the readers move up again. This paragraph ends with the sun "high in the sky."

The general to specific pattern starts with the big picture and pulls readers in by adding more and more detail. The bottom to top pattern creates a world for readers by beginning with the narrator on the boat and moving in a logical pattern upward. (If the narrator had been in a plane, the opposite pattern, top to bottom, could be used.)

The Amazon surrounds you. You can see it, touch it, smell it, and hear it. The place itself interacts with the characters and therefore the readers. It becomes a character.

PICTURE IT! | *From General to Specific*

In order to see an object clearly, begin with the big picture (the general idea) and then move in closer to see the specifics. Starting with the big picture alerts the readers to "Look at this now." Moving in to see the details makes more sense once you know what you are examining.

Go to the bookstore or library, and read nonfiction books like the ones you write until you find five examples of setting that move from general to specific. Copy the five example paragraphs on your computer or in your writer's journal. Then, number each new picture you see. With a highlighter, mark every word that uses one of the five senses.

List the titles of the books you read entirely in your reading log and write about your findings in your writer's journal. Did the pictures flow smoothly from general to specific? Did you feel there were enough pictures in each selection? Would you have added more pictures? Would you have deleted any?

How many sensory images did you find? Which senses were mentioned: sight, touch, taste, smell, or hearing? Did you find more than one sense in a single sentence? Was appealing to more than one sense effective?

Did the sensory images make the place come alive for you? Did you feel as if you had been introduced to a living, breathing place? Did the setting step forward to interact with you and the narrator? Or did it just fade into the background? ✦

What
What Do You Place in Your Setting?

The props you place in your setting need to be important and accurate. If you are taking the time to draw readers' attention to an item, it must move the story forward. In the picture book biography *America's Champion Swimmer: Gertrude Ederle*, by David A. Adler, the props we see are an important part of the journey.

> At about ten-thirty in the morning, Trudy had her first meal. She floated on her back and ate chicken and drank beef broth. A while later, she ate chocolate and chewed on sugar cubes. Then she swam on.

Trudy Ederle is swimming across the English Channel. It's twenty-one miles from one side to the other. The journey is so long, swimmers need nourishment before they reach the other side. After three and a half hours of swimming, Trudy stops to eat. "At about ten-thirty in the morning, Trudy had her first meal." (This biography has a third-person point of view.)

How do you eat in the middle of the ocean? Trudy "floated on her back" says the text, and then the props come into view. What can you eat in the water? Trudy "ate chicken and drank beef broth." It's like a picnic in the water.

Then the text says, "A while later, she ate chocolate and chewed on sugar cubes." Since these foods are finger foods, you can easily imagine someone eating chocolate and sugar cubes while floating on her back.

This is just enough detail for the picture book reader. In a story for older readers, there would be more props mentioned in connection with the meal. How the support team managed to deliver the food to Trudy would be added. The delivery scene before the meal would show readers the props the team used, whether nets or baskets or bags. The older the readers, the more details you can show. And don't clutter your set with extra props. You want the pictures you write to show the story, not take up space. If a prop slows down the story, don't use it.

PICTURE IT! | *A Recipe*

Props are an essential part of a how-to book. In order to show someone how to do something, you need to let readers know exactly which props they need. Recipes list the "Ingredients" first. Art projects list the "Materials Needed." Sports books specify the equipment needed to play the sport.

Precise detail is important when it comes to specifying props for a how-to piece. Powdered sugar and brown sugar are two kinds of sugar, but they don't taste the same. Just ask a donut. Football cleats and basketball shoes are both sports shoes, but don't even try to wear cleats to a basketball game. You'll scratch the gym floor (and have to deal with an angry coach)!

For this exercise, find five prop lists, whether in cookbooks, art books, or sports. Compare each list with the instructions that follow it. Are the props listed in order? Is the first prop mentioned the first item you will need? Is the second one used second? Does the list match the task one item at a time?

Now check the accuracy of the list. Are all the props listed? Is the list specific enough? Does the list have any unnecessary props?

Don't forget to check the point of view. Does the writer address the readers in the imperative voice, giving commands? Although you don't see the word "you," it is implied with this voice, giving these books a second person point of view.

For your own how-to manuscripts, you can approach the props list in two different ways. You may find it easier to create the props list after you finish the text. Everything will be in the proper order, and you just cut and paste to make the list. Or, you can use the props list as an outline to help you write the text. The ingredients list is shorthand for the recipe.

After you check these props, use three props of your own—your pen, your reading log, and your writer's journal—and write about the prop lists you found. ✦

Why
Why This Setting?

The setting of your story is essential to understanding the topic. If the setting is essential, then the story would change if it took place somewhere else.

The book *What the Dinosaurs Saw: Animals Living Then and Now*, by Miriam Schlein, is a compare and contrast book. It compares the world of the dinosaurs and today's world. You can see why the setting of this easy reader is essential to understanding the book.

> The sun that warmed
> the dinosaurs
> still warms you.

The book begins an invitation. It asks readers to see animals that lived when the dinosaurs were alive. Except for the dinosaurs, all of these creatures are alive today. Back and forth, compare and contrast, this book jumps between two worlds. The dinosaurs saw these animals in their world, and you can see them in your world too. Without these two settings, how can the children understand that these animals are survivors? The settings are essential. They cannot be changed.

What the Dinosaurs Saw: Animals Living Then and Now uses the familiar to unfamiliar pattern. It begins with the child and his world and reaches out to a world the child will never experience, the world of the dinosaur. The first setting, the child and his world, is familiar. The second, the world of the dinosaurs, is not. Yet with these two essential settings, a new concept is learned. Descendents of ancient times still live today. How else could you teach this without these two settings?

When selecting a setting, it should be clear from reading the background material where the book must take place. The setting and the story are inseparable. Don't take the setting for granted. Explore the world of your story and see what it can teach you. Who knows what secrets your setting keeps?

PICTURE IT! | *No Setting at All?*

What happens if you can't find a setting? After all, where does an alphabet book take place or a reference book? Hmm?

If you can't find a setting, the world itself counts as a setting. Some books zoom in so closely on the details that the setting just isn't seen.

If you were to take an alphabet book or a book of baseball statistics to Mars, the facts inside would be classified as Earth facts. Conditions on Mars would change the way a baseball game is played (changing the stats), and the examples used in an alphabet book would be completely different. As discussed earlier, where you live is a part of who you are.

For this exercise, read five nonfiction books like the ones you write and see if you can identify the setting. Write the titles in your reading log and the setting of each book in your writer's journal. Was the setting an essential part of each book? If you changed the setting, would the book change?

What about the settings in your own writing? Are you writing fact books that zoom in so closely they take the world for granted? Or do you write books that show readers a small part of their world?

How does your world affect the choices you make in your writing? Do you find one aspect of the world fascinating? If you could sign a book contract to write a nonfiction book on any topic, what would that topic be? ✦

A New World

When you write nonfiction, you create a new world on a smaller scale. What you include in that world depends not only on the idea or event itself, but also on the age of your readers.

You may write a book where the setting seems invisible. An alphabet book, after all, doesn't go on about the setting. The *props* in the setting are the topic of an alphabet book. In a fact book about baseball stats, the results of *action* in a setting (a baseball field) are recorded. The setting seems invisible, and yet it is there.

The real world is an essential part of nonfiction. Bring readers into the world of the story with sensory detail. Write pictures! Specific and concrete language adds to your readers' understanding of your world without taking up a lot of space.

Keep your readers in mind as you write about the world of your story. For the youngest readers, everything is new. Their world does not extend beyond home and family. As readers grow, they move out into the world to explore. Use the familiar to unfamiliar pattern to bring your readers into new worlds.

Chapter Ten

Poetry Settings

 Like the onion, poetry is constant discovery. Peel the onion, layer after layer, until the very heart is reached; every cell contains myriad worlds.

—RUTH GORDON, *Peeling the Onion: An Anthology of Poems*

By pulling you inside, a poem takes you to another place. Setting is that place. As you move through a poem, the pictures in the writing should flow one into the other. A well-written poem brings you inside itself and shares a secret with you. You may laugh, you may cry, you may learn something new.

Are you ready to learn about how setting influences poetry? As you do the exercises and read new poetry books for this chapter, keep in mind that not every collection will have examples of each use of setting. You may find five examples in one book, or you may need to read an entire shelf of books! Once again, reading immersion is your goal. Surround yourself with words and enjoy the journey.

Where
Setting Is a Place

Setting is a place, and sometimes that is the essence of a poem, the place itself. In the poem "Geode" by Barbara Juster Esbensen (from her collection *Who Shrank My Grandmother's House?: Poems of Discovery*), the places the poet sees inside the rock are the topic of the poem. Although you don't see it in this excerpt, the poem begins with "I," indicating the first person point of view.

> Here is a city   frozen
> in a hollow
> stone

With one well-chosen word, the world of the poem changes. After introducing the city picture, the poem adds a space, a pause, between the word "city" and the word "frozen." This pause adds drama to the poem. At the same time, it causes readers to see the setting in a new way.

Poetry is spoken music. Did you hear the echo of an o? The city words in this stanza have long o sounds: frozen, hollow, and stone. As you read the stanza aloud, you can hear the echo. Even the geode itself looks like an o.

With different words, the place in the poem would feel different.

> I
> see a city
> hiding
> inside

The long i doesn't echo. It makes you look up, to see how high (another long i word) the buildings are. The tall I reminds you of skyscrapers. With different words, you hear different sounds, you feel different feelings, you see different pictures. When you are writing about place, the words you select are crucial.

PICTURE IT! | *Vacation Slides*

Go to the bookstore or library, and take a poetry vacation. Read until you find five poems with names of places in the titles. You're looking for poems with "pictures" of places. Once you find the poems, write the titles of the poetry books you read in your reading log. Then prepare the poems for note taking. Type them on your computer or write them in your poetry journal. (Remember to record where you found the poem.)

If you were going to read this poem aloud as you showed vacation slides, where would you change the slides? Every time you see a new picture in the words, draw a star. Click! Click! Click! How many slides would you need for each poem? How many pictures did you see?

Don't forget your other senses. When you visit a place, you experience it with more than your eyes. If you touch, taste, hear, or smell something on your poetry vacation, make a note of that too.

Write about your poetry vacation in your writer's journal. Did you find enough pictures in the poems? Did the poems use all five senses? Did your poetry vacation take you to another place? Or do you want to ask the travel agent for a refund? ✦

When
Setting Is Time

As we've discussed with both fiction and nonfiction, when the story takes place is part of the setting too. The poem "The Birth of Fernandina Island," from Tony Johnston's collection *An Old Shell: Poems of the Galapagos*, begins with the when of it all.

> One molten morning
> the world
>
>   explodes

Two kinds of time are addressed in this brief excerpt. The first is time in history. The title of the poem, "The Birth of Fernandina Island," indicates to readers that this poem retells an event from the past. The opening line, "One molten morning," shows readers the time of day and introduces the volcano.

Both time in history and time of day anchor the poem in a specific place. History settings need to be accurate in their detail. Careful research gives you the details you need to make the past come alive. This island was created by the eruption of a volcano, and the details of that eruption are the history of this place.

Setting a poem during a specific time of day gives readers a reference point. Morning, noon, and night are familiar to readers. This poem begins with the familiar reference point of morning to show the birth of an island. The picture in the words is quite specific. "One molten morning" is not just any morning. A big change is about to take place. Specific setting details make all the difference.

How time progresses in a poem is another aspect of "when" you need to consider. Moving from beginning to end, in a sequential manner, is the simplest way to organize time. For younger readers, a sequential time pattern is best. Moving back and forth in time confuses the youngest readers. Remembering an object or an event from the past partway through a poem is fine for older readers, as long as the connection between the two word pictures is clear.

"The Birth of Fernandina Island" uses the omniscient point of view. Readers see the island form from on high. This poem recounts the actions of the volcano that day, not the emotions of a single character. Bit by bit, picture by picture, readers see the birth of an island.

PICTURE IT! | *Watch the Clock*

For this exercise, read several new poetry collections until you find five poems that mention time somewhere in the poem. After you write the poetry book titles in your reading log, go back and look at the poems again. How much space in the poem is given to the mention of time? Out of the fifteen lines in Johnston's poem, "The Birth of Fernandina Island," only one line specifically mentions the time. The rest of the poem *shows* time in the birth of the island.

List the title of each "time" poem in your writer's journal, then write the time details after it. How many words or lines mentioned time in each given poem? Did the poem mention time of day or a time in history? Did time pass in the poem? If so, did it pass sequentially, or did the poet use flashbacks? How do you feel about the poet's use of time? ✦

Who
Setting as Character

The setting itself may act as a character in a poem. In the poem "Invitation from a Mole," by Alice Schertle (from her collection *A Lucky Thing*), the mole invites readers to come into his world. As you go deeper and deeper, the mole says,

> wear the earth like a glove
> close   your   eyes
> wrap yourself in darkness

In this poem, the earth is more than a place, a mere location. In "Invitation from a Mole," the earth interacts with the narrator of the poem. The earth becomes a character.

Under the ground, the mole shares his world. Readers see the setting from his point of view. The words chosen here reflect the mole's emotions.

Once the mole invites you to "close" (heartbeat) "your" (heartbeat) "eyes" (heartbeat), your eyes are out of the picture. You must use your other senses to experience the earth, and the poem.

When the place in your poem is a vital part of the experience, allow that place to come alive. Use your senses to draw your readers into your setting. Let them feel it, touch it, taste it, smell it, see it.

In "Invitation from a Mole" the setting is an essential part of the poem. In fact, without the setting, there wouldn't be a poem! How can the mole invite readers into his world if he cannot describe it? How can the mole share his relationship with the earth without making it a living, breathing character?

Move beyond clichés like the mole did when he invited you to "wear the earth like a glove." One of the gifts of poetry is creating a new picture by connecting two unrelated images. With simile and metaphor, show your readers something familiar in a new way.

PICTURE IT! | *Talking Trees?*

When you think of character, the idea of talking comes to mind. In the case of setting, however, a speaking part isn't always necessary. Do the trees have to talk to be considered a character in a poem? Not really.

If the setting interacts with someone or something in the poem, then the setting is acting as a character. *Acting* is the key word here, not talking. You can act without speaking.

The true test is, if you take the setting out of the poem, does the poem change? Let's say you have a poem about an argument between two friends that takes place in a school. Is the school essential to the poem? Not if the argument could have also taken place over the weekend. The setting of the school is the backdrop, not a character.

On the other hand, if you take the setting out of "Invitation from a Mole," there wouldn't be any poem at all. The interaction between the narrator and the setting *is* the poem. Thus, in this poem, the setting acts as a character.

As you read more poetry books for this exercise, look for poems where the setting interacts with the other characters in the poem. Once you find three examples, write the titles of the books you read in your reading log. Then write about your search in your writer's journal. Did you find any poems where elements of the setting had a speaking part? Or did your setting act as a silent character? How many poems did you have to read to find three examples of setting as character? ◆

What
What Do You Place in Your Setting?

What you place in your setting is also a part of the world you create in a poem. How the characters in your poem interact with the props you place in their world becomes part of the poem's movement. What you place in your poem is up to you and the needs of the poem. Here is one example from a poem titled "Mrs. McUnder" by Jeff Mooo (from his collection *The Butterfly Jar*).

She watched the bright moon shining *under* her head
And found her lost shoes hiding *over* her bed.

Mrs. McUnder is finding things in all the wrong places. She has her "under" and her "over" reversed. These spatial concepts are opposites, and in this poem, the words are typed in the opposite places, too! The poet's use of italics draws the reader's eye to the situation.

With each line, the concept is clearly shown with the props that the poet selects. "She watched the bright moon shining *under* her head," says line four of this twelve-line poem. Now every child knows that the moon shines up in the sky, so the word that should be there is *over*. The moon is over your head, not under it.

The next line of the poem has the opposite problem. "And found her lost shoes hiding *over* her bed." Although the words are reversed here, the word in italics is still the wrong word. One prop used here is a bed, something very big. Shoes, on the other hand, are small. If you place shoes over a bed, they don't hide. The shoes would be in plain sight. The props used here show the concept quite clearly.

Over and under are opposites, and in this poem these words are used in the opposite places. It's a double opposites' poem. With the right props, the opposites are clearly demonstrated. The opposites concept drives this poem, not the character's point of view. This poem is *about* Mrs. McUnder, not *by* Mrs. McUnder. It is told from on high, in the omniscient point of view.

PICTURE IT! | *The Props*

When it comes to writing, you are the prop master. You decide which props to use and which props not to use. Read new poetry books for this exercise, and look for five poems with props in them.

After you write the book titles in your reading log, copy the five poems on your computer or in your writer's journal, so you can rewrite them. Now, highlight the props in each poem and *change* them. That's right! Try to rewrite each poem with different props.

Did it work? Could you rewrite the poems using different props? Or did the poems change when the props changed? (If you can successfully fill in the blanks with another prop, then the details in the poems aren't specific enough.)

After you finish your rewriting (and possibly a new poem or two!), write about your day as a prop master in your writer's journal. ✦

_____

Why
Selecting Your Setting

If you mention a setting in your poem, that setting must be essential to the understanding of a poem. In an untitled poem from *Drat These Brats!* by X.J. Kennedy, the last two lines of the final stanza read:

> "Gosh, but aren't golf courses fun?
> See, I've made a hole in one!"

The point of view in these two lines is first person. Gertrude says, "I've made a hole in one!" Readers see the golf course through Gertrude's eyes.

This poem *must* take place on a golf course. Without the golf course, the "hole in one" at the end of the poem doesn't make sense. A "hole in one" in another setting doesn't mean quite the same thing.

When writers talk about *organic* settings, they mean that the setting itself cannot be separated from the character or the story. A golf course poem belongs on a golf course. That's organic.

PICTURE IT! | *Feel the Dirt*

Take out your sticky notes for this final exercise, and go to the bookstore or the library. Select five new poetry books and look for poems with organic settings. You want to find poems where the setting cannot be changed, where the character, the action, and the setting are inseparable. Once you find an organic poem, put a sticky note on the page, and keep reading. After you have finished reading all five books, write the titles in your reading log. Now take a tally. How many poems in each collection were organic? How many poems in the collection even mentioned setting? Do a little math and see what percentage of the poems with settings had organic settings. Write about your tally in your writer's journal. ✦

Earth Mother

In a poem, the setting details are connected to all of the other parts of the poem. The character and the action cannot be separated from the setting. The place where the character lives and moves is a vital part of any poem.

As the poem moves from picture to picture, the setting may change. The setting itself may cause a change, as storm clouds bring rain. The character may makes changes to the setting or even move to another setting. Poetry isn't static.

Changes in a poem need to come from inside the poem, not the poet's hand. A poem is not a marionette, waiting for you to move it around. Allow your poems to grow organically.

Setting can be established in a poem with just a word or two. Selecting a word that conveys the feeling of a place is your challenge. The words will come in due time. Be an earth mother and wait for the seeds to grow. If you have patience, oh, the pictures you will write!

PART V

Putting It All Together

Chapter Eleven

Your Fiction Manuscript

 The best book begins with characters, characters who want
something. They spend the rest of the book trying to get it, while
other people and events conspire to keep them from getting what
they want.

—OLGA LITOWINSKY, *Writing and Publishing Books for Children in the
1990s: The Inside Story from the Editor's Desk*

You've learned how to create vivid pictures of stories, characters, and
settings. Once you have your first draft on paper, it's time to look at
your story with new eyes. Two things happen to you fiction writers after the
first draft stage. You discover that you don't say enough about your character
and you say too much about your character. This paradox appears in the
very same draft.

After living with your characters for quite some time, you see every aspect
of the story in your head. The question is, Did everything in your head travel
down your arm and make its way onto the page? After your first draft has cooled
down, after you have set it aside for a time, it's time to come back to it and
find out what you really wrote.

At the same time, you probably have written too much story. Because you
know so much about your character's world, you add it to your manuscript.
And writing down everything that comes to you *is* your task with a first draft;
it is not a mistake. However, after you let your manuscript cool down, you
must return and shape your story.

Shaping your story is what you will do in this chapter. If you do not have a
fiction manuscript ready to edit, study someone else's book as you read this
chapter. Find a used book that you can write in, and edit it as you work through

this chapter. As you "deconstruct" your example book, you can learn how to edit your own manuscript.

Define the Genres

In order to shape your fiction for the marketplace, you need to define it. Write the title of your manuscript in your writer's journal. Under the title, list each genre as you define it. First consider the make-believe factor. Is your book:

A. *fantasy*—something that could *not* happen in real life
B. *reality*—something that could happen in real life

Next, look at the time period. Did the events in your story happen:

A. twenty years or more in the past—making the book *historical*
B. in the present—making the book *contemporary*
C. in the future—making the book *futuristic*

Third, decide on the topic. Is the book:

A. adventure
B. sports
C. mystery
D. suspense
E. horror
F. sci-fi
G. humor
H. animal story
I. family story
J. peers /school story
K. growing up or coming of age

List every genre that applies.

Now, look at the age range and reading level of your manuscript. Which age range is your book targeting? Is it one of the following:

A. a board book for infants and toddlers
B. a picture book for preschool or early elementary school
C. an easy reader for beginning readers
D. a transitional reader or chapter book for second and third graders

E. a middle-grade book for fluent readers in upper elementary school

F. a young adult book for middle school and high school students

Knowing the age of your audience will help you in two ways. First, the age range will determine the format you use. If you know you are writing a picture book, you know you have thirty-two book pages to cover. On the other hand, if you are writing a YA novel, you have two hundred pages to fill. Knowing the length will help you in the writing process.

Secondly, knowing the age of the readers will also help you with vocabulary. Although you do not need to work from a vocabulary list, keeping your readers in mind as you write is helpful. The words that toddlers and teens use are not the same. Children see the world differently as they grow older. You need to use language that your readers understand.

Add the age range of your manuscript to your genre definitions in your writer's journal. For example, *The Folk Keeper*, by Franny Billingsley, is a YA fiction book that is a fantasy about Selkies. Stop and write for a few minutes about your genre choices and how these choices fit the needs of your audience.

The One-Line Summary

When your book is published, the Library of Congress will list your name and the title of your book with a one-line summary on the copyright page. The formal name for this information is the "Library of Congress Cataloging-in-Publication Data" (also known as the CIP). In a single (albeit long!) sentence, the book is summarized.

For *The Folk Keeper*, the Library of Congress summarizes: "Orphan Corinna disguises herself as a boy to pose as a Folk Keeper, one who keeps Evil Folk at bay, and discovers her heritage as a seal maiden when she is taken to live with a wealthy family in their manor by the sea." Here is a 162-page book captured in a single sentence. It doesn't tell you everything that happens. It is only a summary.

Why do you need a one-line summary? When you are revising, you must sum up your book in a single sentence so you know which direction your book is headed. You must always keep in mind the focus of your book.

How do you find the focus of your book? Ask yourself the one thing your readers need to know to understand your book. In a work of fiction, it is the main character that dominates the summary. Fiction is about character.

A one-line summary is both short and comprehensive. The CIP for *The Folk Keeper* tells us where the book began: "Orphan Corinna disguises herself as a boy to pose as a Folk Keeper, one who keeps Evil Folk at bay." It also tells us where the book ended, with Corinna's discovery of "her heritage as a seal maiden." Where she makes this discovery is also mentioned: "in their manor by the sea." In one line, you have it all: plot, character, and setting.

What will your summary say? Write your own CIP summary under the title and genre definitions in your writer's journal.

Storyboarding

> Every scene that precedes the climax must logically build toward it, and every scene that follows the climax to the end of the story must be a logical result of it.
>
> —JAMES V. SMITH JR., *You Can Write a Novel*

Storyboarding, which we discussed in the Seeing Fiction chapter, is a visual technique that enables you to see your entire manuscript at a glance. When you storyboard, you create a visual outline of your story. With this picture outline you can examine one element of your story at a time.

Plot

Start with the action. Make a *plot storyboard* for your manuscript in your writer's journal. The age range will help you decide which type of storyboard to use. For short illustrated works, like picture books and simple easy readers, use the Picture Book Storyboard on page 25. Draw page squares and write a short phrase describing what happens to the main character on that page.

Since you don't know how your book will be illustrated, start a new square every time you see a new action picture in your manuscript. See if you have enough action pictures to fill an entire book.

For longer works, use the Chapter Book Storyboard on page 38. In your writer's journal, draw 2" or 3" squares on facing pages so you can see the entire book at a glance. Start with chapter one on the left-hand side and work your way over to the right-hand page. Make a square for each chapter of the book.

Inside the square for each chapter, list the key words and phrases that summarize what happens to the main character in that chapter. The idea is to write tight and short, not to include every detail. You want to see your entire story at a glance. Stick with the highlights, and don't forget to number the chapters.

Character

After you see the action pictures, it's time to assemble the cast. Who is in your book? Turn to a new page in your writer's journal to create a *character storyboard*. For picture books and easy readers, draw little squares to represent the pages. For longer works, draw a large square for each chapter.

To fill in this storyboard, write the name of every character you see in your manuscript. If a character acts on page 5 of your picture book plot storyboard, write his name on the square for page 5. If a character is mentioned in chapter seven of a novel, write his name in the square for chapter seven.

You don't need to write what each character says, or perhaps doesn't say if he doesn't have a speaking part. Simply list each name. The idea behind a character storyboard is to see at a glance where each character appears in a book.

CHARACTER STORYBOARD for *Freckle Juice*, by Judy Blume
ch 1 Andrew, Nicky, Andrew's mom, Miss Kelly the teacher, the reading group, Sharon
ch 2 Andrew, Sharon, Andrew's mom, Mrs. Burrows, Miss Kelly, the class
ch 3 Andrew, Mrs. Burrows, Andrew's mom, the ladies, Sharon
ch 4 Andrew, Andrew's mom, Mrs. Burrows, Sharon, a big green monster
ch 5 Andrew, Nicky Lane, the class, Miss Kelly, Lisa

With the younger books, the character storyboard will help you see if the main character really is the star of the book. Does the main character appear in every square? Does the action in each square center around that main character?

If you have written a book with subplots, the character storyboard can help you keep track of who does what when. The plot storyboard needs to focus on the main character. Use your character storyboard to help you see the subplots at a glance.

Add a brief summary of the subplot action chapter by chapter next to the character's name. Highlight the subplot phrases using a different color for each character. Who does what when is now easy to see.

Setting

Once you know who the actors are and what they do in your book, it's time to look at the sets. Where does all of this action take place? Where do the characters move around? Turn to a fresh page in your writer's journal, and draw the squares for a *setting storyboard*. Draw small squares for the short books or large squares for the long books.

The setting storyboard is the simplest of the three. Take a blank storyboard, and simply write the name of the place where the story happens in the squares. For the shorter books, make a page-by-page list of squares. For the longer books, list the settings you find in each chapter in every chapter's square. Write the name of the place in each square.

If you have the setting in your head but it's not in the manuscript yet, this is where you find out. Add the location to the storyboard, and make a note on your manuscript to add more setting pictures when you rewrite.

Story Arc

> Events in a story don't happen by chance. In fiction every event must *logically* follow another.
>
> —RONALD B. TOBIAS, *Theme and Strategy*

The story arc is an organizational pattern that brings readers from one place to another. Now that you have created the three storyboards for plot, character, and setting, you can use them to look at your book in more detail. This time around you are looking for the story arc in each of the three elements. You want to see how the story flows.

Plot

To see the story arc, you must first identify the *main story problem* in the book. Turn back to your plot storyboard. What does the main character want? This is your main story problem. Write "Main Story Problem" at the top of the page and summarize the problem in a sentence.

As the character works to solve his main story problem, he overcomes obstacles. In a short book, one without chapters, there are often three obstacles that arise during the course of the story. Circle the page where the first obstacle arises and write "Problem #1" over that square. Summarize the problem in a single sentence. Find the other two story problems. Number each one and summarize it with a single sentence. If your book has more than three story problems, number and summarize any other problems you see.

A chapter book usually has one obstacle per chapter. At the same time, if you look carefully, you can see a larger obstacle that stretches across several chapters. First, write the obstacles that occur in each chapter. (You may have already written these when you created your plot storyboard.) Now look at the character's actions over several chapters. Do two or three or more chapters form an act? Does the character work to solve different aspects of the same bigger problem in these chapters? If so, write "Problem #1" over the first chapter in the act. Then summarize that bigger problem with a sentence. Continue through the story, identifying the second and third acts. Label "Problem #2" and "Problem #3" and summarize each. Continue throughout the story as needed.

At the end of the story, you should see a chapter that shows the climax of the book. Things are as bad as they can be, and then the character takes action to solve his problem. Write "Climax" over this square. This should leave you only a chapter (or two) for the resolution, for tying up loose ends. Write "Resolution" over this square.

How did the story arc? Did it rise and rise and rise until the very last minute, until the climax? As soon as the character solved the problem, did the story tie up the loose ends and then stop?

What is the pacing like? Are the obstacles in your story evenly spaced? Does the first obstacle occur right after the characters are introduced? Does the second obstacle arise after a few pages (for a picture book) or after a few chapters (for a chapter book)? Was this pattern repeated after a few picture book pages or a few chapters for the third obstacle? Or are the obstacles bunched together, at the beginning, the middle, or the end of the book?

Pacing is very important. Although episodic books rise and fall within each chapter, overall the tension in the story should rise. If it does not, you need to move things around. In *Children's Book Insider*, Publisher Simon Boughton says, "Begin with Chapter Four. Get readers into the story right away, revealing what they need to know, instead of setting it up with the first three chapters."

If your character solves the story problem in the middle of your picture book, lop off the end. If all of the action happens in the middle of your story, make the middle your story. You need to know what happens before and after your story takes place, but your readers do not. Use the story arc so you can see where your story really is

STORY ARC GRAPH

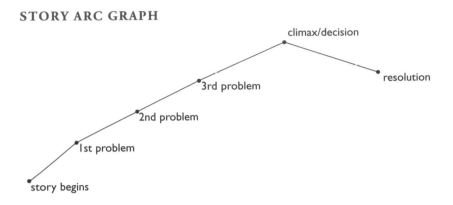

Character

The characters in the story play a vital role in shaping how readers see the story. Turn to your character storyboard and see where the characters are. Who is the first character readers meet? Who is the last character readers see? Are these characters the same? Is it the main character? If not, why?

How do readers experience your story? Is the main character also the narrator, so that the book uses the "I" voice of first person? Are readers the main character, with the "you" voice of second person? Or are the readers and the narrator both on the outside looking in, with the third person "he, she, or they" voice? Write the main character's POV next to his name on your character storyboard.

Once you start a story with a certain point of view, you need to keep that point of view throughout the book. If you use alternating narrators, these narrators need to keep their voices consistent also. This is a part of the promise you make to readers on the very first page. If readers see the character's world in first person in chapter one, you can't switch that character to third person in chapter three and second person in chapter five. This is too confusing for readers, especially the younger ones.

Look over your character storyboard and see who is where in your book. Then look at the manuscript itself to identify the point of view used for each character. Write the POV for each person on your character storyboard. Write a 1 for first person point of view, a 2 for second person, and a 3 for third person. Proceed square by square through your manuscript.

Did the viewpoint for each character stay the same throughout your book? If you find this is not the case, mark those sections for revision. Think about which point of view works best and then make that point of view the only one you use.

Setting

How your readers see the setting is directly connected to the point of view. Some writers show their readers the world of a book entirely through the eyes of the main character. Other writers alternate between the omniscient point of view and the character's eyes.

The omniscient, or all-knowing third person, POV is generally used at the beginning of a new section. This may be a chapter opening, or a scene transition within a chapter. Looking carefully at published books, you will see white space before most of the omniscient POV transitions. This lets readers know that change is coming. Then you, the writer, fly up into the sky and see a world that the characters can't see. You describe it quickly in a line or a paragraph of summary. The story resumes when you jump back to the character and move on with the action.

Chapter eight of *Belle Prater's Boy*, by Ruth White, opens this way . . .

> Coal Station Elementary and Coal Station High School were both located a little piece up Slag Creek at the end of Residence Street, just before the road started getting narrow and wound up Cold Mountain toward Kentucky.
> Woodrow entered the elementary school with me . . .

In one sentence, the writer describes the world of the story. The readers find out where the school buildings are in the town. The next setting is introduced by comparing it to sites the readers already know. For the rest of that scene, readers see only what the character sees through the first person narrator.

Seeing the world through the character's eyes means noticing things that have an emotional impact on the character. Follow Maud (who cannot swim) over the ship's rail in *The Pirate's Son*, by Geraldine McCaughrean:

> And because her brother was up to his chest in water, and because the green transparent water was filled with dark and unidentifiable shapes, she was quick and nimble, chanting as she went, on and on: *sharks, sharks, sharks, sharks, sharks.*

The character sees his world through the filter of his feelings. Just like you, the character notices two or three things at the most at any one time. When you see the world through the character's eyes, make it an integral part of the story. Add a sentence here and a phrase there. Don't dump clumps of setting description. Have it occur naturally, in small bites, just as it does in real life.

Open your writer's journal to your setting storyboard. It shows you the settings the characters visited. Revisit each setting in your manuscript. Which point of view did you use to describe that setting? Do readers see the world from up high in the omniscient POV? Or do readers see the world through the eyes of the character? On the storyboard, write an O next to each omniscient view of the setting and a CH for each character view of the setting. (For a longer book or one with many scene changes, you may wish to write these labels next to the setting descriptions in the manuscript as well.)

Did you find any setting descriptions that need rewriting? Do you need to move your omniscient point of view descriptions to transitional moments when the setting changes? Did you find any clumps that you need to break up? When you see the setting through the character's eyes, does the setting happen as a part of the action? Or does the action screech to a halt? Can you move setting words in the action sentences? Rewrite as necessary.

Technique: Character, Character, Character

> Make sure your main character wants something, and make sure somebody is keeping him from getting it.
> —LAVONNE MUELLER

The focus of fiction is the main character. How the main character feels shapes the story. What the main character does shapes the story. What the main character sees shapes the story. The character's world *is* the story.

Character and Plot Are One

Because who the main character is and what the main character does are inseparable, the character and the plot cannot be separated. What the main character wants must be the driving force of the story. Ask yourself if this is true in your story? Does everything in the story center around the main character's driving need? Are the main character and the action in the story inseparable? Do the actions in the story flow out of the wishes and desires of the main character? Do the events in the story occur because of who the character is?

Start a new page in your writer's journal, titled *Character Study*. Write down everything you see in your manuscript on the page about your main character. Did you mention the ordinary things like name, age, and gender? Did you move deeper into the character and show her likes and dislikes, her relationship with family and friends? Most importantly, did you show the readers what the character wants?

You might know the character inside and out, but did all of that information make it onto the page? When you create an "after the fact" character study for your own manuscript, you can compare it to any earlier character studies you created. Did everything in your head make it onto the page? If not, revise until you share enough with your readers so they can live inside of the character.

Is It Believable?

Believability is the next thing to check. Although you write a great scene, it may not be believable. Ask if your character would really do that? Believability hinges on the character. If readers know what a character wants, they are more apt to believe the actions that the character takes. Knowing the character helps the readers believe in that character.

The writer must establish belief in the character by revealing the character to the readers. Main characters that are flat are not believable, so it is essential for you to create well-rounded characters. The more readers know about the main character, the more they believe in him, even if the character does something outlandish.

If the actions that the character takes don't match his personality, the story breaks down. The spell is broken. Suddenly readers are aware of you, the writer. When you do not allow the character to move from within, readers see the strings you have attached to the character. Your character becomes a puppet, a wooden marionette.

Did you add something to the story because you wanted it to happen? Wanting something to happen and having something happen because it needs to happen are not the same. If the action in the story doesn't flow out of the desires of the main character, you are in charge, not the character. The character needs to be the reason the events in the story take place. The character *is* the story.

Adding elements or events to the story that move the plot forward yet are physically impossible also breaks the spell. Unless you have created a world where people fly, your characters can't jump off tall buildings and survive. Your character's world is assumed to be the real world unless you have clearly established that it is not. The world of your story has to be believable too.

Entire genres are built around believability. Science fiction, fantasy, and historical fiction all require the writer to take readers to a place neither has ever visited. The world of these books is clearly established from the start. On the very first page, readers know they have entered a different place. Setting details show readers this new world, and even though it is not our world, there are rules you must follow.

If a planet does not have gravity, how do the characters move? You must figure it out before you write that scene and impart that knowledge to readers without lecturing them. Once readers have the details, they follow willingly because they believe.

Readers are willing to follow a character to the end of the universe *if* you can make them believe that the character knows the way. Check your manuscript for believability. Go over your story scene by scene, and ask yourself, Would the character really do that? Does it help the character solve his problem? Is it physically possible? Does it break any laws in the world of this story? Rewrite as necessary.

Growth and Change

The third essential character ingredient is change. After all of this action, after all of these feelings, does the character grow and change? If not, why lead readers on this merry chase? What was the point? Stories are about life, and life is about change.

Even if the story needs an unhappy ending (and many YA stories do), the character still needs to grow and change as a result of living that story. Your story must ring true.

How do you know what needs to happen? Look at what the character wants, at what the character needs. The growth and change in the story need to come from inside the character. It needs to be organic.

What the character wants is also a promise the writer makes to the readers. The readers find out what the character wants at the beginning of the book. Satisfaction comes—for the readers and the character—when after all of the struggles of the book, the main character makes a decision to change and, in so doing, achieves his heart's desire. Was the promise kept? Did the character get what he wanted? In other words, did the story end with a promise fulfilled?

Turn back to the story arc and look at the promises made. How was the character introduced to the readers? What did the character want?

Now look at the climax of the story. Does the character make a decision to change? How does that decision affect what the character wanted all this time? Are the two related? Does the change come from inside the character? Is it organic? Or does time simply pass as the pages turn?

Make your story stronger by focusing on the character inside and out. Who the main character is and what that character wants should drive every action in your fiction manuscript. Revise until character *is* plot.

Picture Writing

With the story tightly focused on the character, the next step is to look at the character's pictures. In each scene, what is the picture that readers see? For this section, write directly on your manuscript pages.

How Many Pictures?

Start at the beginning of your story. Draw a star after each word picture you see. Draw a star when you see a new character. Draw a star each time a character moves. Draw a star each time you see the setting mentioned. Draw a star each time you see a new picture.

3, 2, 1, Action!

Using a highlighter pen, capture the action. Mark every verb that you see. Draw a line under the active verbs. Make a dot over passive verbs. How active is the action?

Color It In

With a second highlighter, capture the scene. Mark all of the description with a different color. If it's just a single adjective, highlight it. If it's an entire phrase, highlight it. Watch for use of the five senses. How do readers see, hear, touch, taste, or smell the pictures in your story?

Scene by Scene

After you highlight and star the picture words in your book, after you see the action and the description, look at the white spaces. Do you really need these words? If they don't show a picture, why are they in your book?

Start at the beginning of your manuscript and, scene by scene, cut the extra words. Don't distract readers by using words that aren't working. If they don't show a picture, out they go!

No one expects you to write pictures in one take. Movie directors shoot every scene over and over, but not every frame makes it into the final edit. Give yourself room to explore your vision; and after you see what you really want, take out the rest. Cut out everything that doesn't show a picture.

Picture writing is picture *re*writing.

Final Decisions

> Remember, what lasts in the reader's mind is not the phrase, but the effect the phrase created: laughter, tears, pain, joy.
>
> —ISAAC ASIMOV

Before you send your manuscript to a publisher, you must answer two questions: Does the form you selected fit the main character? Did you meet your goals for this book? To answer these questions, step back and look at the manuscript as a whole.

Form

After all is said and done, was the fiction genre the best choice for this book? Or could this material have been better expressed in nonfiction or poetry?

Did the material match the age of the intended readers? Were the other genre choices a good match? Was this a fantasy story that needed to be a reality story or vice versa? Did the attitudes in the story match the time period, whether past, present, or future? Did the topic genre (adventure, sports, mystery, suspense, horror, sci-fi, humor, animal story, family story, peers/school story, growing up or coming of age) seem appropriate?

Asking these hard questions about your manuscript can save you a lot of grief later. If the answer to any of these crucial questions is no, it is better to rewrite now than to collect rejection letters and not know why.

Give Me Five

You're almost done, so now it's time to "give me five." Find a fresh page in your writer's journal and write:

GIVE ME FIVE

1. _____
2. _____
3. _____
4. _____
5. _____

After each number, list one goal that you had for your book. These goals can vary greatly, depending on the character and the genre choices you made.

The easy reader mystery, *Buzby to the Rescue*, by Julia Hoban, met these goals:

1. focuses on Buzby
2. uses simple language
3. shows the clues clearly
4. is funny
5. has a happy ending

The Shakespeare Stealer, a historical novel by Gary Blackwood, on the other hand:

1. uses Widge to show Shakespeare's company
2. is filled with historical details
3. uses language to show the time period
4. shows life and death situations
5. has a realistic ending

The mysteries solved in each of these books match the age of the readers. The changes each character goes through are also age appropriate. One size doesn't fit all when it comes to fiction.

What are your goals for your fiction book? Give yourself five and write them down. You know your book is finished when, after writing and rewriting, you have reached all of your goals. Only then do you send it to an editor.

Chapter Twelve

Your Nonfiction Manuscript

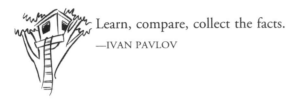 Learn, compare, collect the facts.
—IVAN PAVLOV

Nonfiction manuscripts go through many steps on the way to publication. Many writers begin with a proposal. They do the initial research and outline the book. When a publisher accepts the book proposal, a contract is written and work begins in earnest. As the writing and the research interact with one another, the book grows and changes.

After the first draft is completed, step back and look at the book with new eyes. That is exactly what you will do in this chapter, look at your first draft so you can edit it.

If you do not have a nonfiction book ready to edit, find a published book you can study. You want to find a book you can write in so you can analyze the different elements and keep it for future reference.

Define the Genre

How you edit your book depends on what type of book it is. Open your writer's journal and write the title of your manuscript on a fresh page. Underneath the title, list the genre as nonfiction. Then look a little deeper.

Is your nonfiction book:

A. an information book

B. a biography

If the book is an information book, what is the topic? Where will it fit in the Dewy Decimal system?

A. 000 Generalities
B. 100 Philosophy & psychology
C. 200 Religion
D. 300 Social sciences
E. 400 Language
F. 500 Natural sciences & mathematics
G. 600 Technology (Applied sciences)
H. 700 The arts
I. 800 Literature & rhetoric
J. 900 Geography & history

If the book is a biography, is it:

A. one person's life story
B. a collection of biographies

Now, look at the age range and reading level of the book. Which age range is the book targeting? Is it:

A. a board book for infants and toddlers
B. a picture book for preschool or early elementary school
C. an easy reader for beginning readers
D. a transitional reader or chapter book for second and third graders
E. a middle grade book for fluent readers in upper elementary school
F. a young adult book for middle school and high school students

Write all of the genre labels that apply to your book under the title. For example: *The Amazing Potato: A Story in Which the Incas, Conquistadors, Marie Antoinette, Thomas Jefferson, Wars, Famines, Immigrants, and French Fries All Play a Part*, by Milton Meltzer, is a middle-grade nonfiction information book about the history of the potato and how it affected society. At the library, it is shelved in the 600s, the Applied Sciences section.

The One-Line Summary

Vigorous writing is concise.

—WILLIAM B. STRUNK JR., AND E.B. WHITE, *The Elements of Style*

The genre labels lead you to the next step, which is a one-line summary of the book. When your book is published, the copyright page will summarize your book in a single sentence. Under the author and title listing, you will find the "Library of Congress Cataloging-in-Publication Data" (also known as the CIP).

What does the summary look like for a nonfiction book? For *Christopher Columbus: Voyager to the Unknown*, by Nancy Smiler Levinson, the summary reads, "A biography of the fifteenth-century Italian seaman and navigator who unknowingly discovered a new continent while looking for a western route to India." Here the plot of the book is summarized in a single sentence. The main character ("the fifteenth-century Italian seaman and navigator") and the setting ("a new continent") are also included. Even the type of book ("biography") is categorized. One hundred eighteen pages are condensed into a single line.

Write your future CIP summary into your writer's journal. This will help your writing as you revise. It will also help you summarize your book in your cover letter when it's time for you to submit it to a publisher.

Storyboarding

It is a bad plan that admits of no modification.

—PUBLIUS SYRUS

After you have defined your book and summarized it, look at the sweep of the entire book. Begin by looking at the big picture.

It is with storyboarding that a line is drawn in the sand between character-driven books and concept-driven books. If your nonfiction book follows a real-life character, you must use both the fiction manuscript chapter and this one. Use the storyboarding and story arc approaches in the fiction manuscript chapter to help you develop your character. Then come back to this chapter for the nonfiction elements.

In an information book, the information itself is the star, not a character. The focus on information rather than character requires a different approach to storyboarding.

Open your writer's journal, write "Storyboard" at the top of a new page. If you are storyboarding a short book, such as a picture book or a young photo-essay without chapters, draw a square for each page in the book.

If you are storyboarding a longer book with chapters, draw a large square for each chapter. If the book has numerous chapters, you may need to use two pages for your storyboard, one on the left and one on the right. Your goal is to see the entire book at a glance.

Think of your storyboard as a visual outline. Inside each square, write what you see in the text on that page or chapter, and include each topic you discussed. For longer books, you may have to create a tiny outline in each chapter square. Use key words and phrases to summarize the information. Remember to include chapter titles, as well as any sidebars, charts, or other nonfiction elements.

Story Arc

It's not enough for a nonfiction writer to just write good, clean sentences; he must organize those sentences into a coherent shape.
—WILLIAM ZINSSER, *Writing to Learn*

Now that you have created a storyboard for your book, look deeper to see how the information inside the book is organized. How the information flows from one idea to another is the story arc for nonfiction.

First look at the general pattern for the book. Look back at your storyboard and analyze it. From chapter to chapter, did you use the journalist's pattern, moving from general to specific? Or did your material require that you use the scientist's pattern, moving from simple to complex? With either of these approaches, you could also have used the familiar to unfamiliar pattern.

If your story doesn't use one of these common story arcs, that doesn't mean that it doesn't have an arc. There are many, many ways to organize ideas. The key is to find an organization pattern that works with the material. You want to find a logical way for one idea to flow to the next.

OTHER NONFICTION STORY ARCS
Sequence (numbers, letters, days of the week)
Question and Answer (a variation of the problem–resolution pattern)
A Day in the Life (begins in the morning, ends at night)
The Journey (travels from one place to another)
Predictable (a clue in the text tells you what happens next)
Cumulative (repeats and builds, like The House That Jack Built)
Cause and Effect (one thing leads to another)
Compare and Contrast (an elephant is big, a mouse is small)
Definition (tells what something is)

A book may use one or more patterns to organize its ideas. *Saving Endangered Birds: Ensuring a Future in the Wild*, by Thane Maynard, not only defines endangered birds, it lists them in alphabetical order. Using the alphabet as a sequencing tool helps readers find their way around the book.

Some story arcs, such as "A Day in the Life" or "The Journey" blend nicely with the narrative traditionally found in fiction, only the readers follow a real-life character in a real-world setting instead of an imaginary one. The CIP for *Six Words, Many Turtles and Three Days in Hong Kong*, by Patricia McMahon, says: "Describes the daily activities, school work, and family life of an eight-year-old girl in Hong Kong."

Chronology

Chronology is a variation of the sequence story arc. As you organize the rest of your story arc, from general to specific or simple to complex or familiar to unfamiliar, you can also organize the items in your story chronologically. *Secrets of the Mummies*, by Harriet Griffey, uses the general to specific pattern. At the same time, the events in the book are organized by date. The oldest mummies are discussed first. The book begins with the Egyptian mummies and ends with "Mummies Today."

How-to books also use chronology as a story arc. The task itself will be organized step by step. That's one chronology. How the tasks are listed in the book is another chronology. In *Clueless in the Kitchen: A Cookbook for Teens*, by Evelyn Raab, the order of the recipes follows the order of the meals in the day. Breakfast recipes are found at the beginning of the book. Desserts are at the end.

How Many Arcs?

As you look at your storyboard, how many arcs do you see? Does your book have just one organizing pattern, or does it use several? Write "Story Arc" on your storyboard page and name all the story arcs you see.

If your manuscript doesn't have an arc yet, add one now. How readers move from one idea to the next is crucial. Test potential story arcs by creating new storyboards. Don't rewrite the entire book; just test the outline with a new pattern. If one pattern doesn't work, try another. Once you find an arc that works, open a new file and cut and paste to reorganize your book. Without a spine to hold the bones of your book together, your book won't stand up.

Nonfiction Techniques: Logic

Internal Story Arc Logic

Once you have seen the story arc for the entire book, move in closer to see how the story flows from paragraph to paragraph. On the first page of your manuscript, underline each topic sentence with a red ink pen.

The topic sentence summarizes the key information in the paragraph. Often the first sentence, the topic sentence, shows readers where the writer is going next. By underlining the topic sentences, you can see the internal story arc.

INTERNAL STORY ARCS
Cause and Effect
Compare and Contrast
Problem–Resolution

Which internal story arc does your story use? Does it show one thing causing another? Does it compare and contrast two different items? Does it show a problem and efforts to resolve that problem? Write "Internal Story Arc" on a new page in your writer's journal and list the arc you used.

Balance

Once you have determined your internal story arc, you need to check for balance. In *cause and effect* story arcs, the cause and effect need to be directly related. A sneeze does not cause a solar flare. If you are linking two items with cause and effect, you must show a direct relationship between the cause and the effect.

Balance is especially important in *compare and contrast* story arcs. If you say three things about one side of the story, you need to say three things about the other side of the story. You can't expect readers to already know both sides of the story. Children don't have enough life experience yet. Stacking the deck on one side isn't fair. If you don't really want to present the other side's view, then don't use this story arc technique. Use the cause and effect or the problem–resolution story arc instead.

Problem–resolution story arcs are the same story arcs used in fiction narrative.

Balancing this story arc requires that you state the problem and the search for a solution. Finding the answer without understanding the problem shows readers only half of the story. How can there be an accomplishment without any struggle?

In fiction narratives, the struggle itself takes up most of the story arc. One problem leads to another as the tension builds throughout the story. Spacing out these problems so that they appear at regular intervals balances the story, whether you are writing fiction or nonfiction. Too much at once can overwhelm readers. Too little can bore them.

Balance is the key to making the most of a problem–resolution story arc. How much of the text did you use for each new problem? Does each problem carry equal weight? Or does one problem dominate the text? If you found one problem more interesting than the others, consider focusing your book on that problem alone. If changing the focus isn't possible, remove the extra material and save it for another book or a magazine article. Research is never wasted.

POV Check

Now that you are examining the story page by page, this is a good time to check the POV. Which point of view does your story use? Is the text written in first person, using the "I" voice? Does it use second person, the "you" voice? Or is the story written in third person, the "he or she" voice?

The voice you use depends on the type of book. Books with instructions are often written in the "you" voice, even if you don't see the word "you." The imperative voice is the one that gives commands ("Add three eggs."), and with this voice, the "you" is implied.

Write the POV on your internal story arc page. Did you find any POV changes as you went paragraph by paragraph? If so, you should rewrite. Changing the narrator's POV in the middle of the book confuses readers. (Using a new POV in a quote or a sidebar should be fine.)

Picture Writing

Now that you have organized your ideas, it's time to move closer and look at the pictures you are sharing with readers. In this section you will be working with words one line at a time.

USE THE ELEMENTS

Nonfiction elements, such as tables, charts, graphs, and sidebars, can help you balance your book, regardless of the pattern. When the book is designed, these nonfiction elements are set aside visually to separate them from the body of the text. This breaks the text into chunks, making it easier for readers to digest. It also gives you a place to add interesting information that doesn't fit into the body of the text.

Extending your research beyond the text adds interest for readers. You can add tidbits and kid-friendly trivia in sidebars, charts, graphs, maps, and more. The "oh, by the way" information that readers love fits nicely into these elements. A *sidebar* acts like a small magazine article with a title and a focus of its own. *Diagrams, graphs, charts, and maps* can show readers visual information that can take pages to explain. The captions you write for these elements sum up important facts in just a few words.

Sidebars and other nonfiction elements give you the best of both worlds. They allow you to keep the body of the text balanced. At the same time, you can share all of the exciting tangents you found. No one said that you had to share all of your information in the body of the text. Put your research to work and add another layer of meaning to your book. Balance your book by adding nonfiction elements.

How Many Pictures?

How many pictures did you write? Turn to the first page of your manuscript, and start hunting. Draw a star in your book each time you see a picture in the words. Draw a star each time you see a character, a movement, an idea, or a place.

3, 2, 1, Action!

Test the action in your words. With a highlighter pen, mark every verb that you see. Make a dot over passive verbs. Draw a line under the active verbs. How alive is the text?

Color It In

Check the details with another highlighter pen. Using a different color, mark all of the descriptive words. Underline both single words and phrases. Focus on the five senses. Do you help the reader see, hear, touch, taste, or smell the details in the story?

Gaps

Now that you've seen pictures, action, and details, what is left? Do you have a lot of words in your text that aren't doing anything? Do you really need these extra words?

The white space you see shows you the gaps in your manuscript. If the words don't show the readers a picture, the readers have a gap between one picture and the next. Your task is to eliminate those gaps.

James V. Smith Jr., author of *You Can Write a Novel,* uses the GAP method for line editing. "GAP stands for 'gain a page.' You try to shorten every chapter by one page," says Smith. "Shorten every paragraph by at least one line."

Turn on your computer and make a new file for your manuscript, a GAP file. Then start cutting. Take out every word that isn't working. Smith recommends repeating this process three times. "Come back to it in a week or two, when your blood is running cold."

If you eliminate every word that doesn't show a picture, only the picture words will remain. All you'll have left is Picture Writing!

Final Decisions

> Get right to the heart of what readers want and need to know
> —SAMM SINCLAIR BAKER, *Writing Nonfiction That Sells*

Before you send your work to a publisher, you must answer two questions: Is the form you selected the best choice for your topic? Did you meet your goals for this book? To answer these questions, step back and look at the manuscript as a whole.

Form

Now that you have poked and prodded your way through your manuscript, do you think that the nonfiction genre was the best choice for this material? Or could your ideas have been better expressed as fiction or poetry?

Does the information in your book match the age of the readers? Does it cover topics that children learn in school at that age? Would your biography work better as historical fiction?

Knowing where to begin is not automatic. Finding the right form for your ideas takes time and thought. Your preschool concept book idea may work better as an information book for second grade. The biography you are researching may interest you (and your readers) more as a work of fiction. Can you accept the change and allow your material to find the form it needs?

Give Me Five

The final step in the revision process brings you back to the beginning of a project. You know your project is complete when it has reached its goals. Every project has its own parameters. The age of the readers and the topic itself will influence those goals. Open your writer's journal and make a chart:

GIVE ME FIVE

1. _____
2. _____
3. _____
4. _____
5. _____

Now consider your goals. What five goals do you have for your nonfiction project? Here are two examples to guide you:

Charles A. Lindbergh: A Human Hero, a biography by James Cross Giblin:
1. Is a birth to death account of Lindbergh's life
2. Uses quotations from primary sources
3. Details Lindbergh's life with narrative passages
4. Shows both triumph and tragedy in Lindbergh's life
5. Has an extensive bibliography

How Come?, a science information book by Kathy Wollard:
1. Is a question-and-answer book
2. Types difficult words in italics and then defines them
3. Uses sidebars
4. Quotes experts
5. Has a complete index

Write your goals on the chart. Next, ask yourself if you have accomplished these goals. When your answer is yes, send your work to a publisher.

Thirteen

Your Poetry Manuscript

 Poetry is really the fusion of three arts: music, storytelling, and painting.

—MOLLY PEACOCK, *How to Read a Poem . . . and Start a Poetry Circle*

After you have written a series of poems about a topic, collect them and look at them again. When you send in a collection of poems, each poem must work individually and all of the poems must work together. It's a delicate balancing act.

If you have written a single narrative poem that you intend to send in as a picture book, look at it both as a poem and as a picture book. Read this chapter for the poetry, then read the fiction or nonfiction manuscript chapter for the content of your poem. When you do two things at once, they both need to work if you want to make a sale.

This chapter is intended to help you *after* you have written your poetry. If you haven't written any poetry yet, study someone else's poetry with the exercises in this chapter. Find a book that you can write in as if it were your own manuscript. Reading poetry is one thing. Working with words layer by layer is another.

Define the Genres

Before you can analyze your poetry, define it. What kind of poetry book have you written? Is it:

1. One poem that tells a single story (a picture book poem)
2. A collection of poems on a single topic

Open your writer's journal and write the title of your poetry book manuscript. Underneath the title, list the first genre definition.

Now, look at the age range and reading level of the book. Which age range is the book targeting? Is it:

A. a board book for infants and toddlers
B. a picture book for preschool or early elementary school
C. an easy reader for beginning readers
D. a transitional reader or chapter book for second and third graders
E. a middle-grade book for fluent readers in upper elementary school
F. a young adult book for middle school and high school students

Knowing the age range will help you with word choice. Preschool poetry words and YA poetry words are not the same. Although you don't need to limit the words you use with poetry, you must be aware of the words your audience would use. It's one thing to use a single "fancy" word to expand your readers' vocabulary. It's quite another to write word after word that the readers don't understand at all or conversely words they would think of as "babyish."

When you write the first few drafts, write for yourself. Just let the words come. When you work on the final few drafts, revise with the readers in mind.

Write the age range of your manuscript in your writer's journal. Add a few thoughts about the vocabulary you have used.

The One-Line Summary

A one-line summary of your book is next. When your book is published, the Library of Congress will sum up your book in a single sentence. Open any poetry book to the copyright page and you will see the "Library of Congress Cataloging-in-Publication Data" (also known as the CIP). Under the author and the title is the "Summary." *Adam Mouse's Book of Poems*, by Lilian Moore, has this summary: "A collection of poems about nature written by a mouse named Adam."

What will the summary say for your book when it is published? Write your own summary under the title and genre definitions in your writer's journal. This will help you keep your focus as you revise.

Storyboarding

> For a poem to be remembered, it needs to be fully developed, fully thought
> through, fully expressive of its purpose.
> —PETER SEARS, *Gonna Bake Me a Rainbow Poem: A Student Guide to Writing
> Poetry*

Just as with the other genres, you study poetry by looking at the big picture
first. Storyboard the three main components of the story: plot, character, and
setting. Once again, use a separate page to storyboard each of these story
elements.

Storyboarding is a two-step process. First, you map out your book so you
can see what you have where. Then you examine the story arc. In this section,
you will create three storyboard maps for your poetry: one for plot, one for
character, and one for setting.

Plot

Open your writer's journal to a new page. At the top of the page write "Plot
Storyboard." Now draw a square for each poem in your collection. For younger
collections, you can easily create a storyboard on a single page of your writer's
journal. Collections for older readers will probably fit better on two pages. If
your collection has thirty or forty poems, draw fifteen or twenty squares on the
left-hand page and fifteen or twenty squares on the right-hand page of your
writer's journal. Having the pages face one another allows you to see the entire
collection at once. (If you are storyboarding a novel in verse, use this method
and create a square for each poem.)

Write the title of each poem inside a separate square. Then summarize that
poem with a phrase or a sentence. (You may find that the title is a summary of
the poem.) Number the poems in the order in which they now appear in your
collection.

If you are storyboarding a single narrative poem, like the ones found in
picture books, use the picture book method. Draw thirty-two page squares. Fill
in the squares as you want to see them in a book. Write the action you see in
the lines of the poem in each corresponding page square.

When you storyboard a picture book poem, you want to see if you have
enough action pictures for a thirty-two-page book. If you start your poem on
page 5, this means you will need to have fifteen different action pictures. If you

don't see fifteen different pictures, decide if you want to expand the poem or use it in a collection instead.

Character

The characters in each poem are next. Turn to a new page in your writer's journal and label it "Character Storyboard." Once again, draw a square for each poem (or each page of the book if you are storyboarding a narrative picture book poem). Add the title of the poem to each square. Then look at each poem again and decide who the star is?

Your main character doesn't have to be a human. Not every poem has a person in it. A garden or a dog or a galaxy may be the star of a poem. Write the name of the star of the poem in each square.

Setting

Make a *setting storyboard* on the next page of your writer's journal. In each square, write the places you see in each poem. Some poems move from place to place. They travel with just a few lines. Write *all* of the places you have written, in the order in which they occur. It doesn't matter if the main character or the other characters go to these places. Write them down. Don't overlook common everyday places like a living room or a park. Settings don't have to be exotic to be in a poem.

If the characters only talk about a certain place, but don't visit it, write that down too. A mere mention is enough. You want to create a record of the places in the poem. You don't always have to go somewhere to be influenced by a setting. The mere mention of a place (Siberia, Hawaii, India) evokes feelings in readers even if they have never visited there.

Story Arc

Our words must seem inevitable.
—WILLIAM BUTLER YEATS

Now that you have created three storyboards, one for plot, one for character, and one for setting, look at each of them more closely. This time around you are looking for the story arc in each of the three elements. You want to see how the story flows.

Plot

Although the poems in a collection can (and must!) stand on their own, when they are gathered together, they need to work together. Turn back to the plot storyboard and look for the story arc. The story arc is an organizational pattern that brings readers from one place to another. Poetry collections about nonfiction topics often use nonfiction plot patterns to organize their ideas. Poetry collections about people, on the other hand, often use the plot patterns found in fiction, but not always.

Is your collection really a single story? Do the poems act as chapters, featuring the same cast of characters? A narrative collection, one that tells a single story with the same set of characters, will use the tension-building plot patterns of fiction.

STORY ARC GRAPH

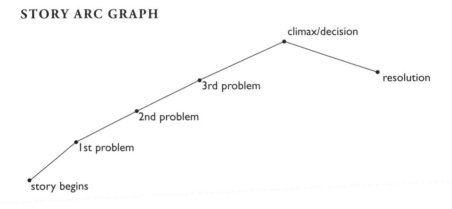

If your collection tells a story, how is that story reflected in the arrangement of the poems? Where does the collection begin? Where does it end? What happens in the middle? How do you travel through the collection from beginning to middle to end? Does the tension build from poem to poem? (If you need more help with fiction plotting elements, see the Your Fiction Manuscript chapter.)

What if your poems about isolated explorations of the same topic? A collection of poems about the same topic, even if they involve people, will probably build with a nonfiction pattern. If so, how should that type of collection move?

Do your poems start small and build to something bigger in the simple to complex pattern? If this is the case, the first poem introduces the topic in simple terms. Each succeeding poem explores the topic in more depth. The most complex poems, in terms of subject matter, fall at the end of your collection. *Flicker Flash*, by Joan Bransfield Graham, for example, begins with a poem about light. Near the end of the collection is a poem about an incubator bulb.

Do your poems start with a big idea and become more specific in the general to specific pattern? The first poem introduces the topic in the broadest terms. Each poem after that shows a specific picture of that same topic. "Cat Tongues," by Eve Merriam, is the first poem in Myra Cohn Livingston's anthology *Cat Poems*. This poem about a cat washing himself can apply to any cat. Other poems in this anthology, such as "My Cat, Robin Hood" and "Miss Tibbles," mention specific cats by name.

Perhaps your poems start with something familiar and then move to a new idea in the familiar to unfamiliar pattern? Kay Chorao's anthology, *Jumpety-Bumpety Hop: A Parade of Animal Poems*, begins with a kitten and ends with an ostrich.

Or did you use another pattern? The pattern in Lee Bennett Hopkins's anthology, *Yummy! Eating Through a Day: Poems*, is visible in the title. It uses the Day in the Life pattern. Check the young nonfiction plot patterns chart on page 50 to see if you are using one.

One size doesn't fit all when it comes to story arcs. Look closely at your poems so you can see which pattern is right for you. If you have written a picture book poem, you may use these patterns too. You must have a pattern that brings readers with you from beginning to end.

Speaking of the end, does your collection reach a conclusion? If the collection is fiction based, are the characters' problems resolved? If the collection is organized with nonfiction tools, does the ending bring readers to a new view of the topic?

Or does your collection simply stop? Does it feel as if the poems could be rearranged without making any difference at all? It may be that the collection doesn't have a story arc yet. If that is the case, try the story arcs mentioned here until you find one that fits your material.

Character

The characters in a poetry collection (whether human or not) also play a part in the story arc. Turn to your character storyboard. Who begins the collection?

Who ends it? Are these characters the same? Is the same character in every poem?

Write the point of view for each poem into the square for that poem. Write 1 for first person point of view, 2 for second person, and 3 for third person. If the point of view changes in the poem, write the new number too.

Does one point of view dominate the collection? Are all of the poems told from the same point of view, or does the point of view change from poem to poem? These approaches can be used for different effects. Sticking with the same point of view can give the collection a unified voice. This is especially effective with narrative collections.

Keeping the same point of view is a must for a narrative picture book poem. Picture book readers cannot switch narrators or points of view in the middle of a story. They don't think that way yet. On the other hand, young adult novels use multiple narrators and change points of view without confusing readers. If you are writing a young adult narrative collection, you may wish to experiment with multiple narrators and multiple points of view.

Using different points of view in a topic-based collection can give the poetry collection a feeling of breadth. It feels as if you have explored the topic fully. You see the topic from many different viewpoints. Variety or unity, which point of view you use for each poem depends on the effect you want for your collection.

Setting

The places in your poetry also play a part in your story arc. This applies to narrative picture book poems and novels in verse as well as poetry collections. Where does the collection travel? Look back at the setting storyboard. Where does the collection begin? What is the setting of the first poem? Where does the collection end? What is the setting of the last poem?

How does the collection move from the beginning to the end? Does the collection begin and end in the same place? If so, do readers gain a new perspective of that place? Even if the place is the same from beginning to end, show readers something new. Why read all of those poems if the pictures don't change?

Or does the collection begin in one place and end in another? If so, are these two places related to one another? Is there a physical or emotional connection between the two? The poems between the beginning and the end must connect the two in some way. If there is no connection at all, find one. Otherwise, you have a pile of poems, not a collection.

Does the movement of the places between the poems feel natural, allowing readers to flow from place to place? Or does the movement between the poems feel forced? If the movement between the poems jars readers, then you have a gap. You must add a transition, another poem between that moves the readers smoothly from one place to the next. You may already have that transition poem somewhere else in your collection. If not, you can always write a new one.

Looking at the Big Picture

After examining the story arc in three different ways, stop and take stock. Move things around. Ask yourself: What does this collection need to work as a book? Where does it need to begin? Where does it need to end? How do you get from the beginning to the end?

Find a plot pattern that works for your collection. Try different patterns until you find one that fits. Decide on your point of view. Do you want the variety that comes with alternating the point of view, or do you want the unity of voice that comes from keeping it the same? How do you want your collection to move from place to place? Do you want your reader to come back to the same setting at the end of the collection or to move to an entirely new place? You want your story arc to flow seamlessly from beginning to end. Now is the time to make that happen.

Revising in the big picture stage allows you to look at the overall picture so you can see the collection as a whole. In order to make the story arc work, you may need to add more poems or take some out. Or you may just need to rearrange what you already have.

Once you determine which poems the collection needs, you can move deeper and edit individual poems. Why spend hours rewriting poems that don't fit in the collection? While certain poems may have helped you develop the idea of the collection, they don't have to stay in the collection. The collection may have grown in a new direction. Or those poems may need to be in another collection. If they no longer fit, you need to let them go. Writing is never wasted. You'll find a home for them somewhere else.

Picture Writing

Poetry for children should catch the eye as well as the ear and the mind.

—DAVID MCCORD, FROM AN INTERVIEW IN *Pass the Poetry, Please!*

Once you have decided where to place each poem in your collection, look at each poem more closely. What are the pictures that you see? How can you make these pictures even clearer?

How Many Pictures?

Reread your poetry manuscript. Draw a star on the manuscript next to each picture that you see. When you see a new character, draw a star. When you see something move, draw a star. When you see a new place, draw a star. Whenever you see a prop, draw a star. Capture every picture on the page.

3, 2, 1, Action!

With a highlighter pen, reread every poem and mark the verbs. Make a dot on the passive verbs. Draw a line under the active verbs.

Color It In

Using a different highlighter, mark all of the descriptive words and phrases. Look for sensory words, words that describe how something looks, sounds, feels, tastes, and smells.

Remove the Scaffolding

When you finish highlighting, your poem should be covered with stars and color. If the words in a line don't show a picture, do you really need them? Can you say the same thing in a more visual way?

Does the poem need the words that aren't highlighted? If the words in a line don't move or describe, why are they in the poem? Take out your thesaurus and hunt for new words.

As you try out new words, remember to delete some of the old words. If you can understand the poem without the nonstarred or nonhighlighted words, you didn't need those words anyway. Those extra words are probably scaffolding. Builders use scaffolding around a house to help them build it. These poles and planks are removed when the house is finished.

Go through each poem word by word, line by line, and take out the scaffolding—those words you needed to help you write the poem. Delete a word or a phrase, and see if the poem still stands without it. If you need the words, keep them. If not, out they go! The pictures in your words will be clearer if you take out the words that aren't working anymore.

Technique: The Three Rs

Being a poet is like being a musician. You get caught up in the music.
—JOHN CIARDI, FROM AN INTERVIEW IN *Pass the Poetry, Please!*

After you look at the pictures in your poems, look at the poem's construction. How did you use the tools of poetry? Are you making the most of the three Rs of poetry: rhythm, rhyme, and repetition?

Rhythm

The best way to test the rhythm of a poem is to read it aloud. You should be able to read each line without emphasizing one particular word or phrase. If you have to emphasize or "stretch" a phrase to make it fit, that line needs rewriting.

Poets spend a lot of time working on the meter, that is, the rhythm of a poem. How the words fit together matters. You may have a natural ear for meter, or you may need to study it.

Meter starts with the word and how it's said. Each word is broken into syllables. Some syllables are stressed and some are not. When the word ends with a stressed syllable, we say that it rises. When a word ends with an unstressed syllable, we say that it falls.

Meter uses the word "feet" to label the different combinations of stressed and unstressed sounds. You can talk about feet using a single word as an example or apply it to an entire line of poetry. Some syllables are accented with stress, and some are not. How these sounds are combined gives poetry a movement we call rhythm.

POETRY FEET IN A SINGLE WORD

2 syllable feet | example words: "today" and "happy"
Iamb: – / | to-DAY | unaccented-accented | stress on last syllable | rising
Trochee: / – | HAPP-y | accented-unaccented | stress on first syllable | falling

3 syllable feet | example words: "tambourine" and "Saturday"
Anapest: – – / | tam-bou-RINE | 2 unaccented - 1 accented | stress on last syllable | rising
Dactyl: / – – | SAT-ur-day | 1 accented - 2 unaccented | stress on first syllable | falling

COUNTING FEET IN A LINE
"Humpty Dumpty"

/   –   /   –   / – – /

Humpty | Dumpty | sat on | a wall,
  trochee| *trochee*| *trochee*| *iamb*

/   – / –   / – – /

Humpty | Dumpty | had a | great fall:
  trochee| *trochee*| *trochee*| *iamb*

/ – –   / – – / – – /

All the King's |horses and |all the |King's men
dactyl | *dactyl* |*trochee*|*iamb*

/   – – / – – /–   – /

Couldn't put |Humpty to|gether |again.
dactyl | *dactyl* |*trochee*|*iamb*

You may or may not consciously use meter when you write. When it comes to revision, however, the more you know about counting feet, the better. If you know the underlying rules of meter, you can understand why a certain word jars your ear when you read it in a poem. If you're not sure of the stress, look up the word in the dictionary. Which syllables are stressed and which are not is shown in the pronunciation for each word. Stressed syllables have heavy stress marks like this ′ that look like accents.

Scan each poem in your collection and mark the feet. Mark each stressed syllable with a / *slash* and each unstressed syllable with a—*dash*. After you scan the entire poem, look for the feet used in each line. Draw a straight line | between the feet so you can see the patterns in the poem.

Once you scan your poems, you can see the rhythm of a piece. The lines in your poems that flow smoothly fit with one another because of the meter. Lines that jar the ear usually have different feet than the rest of the piece. Once you see the feet, you can look for words that fit the pattern you established in the other lines of the poem.

Rhyme

Rhyme is the next poetry tool you check. Once you know the feet, it is easy to check the rhyme. End rhyme is what most people think of when you mention rhyme. In "Humpty Dumpty," the first two lines end with a rhyme. (Two lines that rhyme are called a *couplet.*) The word "wall" at the end of the first line rhymes with the word "fall" at the end of the second line. Both of these words have rising feet, making the rhyme "perfect."

The second two lines in "Humpty Dumpty" also rhyme at the end. "King's men" rhymes with "again." These line endings are also iambs, with rising feet. This couplet also has perfect rhyme. The "feet" and the sounds must match to create a perfect rhyme. Rising feet match rising feet, and falling feet match falling feet.

If the feet at the end of the line match, but the sounds don't, it may be a *near rhyme.* When the end of a line doesn't match perfectly with the end of another line but the sounds in the words are similar, it is called *near rhyme, off rhyme,* or *slant rhyme.* Some words simply don't have a word that rhymes with them perfectly.

Near rhyme uses sound to help it rhyme. When two words share consonant sounds, their rhyme is called *consonance.* When words share vowel sounds, their rhyme is called *assonance.*

In the nursery rhyme "Old Mother Hubbard," the third and sixth line end with words that nearly rhyme. When you look at them on the page, "bone" and "none" appear to rhyme perfectly. When you recite the rhyme, however, the sounds in the words don't match. The word "bone" has a long o, while the o in "none" says "uh." The consonants at the end, however, are identical (n), making this near rhyme an example of consonance.

"Old Mother Hubbard"

Old Mother Hubbard
Went to the cupboard,
To fetch her poor dog a *bone.*
When she got there
The cupboard was bare
And so her poor dog had *none.*

In the nursery rhyme "A Cat Came Fiddling," the word at the end of the first line is "barn" and the word at the end of the second line is "arm." The consonants at the end of these words are m and n, so the words don't rhyme perfectly. The vowel sounds, however, are identical ("ar"), so this is an example of near rhyme with assonance.

"A Cat Came Fiddling"

A cat came fiddling out of a *barn*,
With a pair of bagpipes under her *arm*;

Of course, you may use consonance and assonance elsewhere in your poetry, not just at the end of a line. The words you choose for the beginning and middle of the line are important too!

Some poets even rhyme inside the line. This is called *internal rhyme*. In the nursery rhyme "Higglety Pigglety," the words higglety and pigglety rhyme perfectly with one another. Neither word is at the end of the line, making this an internal rhyme.

"Higglety Pigglety"

Higglety pigglety pop
The dog has eaten the mop
The pig's in a flurry
The cat's in a flurry
Higglety pigglety pop.

Check the rhyme in your poems. Assonance and consonance can occur anywhere in a line of poetry. Write an A where you see assonance and a C where you see consonance. (Draw arrows if needed to link the words.) Write an I where you see internal rhyme. Write an E after each use of end rhyme.

Did you find more rhyme than you expected? You may not consciously think about rhyme when you write a poem, but if a certain word fits just right, it may be because it rhymes! The sound of the music in rhyming words is an integral part of poetry.

Repetition

Repetition is the third poetry tool you can use when you revise. One of the reasons that rhyme is so appealing to kids is that the sounds are repeated. Consonance repeats the consonant sounds. Assonance repeats the vowel sounds.

While end rhyme listens for repetition at the end of the word, *alliteration* repeats the sounds at the beginning of a word.

"She Sells Seashells on the Seashore"

She sells seashells on the seashore,
The shells she sells are seashells I'm sure.
So if she sells seashells on the seashore,
I'm sure the shells are seashore shells.

In the rhyme "She Sells Seashells on the Seashore," the "s" and "sh" sounds are repeated. She, shells, and shore all begin with sh. The word "sure" isn't typed with an "sh," but when you say it aloud, you can hear the sh sound. Sells, sea, and so begin with s. These four lines are filled with alliteration.

Not only are the sounds repeated, but the words as well in this tongue-twisting rhyme. Repeating the words is another way to use repetition in poetry. In the first and third lines, some of the words are repeated in the same order.

Line 1: <u>She sells seashells on the seashore</u>
Line 3: So if <u>she sells seashells on the seashore</u>

The second and fourth lines, however, use the same words in a different order.

Line 2: <u>The shells</u> she sells are seashells *I'm sure*
Line 4: *I'm sure* <u>the shells</u> are seashore shells.

In longer poems, entire stanzas may be repeated. In poetry and in music, a repeated stanza is called a *refrain.*

Reread your poems and check for repeated sounds, words, and phrases. Are any stanzas repeated? Circle any repetitions and mark them with an R.

If you see a place to add more repetition in your poem, try it and see how you like it. If it's just too much, you can always delete it later.

Final Decisions

> I know a poem is finished when I can't find another word to cut.
> —BOBBI KATZ, FROM AN INTERVIEW IN *Poetry From A to Z: A Guide for Young Writers*

Sending a poetry book to a publisher isn't the same as sending a poem to a magazine. The pictures in a poetry book must flow from page to page whether you are sending in one poem for a picture book or many poems for a collection. Before you send out your work, answer the following questions: Is the form you selected the best choice for the book? Did you meet your goals for this book? To answer these questions, step back and look at the book as a whole.

Form

By now your poems are covered with colored highlighters (for action and description) and alphabet codes galore (for the three Rs of poetry). After all is said and done, how do you feel about your poetry? Are the pictures clear? Do the words sing? Did you use the tools of poetry?

Was poetry the best choice for this material? Or do you now think that fiction or nonfiction could have better expressed these thoughts and feelings?

If you feel that poetry was your best choice, look at your form. Which poetic form(s) did you use? At the top of each poem, name the poetry form. Was it free verse, blank verse, haiku, sonnet, or _____ (fill in the blank)?

Use of form is similar to the use of voice. Sometimes you use a variety of forms to give your collection breadth. Other times you use only one form (all haiku, for instance) to give your collection depth. Does your collection have a mixture of forms, or does one type predominate? What do you want for your collection, breadth or depth?

Do you think that a poem needs to be in a different form? Or does the collection require that a poem change its form? You may need to change forms for the unity and balance of the collection. Twelve poems of one type and only two of another may not be enough variety. See what the collection needs as a whole, and rewrite accordingly.

Give Me Five

In your writer's journal, write: Give Me Five. Number the page from one to five. Then ask yourself what you are trying to accomplish with your poetry. What are your goals?

What a poet hopes to accomplish varies with each book. What you want to say and how you say it interacts with your audience and their needs.

For example, *Color Me a Rhyme: Nature Poems for Young People*, by Jane Yolen, is a collection formatted as a picture book. The collection:

1. has one color per spread
2. focuses on nature
3. has a quote for each color
4. lists other color words for the reader to use in writing their own poetry
5. ends with a poem about all of the colors

Polaroid and Other Poems of View, by Betsy Hearne, on the other hand, is a young adult poetry collection. The collection:

1. focuses on different types of sight
2. is divided into chapters by types of sight
3. looks at a wide variety of subjects
4. sees the world through a teen's eyes
5. ends with a chapter of good-bye poems

As you write your own poetry, you too have goals in mind. You know if you want the poems to be silly or serious. You know who your audience is. Being conscious of what you are trying to accomplish can help you as you write and revise. What five things do you want to see in your current poetry project? Write down your goals. After you revise, see if you met these goals. When you have met all of your goals, you are ready to send your work out into the world.

PART VI

Look Again

Chapter Fourteen

Other Viewpoints

 If there isn't enough to a story to entice us to read it a second time, it's a pretty good bet it won't open up any new doors to a kid's imagination, either.

—MELANIE CECKA, SENIOR EDITOR, *Viking*

How Others See Your Work

After you revise until you can't revise anymore, send out your work and let other people see it. At this point, the art of writing turns into the business of writing. How other people see your work depends on what aspect of this business they are coming from.

Your book must sell to people you will never see, never speak to, and never meet. When you send your work, all of the pictures must be in your words, so your work can speak for itself, whether the person seeing it is a young reader, an editor, or a bookseller.

Your book must be vivid and full of Picture Writing to appeal to all of your readers—and all of your readers have different expectations of your book. This is true for the children and young adults who will be your readers. This is also true for all of the people in the publishing industry who act as gatekeepers. In order to reach your child or young adult reader, your work has to pass many tests. At each step, a new gatekeeper has questions to ask.

The editor is the first gatekeeper. Does she see the pictures in your words? If she likes what she sees, she opens the gate and takes your words to the publisher and the acquisitions committee. Will they open the gate? Do your words pass the test? The committee wants to know if they can sell your book. Will the publishing company make money with your words? If the answer is yes, your writing passes the test, and another gate opens. All of this happens before you are even offered a contract!

After the contract, revisions begin immediately. In the development phase, the editor helps you fine-tune the pictures in your words. Your writing comes into even sharper focus. When the editor is satisfied, another gate opens.

As your book moves into production, your words arrive at gate after gate. The marketing, sales, and publicity departments figure out how to sell your book. Will your book be one they target for special attention? Will the sales rep convince the bookstore buyer to carry your book? Will the reviewers write a favorable review? Gates open or close as your publication date draws near.

All of these gatekeepers stand between you and the child or young adult who would read your book. If the pictures in your words open gates, then you can reach your reader.

Editors

Editors want to see pictures in your words. They want to see a story they can fall in love with, a story they cannot stop reading.

One of the editor's jobs is to acquire manuscripts. What you need to know is that acquiring new manuscripts is not an editor's only job. In fact, acquiring new manuscripts is often the last thing an editor does on a typical day. The books in development and production take up most of the day. Editors read new manuscripts in their "free" time, on the train, late at night, or on the weekend.

Once you've "sold" the editor on your story, the editor can do one of two things. She can call or write asking for revisions without offering you a contract. Or she can take it to an acquisitions committee and try to "sell" the book to the committee.

Once you "sell" the editor, she has to sell your book to the acquisitions committee. The publisher, the other editors, and the marketing department staff are on the acquisitions committee in many publishing houses. Each person on the acquisitions committee has her own likes and dislikes. The company also has its own personality.

After your book sells to editorial and marketing, it must also sell to sales and publicity. Then, once it actually leaves the four walls of the publishing house, it has to sell to bookstore buyers and reviewers. If the reviewers don't like your book, libraries may not buy it. Many libraries are required to have three positive reviews before they buy a book. Bookstore buyers have thousands of titles to choose from, so they can pick and choose which books they buy for their store. The editor knows all of this, and this influences how she looks at your manuscript.

An editor may request revisions before or after taking your work to the acquisitions committee. Revisions requested without a contract are done for free, on your time and your dime. If you are offered a contract first, you are paid to rewrite the book.

Should you rewrite without a contract? It depends. If the editor's vision for the book matches yours, why turn down free advice from a seasoned pro? The editor can be your mentor. She can help you write pictures in your words. If the book ultimately sells to the editor, fabulous! However, if the book doesn't sell to that company, you can take that editor's advice and send your professionally edited manuscript somewhere else. The advice was free, and the book is still yours. Now that you know what the editor likes, send her another manuscript.

PICTURE IT! | *In the Book Catalog*

In order to sell your manuscript, you must find the right publisher. Not every story can sell at every publishing house. You could send your story to every publishing house in the United States, but is it practical? Why fill up the editor's mailbox with a book that isn't right for her? Writers who don't do their homework send YA manuscripts to picture book publishers and poetry manuscripts to reference publishers. Mass mailings waste everyone's time and are the reason why many publishers don't read unsolicited manuscripts.

Your book is your pride and joy. This manuscript is your baby, all grown up and ready to leave home. Be a matchmaker. Find a match between your story and a publishing house that can fall in love with it. Don't send your manuscript out willy-nilly. Narrow your search by focusing on publishing houses that match your book.

How do you find the publishing houses that publish books like yours? Just like any other matchmaker, you have to look around. Look at the books a company publishes to find out what each house likes. Read their books, just as you did for the exercises here.

Visit the bookstore and look for books like yours. You've probably read a

THE P&L

Before the editor can call you and offer to buy your book, the publisher has a P&L sheet prepared. The Profits and Loss statement calculates how much the company will profit or lose by publishing your book. "When you're part of a big corporation that demands X percent gross every year, you have to meet that gross," says Atheneum Associate Publisher Ginee Seo in *Publishers Weekly*. The type of book, whether picture book or novel, affects not only the size of the finished book, but also the type of paper and the amount of color to be used in the book. The number of copies to be printed is figured in, as is your name recognition. Everyone has to start somewhere, but famous writers will probably sell more copies, necessitating a larger print run, and that needs to be calculated into the P&L. The bottom line is, can the publishing company afford to publish your book?

good number of books doing the exercises in this book. Read as many books in your genre and age group as you can. Write down the titles and the publishers' names in your reading log. Notice which publishers' books appeal to you. See what kind of "word pictures" they publish. Then go to the library and repeat the process.

After you have collected at least ten potential publisher names, hunt down the catalogs for those publishers. Before you request a catalog from the publisher by sending a letter and a self-addressed, stamped envelope, see if your library is on the publisher's mailing list. If your library subscribes to *Publishers Weekly*, read the Children's Announcement issues. The spring listings are published in February, the fall lists in July. Children's Announcement issues list new books in alphabetical order by publisher name. Each listing includes the title, author and illustrator, price, intended age range, and a sentence describing the book.

Publishers also have their catalogs on their Web page. Type the company name into any search engine. Or go to Amazon.com and click on "Search Books." Type the company name on the "Publisher" line and click! Book titles, publication dates, age levels, reviews, and more all appear at your fingertips. Print a record for yourself.

Read between the lines. See what the catalog says the publisher buys. Save yourself time and heartache, and check before you mail. ◆

Marketing, Sales, and Publicity

Before your book "sells" in the acquisitions meeting, the publisher wants to know how marketing thinks your book will sell to the general public. The bottom line in publishing is the bottom line. In *Children's Writer's and Illustrator's Market,* Roaring Brook Press executive editor Deborah Brodie says, "Publishing has always been a business, even in the old days when it was a 'gentlemen's business.' " The publisher is not going to buy books they don't think will sell.

Marketing, sales, and publicity look at your book quite differently than editorial does. Although everyone at the publishing house wants to see a strong, well-written story, marketing, sales, and publicity are not involved in book development. That's the editor's job. Instead, these departments bring your book into the public eye. At an acquisitions meeting, marketing wants to see books they can sell.

Marketing loves books that can sell in more than one place. Will your book sell in schools? Will it sell in libraries? Or even better, will it sell in both? Does your topic fit in the school curriculum? Does it relate to a holiday? Or is it an evergreen topic, like friendship or counting to ten? *Brown Bear, Brown Bear, What Do You See?,* for example, is a question-and-answer book with colors, animals, and a simple easy-to-read text. Teachers, librarians, *and* parents buy this book.

If marketing thinks they can sell your book at a profit, the acquisitions committee will buy your book. Another gate has opened. You see this gate swing open when the editor makes "The Call" to offer you a book contract!

Once the offer is made (and you say yes!), your book is acquired. Now your book goes into development. This is the infamous revision stage. For a novel, development may last as long as a year; for a picture book, as short as three months. When the writing for your book is completed, it moves into production, unless it needs illustrating.

If your book needs illustration, it may be a year or more before your book goes into production. Illustrating a picture book takes six months to a year, and illustrators are often booked years in advance. If your book simply must have a certain artist, it will wait in line behind the other books the artist has signed up.

Season by Season, Step-by-Step

Once your book moves into production, the marketing department steps back in. Now that all of your pictures are in the words, it's time to bring the book out for your readers. It usually takes a year to move a book from scheduling to the bookstore. Let's follow a book through the marketing, sales, and publicity departments. (Imagine your name on it!)

TIMELINE: YOUR FALL 2008 BOOK
October 2007: Scheduling: Your book is placed on the Fall 2008 schedule. Target titles are selected (big names, timely topics).
November and December 2007: Concept meetings take place.
January 2008: Launch: Your editor pitches your book in-house.
April 2008: Sales Conference: Your editor pitches your book to the sales reps.
May 2008: Key Reviewers: Book copies mailed to key reviewers.
October 2008: Publication: Your book is now available in stores.

Step 1—Scheduling

A year before your book is introduced to the public, it is placed on a schedule with other books that will be coming out at the same time. These books are collectively called the *list*. Books that will come out in the fall are called the *Fall List*, and books that come out in the spring are called the *Spring List*. Some publishers also have summer and winter lists.

Step 2—Target Titles

On each list, certain books are targeted for additional attention. Books by big-name authors tend to be targeted, as the company will probably earn more revenue from these books. Books on timely topics are also targeted. In an interview for *SCBWI*, Puffin executive editor Kristin Gilson says, "Sometimes events in the world determine what we print."

If an anniversary is coming up, such as the one hundredth anniversary of flight, it makes sense to give additional attention to a book that ties in with that anniversary. TV news, documentaries, magazines, and newspapers will focus on the anniversary. The publisher wants to strike while the (media) iron is hot.

Step 3—Concept Meetings

The marketing plan for your book is developed while the book is being manufactured. During production, the members of the marketing, publicity, and sales department meet with the publisher and members of the editorial department to discuss the books on the upcoming list.

Step 4—Launch

Your editor formally introduces your book in a presentation to the entire in-house marketing and sales staff. The book is not completed yet, so a preview of the book is presented. A TI sheet (Title Information) for your book gives the pertinent facts: title, author, illustrator, topic, and trim size. The TI sheet also includes specialized information about you and your book that will help the sales department sell your book.

Step 5—Sales Conference

Sales reps from around the country come to see the new books. This is like a launch, only now the information is presented to the entire sales force. At this meeting, preview materials are distributed to the sales force. Novels are printed as paperbacks called *advanced reading copies* (ARCs). Illustrated books appear in loosely gathered *F&Gs* (folds and gathers). F&Gs are printed in full color so buyers can see how the finished book will look.

Step 6—Key Reviewers

Four to six months before your book appears in stores, copies (ARCs or F&Gs) are sent to key reviewers. This allows the reviewers time to read and review your book before publication. Ideally, a review of your book appears in a magazine or newspaper just as the book begins to be sold in the bookstores. Now a reviewer shares your word pictures with the public.

Step 7—Publication

At last, your book is available to the public. Your readers can see the pictures in your words for themselves. Success!

Time Zones

Marketing generally concentrates on the season at hand—the months leading up to publication and the two or three months after publication.

—DONNA SPURLOCK, CHARLESBRIDGE PUBLICITY/PROMOTIONS ASSOCIATE, FROM AN INTERVIEW WITH *Children's Writer's and Illustrator's Market*

For the people in marketing, sales, and publicity, the seasons overlap. When the forthcoming fall books are in one stage, the forthcoming spring books are in another. If your publisher has three or even four publishing seasons, all of these forthcoming seasons are simultaneously in progress.

Marketing, sales, and publicity also go out on the road to create a buzz about their books. Most of this work is done just before or just after a book is published.

ON THE ROAD
Marketing: exhibits at school and library conventions
Sales: exhibits at bookseller's conventions, makes bookstore sales calls
Publicity: conducts author tours

Marketing, sales, and publicity are always working toward the future. When a book is new, when it's on the way out, or has just been published, that's when these groups focus on it. "The day after one season ends, the next season begins," says Penguin Putnam Library marketing coordinator Sarah Henry. Forthcoming lists are always in the works, demanding attention.

PICTURE IT! | *The Pitch*

Although your editor may work on six to ten books a year, the marketing, sales, and publicity departments handle every book that the company publishes. The larger the company, the more books they need to remember. With all of these books to remember, how can you stand out? It depends on your pitch.

Can you summarize your book in a *pitch*, that is, a single sentence or a phrase? What is the picture in your story? When a sales rep visits a bookstore, your book may have thirty seconds to make a sale. Remember, the rep is there to sell all of the other titles in the catalog that season, and the bookseller is a busy person. "This book is about _____ (fill the in the blank)," may be all you have to impress a bookseller.

In a busy world, "It's a book about X" is what the buyer wants to know. It is essential that you know your book inside and out, so you know not only the pitch but also the spin. Your *spin* on the topic is what makes your book different from all the rest. In *Children's Writer's and Illustrator's Market*, author Seymour Simon says, "You're not going to come up with a topic nobody's ever thought of before. The slant is what's important." To stand out in the crowd, your book needs to be different in some way. Why is buying your book a must?

The book jacket copy is an expanded version of a pitch. Go to the bookstore or the library and take ten minutes to read the back covers and inside flaps of several books. The copy in these two locations pitches the book. Did the words grab you? Did you see a picture? Did you want to read more?

If you were a bookstore buyer or a librarian, which books would you select? Why? Did the books have pictures in their pitches? Write down your reasons in your writer's journal. Record the titles of any books that you read from beginning to end. ✦

Reviewers

> The old publishing model for children's books based on serving the libraries has been replaced by the "media" industry model, selling "entertainment" to the masses.
> —STEPHEN ROXBURGH, PUBLISHER, FRONT STREET BOOKS, IN AN INTERVIEW IN *Publishers Weekly*

As discussed earlier, four to six months before publication, copies of your book are sent out to key reviewers. Reviewers don't see a finished book, but a work in progress. When you send your manuscript to the publisher, the text is *paged*, typed onto book pages. Galleys with loose pages are called *unbound galleys*. Galleys with bound pages are also called *advanced reading copies* or ARCs.

Some reviewers will not accept unbound galleys, and you can't blame them. How would you like to receive fifteen or twenty unbound galleys? At 150 to 200 pages each, that's a lot of loose paper! A bound galley is a lot easier to read.

Advanced reading copies are bound, but that doesn't mean the manuscript is finished. If a book is late, reviewers see an early draft. Here is one ARC disclaimer:

DISCLAIMER
ATTENTION, READER:
   This is an uncorrected proof derived from a computer disk. It is not a finished book and should not be expected to look like one.
   Typographical errors, pagination, format, artwork, etc., will be corrected before the book is published.
   Thank you.

ARCs may have plain paper covers with no art or text on them other than the vital statistics needed to identify the book: the author, the title, and the publisher's name. Or ARCs may have full-color art on the cover and look just like a paperback book. What goes in the mail depends on how far along the book is when the review deadline arrives.

Picture book art can make or break the sale, so review copies of picture books are always sent illustrated with full-color art. Depending on how far along in the production schedule the book is, the reviewer may receive proofs or F&Gs. A *proof* is a color copy of the book straight from the printing press. The press sheet has been cut into pages, but the pages are not folded or bound together in any way. When proofs are made, the press sheet is only printed on one side. Reading proofs is like looking at a pile of paintings.

After the proofs are checked and the color and text are corrected, the next print run is more refined. Now the press sheets will be printed in full color on both sides. After cutting, the pages are folded and gathered, hence the name F&Gs (folded and gathered).

Although F&Gs are not bound, they are printed on both sides, so their pages turn like a book. One press sheet covers sixteen pages, so a thirty-two-page picture book needs two press sheets. The two folded sheets may be stapled or held together with rubber bands. The first page of the first press sheet and the last page of the last press sheet are tucked inside the flaps of the dust cover or book jacket.

Review copies go out with promotional material printed by the publisher. A letter from the publicist may be accompanied by a plot summary or information about the author. Review copies are sent months in advance to give the reviewer time to read and review the book before his deadline and the book's publication. Ideally, the printed review will appear in the reviewer's magazine or newspaper just as the book is published.

The Reviewer's Audience

When your book reaches a reviewer, you have another sale to make. The reviewer has to decide whether or not she can recommend this book to her readers. The reviewer's audience varies depending on the publication. Some reviewers write for parents, some for educators, and some for librarians. All of these audiences read children's books, but each audience has different needs. Librarians want books that serve a wide cross-section of their population. Educators need books for the classroom. Parents buy books for individual children.

The reviewer also has an editor to please. Each publication has its own style and review criteria. Most publications have limited space and so print only positive reviews. Other publications are comprehensive and print both positive and negative reviews.

Reviews for Parents

Reviews for parents appear in the newspaper and in parenting magazines. Since space is limited, only positive reviews are printed in these publications. Not every word about your book will be positive, but the overall tone is one of recommendation. Parents are busy, so the reviews are short, to the point, and organized by the child's age.

Reviews for Teachers

Teaching magazines also review children's books. Educators focus on books that can be used in the classroom. There is more plot summary, and reviews end with a classroom activity for the book(s). Book review columns focus on new books, and lesson plan articles sent in by teachers mention old favorites. Book review columns for teachers emphasize themes such as "Great Stories in History" or "Animals" rather than the books published that month. Reviews list the books by grade level (primary, intermediate, etc.). Teaching magazines recommend books for classroom use.

Reviews for Librarians

Magazines for the library market treat book reviews as breaking news. Reviews of the latest books are printed on or before their date of publication. (The same applies to *Publishers Weekly*, the trade magazine of the publishing industry.)

Librarians buy books for their patrons based on reviews and the catalogs they receive from the publisher. Library books are purchased without being read ahead of time, so reviews are crucial.

Reviews make up a substantial part of many library magazines. The reviewer often compares your book to other books like it and then recommends for or against purchase.

The Reviewer's Criteria

What are the reviewers looking for when they read a book? They want to see pictures in the words, just like the editors do. Let's look at the policies of three highly esteemed review magazines and examine their criteria. *School Library Journal* is considered a comprehensive review magazine, meaning that it reviews across the publishing spectrum. In the year 2000, *SLJ* reviewed more than four thousand books. *SLJ*'s Book Review Policy Statement says that they "evaluate books in terms of literary quality, artistic merit, clarity of presentation, and appeal to the intended audience. They also make comparisons between new titles and materials already in most collections and mention curriculum connections. Our reviewers recommend purchase, or advise against it."

The Horn Book Magazine reviews selectively. In order to be reviewed in *The Horn Book Magazine*, a book must "achieve high standards of plot, theme, characterization, and style." *The Horn Book Magazine* estimates it reviews only four hundred titles a year. *The Horn Book Guide*, on the other hand, is comprehensive. Published twice a year, the *Guide* "contains brief critical reviews of all hardcover trade books for children and young adults published in the United States by publishers listed in *Literary Market Place*." The Fall issue of the *Guide* reviews books published from January to June, and the Spring issue reviews books published from July to December.

Booklist evaluates books "for acceptable literary quality according to standard criteria for different types of writing: for fiction, characterization, point of view, setting, plot, theme, and writing style; for nonfiction, content, organization, balance, format, style; and for picture books, style and quality of the art, relationship of art and text, and suitability of the whole to the intended audience." *Booklist* assigns an age or grade level listing based on the book's "format, reading level, style, subject interest, and appeal." The age level selected may not always agree with the age level listed on the book jacket. Although *Booklist* has a "recommended-only policy," if the reviewer anticipates public demand for a book, that book will be critically reviewed with "comments on weakness and limitations."

Reviewers are looking for the very best. If the review magazine is selective, books that are not deemed as "quality" simply aren't mentioned. Only the cream rises to the top. In comprehensive review magazines, if the reviewer doesn't like your book, they say so in no uncertain terms.

It used to be that only a select few read book reviews, but with the advent of online bookselling, anyone with an Internet connection can read reviews of your book. Amazon.com prints reviews from *The Horn Book Guide* and other review sources on each book page. Both positive and negative reviews are listed under the "Editorial Reviews" on each book page in Amazon. Barnes and Noble calls their review section "From the Critics." In the information age, the reviewer acts as a gatekeeper.

PICTURE IT! | *A Star!*

When doing reviews, *Publishers Weekly*, *Kirkus Reviews*, *Booklist*, *The Horn Book*, and *School Library Journal* star books they consider outstanding. What makes these books different than the rest? Look at a book through a critic's eyes and determine why they see stars when they read certain titles. For this exercise, you will need to find a copy of a review magazine. (Appendix G lists Children's Book Review Magazines.)

Go to the bookstore or the library and look in the magazine section. If no copies are available, ask if you can borrow the staff copy. Skim through the magazine until you find the reviews. Can you see the stars? Read the starred reviews and notice what the reviewer mentions. Why did this book receive a star? What made it rise to the top? Does the reviewer mention vivid and visual language? As you read through the review magazine, make notes in your writer's journal. This is the book you want to write, a book that wins a star. How can you accomplish that?

If you can, take your star search a step further, and read the starred book for yourself. Does it shine? Why? Record your thoughts in your writer's journal. ◆

Booksellers

Depending on the book, Target or Wal-Mart can outsell a Walden or Barnes & Noble.

—ANNE ZAFIAN, DIRECTOR OF SALES FOR CHILDREN'S PUBLISHING, TIME WARNER, IN AN INTERVIEW WITH *Publishers Weekly*

What Is the Bookseller's POV?

What is the bookseller looking for in a children's or young adult book? The bookseller is looking for a good story, one that will sell. To get your book into the bookstore in the first place, the sales rep has to make a sale. This is just one more step in the long selling process required to place your book into the hands of a child or young adult.

A week or two before the sales rep visits a store, he sends the store the publisher's catalog along with ARCs (advanced reading copies) and F&Gs (folds and gathers) for the new season's books. This gives the bookstore buyer time to read the books and make decisions. When the sales rep comes to take the order, the sales rep will mention your book if it isn't already on the buyer's list. Talk about your book may take a minute or less. There are many books in the catalog.

The sales call for a chain bookstore doesn't take place in the local store. Buyers in the corporate office make decisions for the chain nationwide. If your book is not selected, it won't be in any of their bookstores, unless you live nearby or someone orders a copy. In a chain store, even the location of books on the shelves is decided at the corporate level.

Independents are the opposite of chain stores. Indies buy for their local area and make decisions about each book that goes into their store. The store staff decides which books they will buy and how the store will be organized.

What each store buys depends on how they see their market. An independent children's bookstore is a place shoppers go to buy birthday presents. "I'm looking for a gift for a four-year-old-girl," is what the customer says, and the bookseller finds a book that girl will like. In a store with toys, the toys compete with the books for attention.

Independent bookstores also serve the school market. Some indies run book fairs for local schools. The store orders the books and staffs the fair so parents can buy books for their child at school. A portion of the sale benefits the school.

Books for school can be a big seller in the children's book market, for both indies and large bookstore chains like Barnes & Noble or Borders. Parents often buy books for school projects and reports. If your child has a report on penguins, you can buy a book about birds or Antarctica. After the report is finished, you can use these reference books again. If you bought a book about penguins, however, you may never need it again. Books on specialized topics tend to sell better in the library market.

Books read in school are also stocked at the bookstore so that students in middle school and high school can buy a copy to read and study at home. These titles are almost always classic books, such as *The Diary of Anne Frank*. Classic books for children of all ages are also part of a bookstore order when the sales rep comes to visit.

With four thousand or more new children's books published each year, the question is: Where do they all fit? How much can one store hold? The answer is, not everything. The buyer selects a few new titles each season and continues to buy books that are selling well in that store. Your new book is competing for space with *The Very Hungry Caterpillar*, *Ramona*, and *The Wizard of Oz*. Classic books like these have a track record, and the customers who come into the store ask for them by name.

Books that are targeted are also competing against your book. In the chain stores, publishers pay for window and shelf displays. Book placement is a critical issue with so many books competing for attention. The books that the publisher thinks will sell well are put into the prime spaces, and advertising materials for these books are sent as well. Advertising materials include stand-alone displays with the publishers' names on them and shelf-talkers, small signs for the shelf with an advertising blurb on them.

Other Booksellers

Bookstores aren't the places to buy books. Toys R Us, Target, Wal-Mart, and other large chains buy books nationwide through their corporate office. The publisher assigns a special sales rep to these national accounts.

The books in Toys R Us and Wal-Mart cater to children age eight and younger. Board books, picture books, easy readers, and activity books fill the shelves. They also carry big sellers like *Harry Potter* and the *Chicken Soup* titles. Many books have products featuring the licensed characters you see on television and at the movies.

Target carries board books and picture books as well as reprints of best-selling books for the picture book to young adult market. Books with licensed characters are only part of the collection here.

Department stores offer books for infants and toddlers as gift items in the baby department. Board books and classic picture books are the most common offerings.

Books sold in warehouse stores are sold at huge discounts. Some books end up here as clearance, bundled together with shrink wrap, so you buy two or three at a time.

If you write for a school and library publisher, you may never see your books

AWARD-WINNING BOOKS

Awards for literary excellence are regularly given to children's books of all types. Each book nominated for an award must go through rigorous scrutiny. This review process takes place *after* the books have been published.

Award committees can be comprised of three to fifteen people. The Caldecott and Newbery Committees each have fifteen members. The Orbis Pictus committee has eleven members. The Printz Award committee has nine.

One committee member said that it was hard to narrow the list. After a year of reading, each committee member selected just six books to place on the first ballot. When the committee voted, however, they were only allowed to select three. Right away, half of your favorites are out! Only one book wins the award. The runners-up are "Honor Books."

Best book committees select a list of outstanding books. Their standards are just as rigorous. The main difference is that list committees have more choices. After a year of reading, the committee selects ten or more books of distinction.

You don't have to limit your choices when it comes to reading excellent books. In fact, the more you read, the better! Reading a good book can help you grow as a writer. The Appendix lists Children's Book Awards and Best Books Lists.

Knowing the standards of excellence can also help your writing. A closer look at the criteria that several awards committees use can give you insight into their point of view. There it is, in black and white, the standards for literary excellence. While you may not always agree with the committee's final choice each year, there is no arguing with these criteria.

Quick Picks for Reluctant Young Adult Readers Selection Criteria

Fiction:

- High interest "hook" in first ten pages
- Well-defined characters
- Sufficient plot to sustain interest
- Plot lines developed through dialogue and action
- Familiar themes with emotional appeal for teenagers

Sibert Informational Book Award Criteria

- High quality in writing and illustration. Clarity and accuracy of presentation in both text and illustrative material, as well as appropriate documentation, distinctive use of language, excellent artistic presentation in illustration.
- Stimulating presentation of facts, concepts, and ideas.
- Engaging writing and illustration.
- Appropriateness of style of presentation of information for topic or subject and with respect to the different age levels for whom the book may be appropriate.

The NCTE Award for Excellence in Poetry for Children Criteria

- Imagination
- Authenticity of voice
- Evidence of a strong persona
- Universality
- Timelessness

in a store. School and library publishers sell directly to schools and libraries by sending sales reps to visit school and library conventions, calling on customers individually and sending catalogs.

PICTURE IT! | *Count the Ways*

Where do the books go in your local bookstore? Take your writer's journal to a bookstore and make a map of the children's section. Notice where the different genres are—board books, picture books, etc.—and mark each genre's territory on your map.

Visit each genre section and count the shelves. One Barnes & Noble I mapped had two freestanding walls of shelves with board books on them. The first wall of shelves was divided into four units, each with seven shelves. The second wall also had four units, and each unit here had six shelves. There were fifty-two shelves of board books!

Map each genre in the children's section. Count the shelves and look closely at the books. Do you see any licensed characters? If so, mark that on your map too.

Go to the shelf where *your* books would be shelved, and record the copyright dates for all of the books on that shelf. Of the twenty or thirty books there, how many were new titles? How many were a few years old? How many were classics, in print for five years or more?

If your town has more than one bookstore, map another store and see how they compare. How does the chain store compare to your indie? Did you notice any difference between the big chain stores? Write about your experiences in your writer's journal. ✦

The Child

In the long run, your true audience is the child or young adult who is your reader. After all of this selling to the many adults who act as gatekeepers—to the editor and the publisher and the acquisitions committee; to the marketing, sales, and publicity departments; to the reviewers and the libraries and the stores—your book finally reaches its destination, the hands of a child. That child or young adult may find your book in the bookstore, in the library, in the classroom, inside some wrapping paper, or in someone else's backpack. Now that your book has finally found its audience, what does that audience want?

At every step of the way, your readers want a story that speaks to their lives. Whether your readers are two or ten or seventeen, they want a book that speaks to who they are right now. Sharing life lessons only works if you make your words relevant to the child or young adult who is your reader. Children live in the here and now.

As children grow into young adults, their needs and interests change. In *Children's Writer's and Illustrator's Market,* Lee and Low Books Executive Editor Louise May says, "The best advice I can give to children's writers and illustrators is 'Know your audience.' " It is essential to stay in touch with today's children and young adults.

If you want to write for ten year olds, and you don't know what ten year olds love, find out. Hang out with some kids. Study child development. Reconnect with the ten year old inside of yourself. Read your old journals or start a new one and write about what happened when you were ten.

Whether you write for toddlers or teens, you must connect with their lives in your writing. What's important, what's interesting, what's funny (or not)—all this changes as children grow. When you write for children and young adults, connect with that child or young adult in yourself and the children and young adults around you. It's a difficult balancing act, but it can be done.

Read as much as you can, and study other writers. See how they met the challenge of living in two worlds at once. Others did it, so can you.

Live the creative life as fully as you can. Use both sides of your brain. Let the pictures come to you, and allow words to emerge from your pictures. Then write and rewrite until your words are pictures that everyone can see. Be a tortoise and a hare. Become a picture writer, one step at a time.

THREE "CLASSIC" CRITERIA

In Aristotle's *Rhetoric*, he said that in order to make a convincing argument, you needed three things—ethos, pathos, and logos. These three criteria still apply today.

Ethos is the ethics of a book. Does it tell the *truth?* Does the writer make a promise to the readers and keep that promise? Are the pictures in the words true? Regardless of the genre, you need to speak the truth when you write.

Pathos is the *emotion* of a book. What do the readers want? Are you giving them that? Do the pictures in the words touch the readers' emotions? Does the book have heart? Does your passion for the book come through in your words?

Logos is the *logic* of a book. Is the story arc well structured? Does the story flow from one picture to the next? Does the book make sense? You want your readers to be able to follow the story from beginning to end.

These three criteria sum up what readers look for in a book, whether they use these words from Aristotle or not. Use these classic criteria in your own writing. Let the pictures in your words shine through.

The Appendixes

Appendix A

Writing Habits Poll

In the summer of 2000, I sent a questionnaire about writing habits to the many listservs I read. More than one hundred writers responded. Take the poll yourself, then read what these writers said.

WRITING HABITS POLL
1. How often do you write?
   a. everyday
   b. as often as I can
   c. when the muse strikes
   d. only when I have free time
2. What time of day or night do you write?
   a. first thing in the morning
   b. before work
   c. throughout the day
   d. after work
   e. late at night
3. How long do you write each day?
   a. 30 minutes
   b. an hour
   c. 2–3 hours
   d. 4–6 hours
   e. 6 hours +
   Comments?

The replies I received to my poll were as varied as the writers themselves. Here is a sampling:

I'll write like a madwoman for seven hours straight, then not put a thing on paper for two days.—*Dotti Enderle*, author of *The Lost Girl*

As an at-home mother, I've learned to write anywhere, anytime. Whenever I've tried a more rigid schedule (i.e., "I promise to write for one hour, every day, first thing in the morning"), I actually accomplish less. —*Julia Durango*, author of *Peter Claver, Patron Saint of Slaves*

The more I write, the more I find out that I can write anytime. It's just a matter of making myself focus.—*Suzanne Lieurance*, author of *Shoelaces*

I think the key is to be consistent . . . I find I'm more productive if I try to sit down to the computer at the same time each day. —*Trina Wiebe*, author of *Lizards Don't Wear Lip Gloss*

My time and writing habits vary depending on what I'm working on. I spend the longest amounts of time when I'm working on novels. For poetry and picture books, I tend to work in shorter bursts. —*Linda Sue Park*, author of *When My Name Was Keoko*

Because I only write when I have a story that's been germinating in my head for days or weeks, I can put in as much time as I need to write it out once I think it's complete, but most often I write in spurts . . . think the story through first, begin typing it out . . . go off and do the dishes or some other mindless task, during which time I think of my next lines (or verse, if it's a rhyming piece) . . . type in that next portion . . . back to housework, or walking, and thinking again . . . back to the computer . . . and so on. I'm sort of like a jack-in-the-box . . . up and down . . . up and down. I find it easier to think if I'm doing something physical, but boring. If I were to sit and stare at the computer, the blinking cursor would drive me nuts.—*Dori Chaconas*, author of *On a Wintery Morning*

When I'm working on a book, my writing hours each day increase in direct proportion to the due date. When Walter and I were writing our book, I took off the last six weeks from work before it was due and wrote at least eight hours each day. Prior to that it was four or five hours a day, before and after work.—*Valerie Lewis*, co-author of *Valerie & Walter's Best Books for Children: A Lively, Opinionated Guide*

I work long days—ten to twelve hours average. Sometimes, close to deadlines or when I am trying to fit in an unexpected project on top of one already in my schedule, it's more like thirteen to sixteen hours. —*Kathleen Duey*, author of *Silver Bracelet: The Unicorn's Secret*

I write for a living, and I'm obsessed about writing, so I write whenever I can, wherever I can, from the time I wake up until I drift off to sleep. —*Rick Walton*, author of *Why the Banana Split*

I like to write early in the morning, but I made up my mind that I wouldn't limit my writing to that. So, if I am busy in the morning and get home at five, I often start writing at six or so. —*Kay Winters*, author of *The Teeny Tiny Ghost*

I often write between midnight and 6 A.M. because that's when the world quiets down, my cats are at their most productive, and the Union Pacific train whistle blows.—*Cynthia Leitich Smith*, author of *Indian Shoes*

I work part-time as an editor and am also the mother of a young child, but I fortunately have one day per week reserved as my writing day. Thus, one long concentrated session of writing per week. Other times during the week, I jot things down when I can. —*Lauren Thompson*, author of *Mouse's First Halloween*

I run a small mail order business but write at least five days a week, rain or shine.—*Kezi Matthews*, author of *John Riley's Daughter*

Since I work full time, I use vacation periods, about four weeks a year, to write in a concentrated way, in a remote rural distractionless place. —*Susan Patron*, author of *Maybe Yes, Maybe No, Maybe Maybe*

Four hours is about the longest time I can actually sustain writing. Sometimes it is less than that. After four hours, I need to do something else. I usually can't do that every day, but I do it probably four to five days out of seven. —*GraceAnne A. DeCandido*, author of *Literacy and Libraries: Learning from Case Studies*

When I wrote my book, I took one day off a week from my job as a senior editor at Scholastic. I wrote for two to three hours on that day. This worked out to one short chapter a week for about forty weeks. —*Gregory J. Holch*, author of *The Things With Wings*

Because I write for a living, these questions are actually difficult to answer. There are times when I do no composition at all for days at a time, but might be doing research or editing. I can say that I work every day, all day, being a writer, and that I cannot afford to wait for inspiration. —*Jennifer Armstrong*, author of *Becoming Mary Mehan*

Much of my "writing" is a thinking process that occurs during my morning walk or as I fall asleep at night. Reading and interviews supply details for my writing and are part of my work too. Actual, physical, putting down words on paper is probably two to three hours, but all my working/thinking hours would be six hours plus. —*Lee Sullivan Hill*, author of *Roads Take Us Home: A Building Block Book*

I have always worked a nonwriting job along with my writing, so I don't have much patience with people who tell me they don't have time to write. I learned a long time ago you have to make time. I use the time I am riding in van pool, my lunch break, and any other time I can find during the day. Otherwise, I write late at night and on weekends. —*Lynda Pflueger*, author of *Mark Twain: Legendary Writer and Humorist*

I make a rule: an hour a day on weekdays (except Friday) and two hours on weekend days or holidays. But once I'm involved in a project, I write much more than this. I have to stop at 10 P.M. to calm down so I can go to sleep at 11.—*Angelica Carpenter*, author of *Robert Lewis Stevenson: Finding Treasure Island*

I find that the morning is one of the best times to write, as though my

unconscious has been working on trying to solve whatever problems I needed to figure out while I was sleeping. I take a two-mile walk when I get up, jotting down notes for poems as I go, and then when I come home I enter them into my computer and get to work.
—*Sonya Sones*, author of *What My Mother Doesn't Know*

Once I begin a particular writing project, whether it's an article or a book or a review, the only thing I want to do is work on it. I write better with big chunks of time but edit better with small chunks of time.
—*Betty Carter*, author of *Best Books for Young Adults*

I set a goal of thirty to forty hours per week on my writing. That way I never feel guilty about not writing a set amount of hours on any one day.—*Linda Shields*, author of *The Voice That Means Businees*

There's a time to write, a time to read, a time to study, and a time to refresh the mind and gather new material for the next round. The hardest part is finding the time to write because the more you have published, the more other obligations intrude. Authors have to spend more time promoting their new books, their backlist books, and themselves in order to get the next manuscript accepted. It's not an easy business, but the people you meet, the birth of a new book, and the joy that book can bring young and young-at-heart readers makes it all worthwhile.
—*Judith Ross Enderle and Stephanie Gordon*, co-authors of *Where Are You, Little Zack?*

Appendix B

Craft and Creativity:
A Selected Bibliography

Every time you read a book about craft and creativity, you learn something new. Here are a few good books to help you grow.

Adrienne, Carol. *The Purpose of Your Life*. New York: William Morrow and Company, 1998.

Alley, Michael. *The Craft of Scientific Writing*. Englewood Cliffs, N.J.: Prentice-Hall, Inc., 1987.

Alphin, Elaine Marie. *Creating Characters Kids Will Love*. Cincinnati: Writer's Digest Books, 2000.

Amoss, Berthe, and Suben, Eric. *The Children's Writer's Reference*. Cincinnati: Writer's Digest Books, 1999.

Ayan, Jordan. *Aha! 10 Ways to Free Your Creative Spirit and Find Your Great Ideas*. New York: Crown, 1997.

Bickham, Jack M. *Setting*. Cincinnati: Writer's Digest Books, 1994.

Cameron, Julia. *The Artist's Way: A Spiritual Path to Higher Creativity*. New York: Jeremy Tarcher, 1992.

———*The Right to Write: An Invitation and Initiation into the Writing Life*. New York: Jeremy Tarcher, 1998.

Chu, Chin-Ning. *Do Less, Achieve More*. New York: HarperCollins Publishers, 1998.

Claxton, Guy. *Hare Brain, Tortoise Mind*. New York: The Ecco Press, 1997.

Day, Laura. *Practical Intuition*. New York: Broadway Books, 1996.

Dils, Tracey E. *You Can Write Children's Books*. Cincinnati: Writer's Digest Books, 1998.

Ealy, C. Diane, Ph.D. *The Woman's Book of Creativity.* Oregon: Beyond Words Publishing, 1995.

Edwards, Betty. *Drawing on the Right Side of the Brain.* Los Angeles: Jeremy P. Tarcher, Inc., 1979.

Einstein, Patricia. *Intuition: The Path to Inner Wisdom.* Rockport: Element Books, Inc., 1997.

Emmerling, John. *It Only Takes One: How to Create the Right Idea and Then Make It Happen.* New York: Simon and Schuster, 1991.

Forster, E.M. *Aspects of the Novel.* San Diego: Harcourt, Brace & World, 1927.

Gardner, John. *The Art of Fiction: Notes on Craft for Young Writers.* New York: Alfred A. Knopf, 1984.

———*On Becoming a Novelist.* New York: Harper and Row, 1983.

Garland, Sherry. *Writing for Young Adults.* Cincinnati: Writer's Digest Books, 1998.

Gelb, Michael J. *How to Think Like Leonardo da Vinci.* New York: Delcorte Press, 1998.

Gerard, Philip. *Creative Nonfiction: Researching and Crafting Stories of Real Life.* Cincinnati: Story Press, 1996.

Goldberg, Natalie. *Wild Mind: Living the Writer's Life.* New York: Bantam Books, 1990.

Goldberg, Philip. *The Intuitive Edge: Understanding and Developing Intuition.* Los Angeles: Jeremy P. Tarcher, Inc., 1983.

Goleman, Daniel; Kaufman, Paul; and Ray, Michael. *The Creative Spirit.* New York: Dutton Books, 1992.

Grudin, Robert. *The Grace of Great Things: Creativity and Innovation.* New York: Ticknor & Fields, 1990.

Hopkins, Lee Bennett. *Pass the Poetry, Please!* New York: Harper and Row, 1972.

Horning, Kathleen T. *From Cover to Cover: Evaluating and Reviewing Children's Books.* New York: HarperCollins Publishers, 1997.

Jancczko, Paul B. *Poetry from A to Z: A Guide for Young Writers.* New York: Simon and Schuster, 1994.

———*The Place My Words Are Looking For.* New York: Bradbury Press, 1990.

Karl, Jean E. *How to Write and Sell Children's Picture Books.* Cincinnati: Writer's Digest Books, 1994.

Klauser, Henriette Anne. *Writing on Both Sides of the Brain.* San Francisco: HarperCollins Publishers, 1987.

Kundtz, David. *Stopping: How to Be Still When You Have to Keep Going.* Berkeley: Conari Press, 1998.

Lerner, Betsy. *The Forest for the Trees: An Editor's Advice to Writers.* New York: Riverhead Books, 2000.

Litowinsky, Olga. *Writing and Publishing Books for Children in the 1990s: The Inside Story from the Editor's Desk.* New York: Walker and Company, 1992.

Livingston, Myra Cohn. *Poem-Making: Ways to Begin Writing Poetry.* New York: HarperCollins Publishers, 1991.

Lomask, Milton. *The Biographer's Craft.* New York: Harper and Row, 1986.

Maisel, Eric. *Deep Writing: 7 Principles That Bring Ideas to Life.* New York: Jeremy Tarcher, 1999.

———*Fearless Creating: A Step-By-Step Guide to Starting and Completing Your Work of Art.* New York: Jeremy Tarcher, 1995.

Marcus, Leonard S. *Dear Genius: The Letters of Ursula Nordstrom.* New York: HarperCollins Publishers, 1998.

Martin, Rhona. *Writing Historical Fiction.* New York: St. Martin's Press, 1988.

McClanahan, Rebecca. *Word Painting: A Guide to Writing More Descriptively.* Cincinnati: Writer's Digest Books, 1999.

McCutcheon, Marc. *The Writer's Digest Sourcebook for Building Believable Characters.* Cincinnati: Writer's Digest Books, 1996.

Mock, Jeff. *You Can Write Poetry.* Cincinnati: Writer's Digest Books, 1998.

Mogilner, Alijandra. *Children's Writer's Word Book.* Cincinnati: Writer's Digest Books, 1992.

Olmstead, Robert. *Elements of the Writing Craft.* Cincinnati: Story Press, 1997.

Peacock, Molly. *How to Read a Poem . . . and Start a Poetry Circle.* New York: Riverhead Books, 1999.

Perry, Susan K., Ph.D. *Writing in Flow: Keys to Enhanced Creativity.* Cincinnati: Writer's Digest Books, 1999.

Roberts, Ellen E.M. *Nonfiction for Children: How to Write It, How to Sell It.* Cincinnati: Writer's Digest Books, 1986.

Ryan, Margaret. *How to Write a Poem.* New York: Franklin Watts, 1996.

Seuling, Barbara. *How to Write a Children's Book and Get It Published.* New York: Charles Scribner's Sons, 1991.

Sharpe, Leslie T., and Gunther, Irene. *Editing Fact and Fiction: A Concise Guide to Book Editing.* Cambridge: Cambridge University Press, 1994.

Smith, James V. *You Can Write a Novel.* Cincinnati: Writer's Digest Books, 1998.

Vogler, Christopher. *The Writer's Journey: Mythic Structure for Screenwriters and Storytellers.* Studio City: Michael Wiese Productions, 1992.

Wooldridge, Susan G. *Poemcrazy: freeing your life with words.* New York: Clarkson Potter, 1996.

Appendix C

Children's Book Awards

Every year educators and librarians decide on the best books of the year published in their country. Reading these award-winning books can help you with your writing. The awards are listed here by country, title, type, frequency, and year of origin. The Carnegie Award (U.K. 1936) and the Caldecott Medal (U.S. 1938) are the two oldest awards. Generally, the older the award, the more prestige it has.

Schools, bookstores, and libraries often keep a list of the awards given in their country. If you cannot find a certain list, check the Internet. (If the addresses listed below have changed, type the name of the award into any search engine.) Select an award list and read as many books as you can.

Australia

Aurealis Award: Science Fiction, Fantasy, Horror: Young Adult and Children's. Annual. 2001. www.sf.org.au/aurealis/awards.html

Australian Children's Book Awards: Early Childhood, Younger Readers, Older Readers, Picture Book of the Year, Eve Pownall Award for Non-Fiction. Annual. 1946. www.cbc.org.au/awards.htm

Crichton Award: New children's book illustrator. Annual. 1998. http://home.vicne t.net.au/~cbcavic/award.htm

Canada

Amelia Frances Howard Gibbon Illustrator's Medal: Children's book illustration. Annual. 1971. www.cla.ca/awards/afhg.htm

Arthur Ellis Awards: Crime Writers of Canada Best Juvenile Award. Annual. 1994. www.crimewriterscanada.com

Book of the Year Award for Children: Children's book. Annual. 1947. www.cla.ca/awards/boyc.htm

Elizabeth Mrazik-Cleaver Canadian Picture Book Award: Picture book illustration. Annual. 1986. www.ibby-canada.org/cleavpr1.htm

Geoffrey Bilson Award for Historical Fiction: Historical fiction for young people. Annual. 1998. www.bookcentre.ca/bilson.2002.htm

Governor General's Literary Awards: Children's book and children's book illustration. Annual. 1987. www.canadacouncil.ca/prizes/ggla/default.tx.asp

Information Book Award: Nonfiction for children. Annual. 1987. www.library.ubc.ca/edlib/table/index.html

Mr. Christie's Book Award: Best books for young children, middle readers, and young adults. Annual. 1989. www.kraft.com/newsroom/05232001.html

Norma Fleck Award for a Canadian Children's Nonfiction Book: Children's nonfiction. Annual. 1999. www.bookcentre.ca/fleck/norma.htm

Young Adult Canadian Book Award: Novel or short story collection. Annual. 1980. www.cla.ca/awards/yac.htm

Ireland

Bisto Book of the Year: Children's book. Annual. 1990. www.rollercoaster.ie/books/bisto_shortlist_2001.asp

Eilís Dillon Award: First children's book. Annual. 1995. www.rollercoaster.ie/books/bisto01_winners1.asp#eda

New Zealand

Esther Glen Award: Literature for children and young adults. Annual. 1945. http://lib.cce.ac.nz/nzcba/estherg/

LIANZA Young People's Nonfiction Award: Nonfiction for young adults. Annual. 1986. http://lib.cce.ac.nz/nzcba/nonfic/

New Zealand Post Children's Book Awards: Senior fiction (YA), junior fiction, picture books, nonfiction. Annual. 1982. www.nzbooks.com/nzbooks/static/nzpost.asp

Russell Clark Award: Children's or young adult book illustration. Annual. 1978. http://lib.cce.ac.nz/nzcba/clark/

South Africa

Percy FitzPatrick Award: Children's book written in English. Biannual. 1970. www.unisa.ac.za/dept/clru/percyfitzpatrick.html

United Kingdom

Aventis Prize for Science Books: General Award and Junior Award (under 14). Annual. 1988. www.booktrust.org.uk/prizes/aventis.htm

Branford Boase Award: First novel. Annual. 1999. www.booktrusted.com/handbook/prizes/branford.html

Carnegie Medal: Outstanding children's book. Annual. 1936. www.carnegiegreenaway.org.uk/carnegie/carn.html

Children's Book Award: Picture book, short novel, long novel, and overall winner. Annual. 1980. www.booktrusted.com/handbook/prizes/childrens.html

Guardian' Children's Book Prize: Children's fiction (no picture books). Annual. 1967. www.learn.co.uk/childrensfictionprize

Kate Greenaway Medal: Children's book illustration. Annual. 1956. www.carnegiegreenaway.org.uk/green/green.html

NASEN Special Needs Book Award: Children's book for age 16 and younger. Annual 1994. www.booktrusted.com/handbook/prizes/nasen.html

Sainsbury's Baby Book Award: Books for babies. Annual. 1999. www.booktrusted.com/handbook/prizes/sainsburys.html

Saltire Society/Times Educational Supplement Scotland Award for Educational Publications: Nonfiction for Scottish schools. Annual 1996. www.saltire-society.demon.co.uk/teseduc.htm

Scottish Arts Council Children's Book Award: Scottish children's books. Annual 1999. www.booktrusted.com/handbook/prizes/sac.htm

Signal Poetry Award: Poetry for children. Annual. 1979. www.booktrusted.com/handbook/prizes/signal.html

Smarties Book Prize: Fiction and poetry for ages 0–5, 6–9, and 9–11. Children vote. Annual. 1985. www.booktrusted.com/nestle/prize.html

Times Educational Supplement Information Book Awards: Junior award, age 9 and under; Senior award, ages 10–16. Annual. 1972. www.booktrusted.com/handbook/prizes/tes.html

Tir na n-Og Award: Best English (Anglo-Welsh) Book of the Year. Annual. 1976. www.cllc.org.uk/

Whitbread Children's Book of the Year Award: Children's novel. Annual. 1972. www.whitbread-bookawards.co.uk/generic/year_of_books.jsp

U.S. Awards

Alex Awards: Ten adult books that appeal to young adults. Annual. 1998. www.ala.org/yalsa/awards/alextxt.html

Book Sense Children's Book of the Year: Children's Literature and Children's Illustrated. Annual. 1991. http://news.bookweb.org/home/news/307.html

Boston Globe-Horn Book Award: Fiction and Poetry, Nonfiction, and Picture Book. Annual. 1967. www.hbook.com/bghb.shtml

Caldecott Medal: Children's book illustration. Annual. 1938. www.ala.org/alsc/caldecott.html

Carter G. Woodson Book Awards: Elementary, Middle & Secondary social studies (ethnic identity). Annual. 1974. www.ncss.org/awards/writing.shtml#woodson

Charlotte Zolotow Award: Picture book text. Annual. 1998. www.soemadison.wisc.edu/ccbc/zolotow.htm

Children's Books of Distinction Awards: Picture books, fiction, nonfiction, poetry. Annual. 1998. www.riverbankreview.com/bod02finalists.html

Christopher Awards: Human spirit: books for young people. Annual. 1949. www.christophers.org/awards2.html

Claudia Lewis Award: Poetry book. Annual. 1998. www.bankstreet.edu/bookcom/awards.html

Coretta Scott King Award: African-American children's literature: text and illustration. Annual. 1969. www.ala.org/srrt/csking/csking.html

Edgar Allan Poe Awards: Mystery fiction: Young Adult, Juvenile. Annual. 1961. www.mysterywriters.org/awards.html

Ezra Jack Keats New Writer & New Illustrator Awards: Multicultural Picture Books. Annual. 1986. www.ezra-jack-keats.org/Programs/NYPL_Awards.htm

Flora Stieglitz Straus Award: Nonfiction. Annual. 1994. www.bankstreet.edu/bookcom/awards.html

Giverny Award: Children's science picture book. Annual. 1998. www.15degreelab.com/award.html

Golden Kite Award: Fiction, nonfiction, picture book text, and picture-illustration. Annual. 1974. www.scbwi.org/awards.htm

Jane Addams Children's Book Award: Children's book, social values. Longer Book, Picture Book. Annual. 1953. www.soemadison.wisc.edu/ccbc/addams/about.htm

Jefferson Cup Awards: U.S. history, historical fiction, or biography for children and young adults. Annual. 1983. www.shentel.net/handley-library/jefferson.htm

Josette Frank Award: Fiction. Annual. 1943. www.bankstreet.edu/bookcom/awards
.html

Laura Ingalls Wilder Award: Lasting contribution to children's literature. Biannual. 1960. www.ala.org/alsc/wilder.html

Lee Bennett Hopkins Promising Poet Award: Children's poetry book. Every three
years. 1995. www.reading.org/awards/Lee.html

Margaret A. Edwards Award: Lifetime achievement in young adult literature.
Annual. 1988. www.ala.org/yalsa/edwards/

Michael L. Printz Award: Young adult literature. Annual. 2000. www.ala.org/
yalsa/printz/

Mildred L. Batchelder Award: Children's book reprinted and translated into English. Annual. 1966. www.ala.org/alsc/batch.html

Mythopoeic Fantasy Award for Children's Literature: Children's fantasy literature. Annual. 1992. www.mcpl.lib.mo.us/readers/awards/juv/juvmyth.htm

National Book Award: Young People's Literature. Annual. Re-established in 1996.
http://209.67.253.214/nbf/docs/nbf.html

NCTE Award for Excellence in Poetry for Children: Honor a living American
poet for his body of work. Every three years. 1977. www.ncte.org/elem/poetry/
index.html

Newbery Medal: Children's literature. Annual. 1922. www.ala.org/alsc/newbery
.html

Orbis Pictus Award for Outstanding Nonfiction for Children: Children's nonfiction. Annual. 1990. www.ncte.org/elem/orbispictus/

Phoenix Award: Literary fiction classic remembered. Annual. 1985. http://ebbs.eng
lish.vt.edu/chla/Phoenix.html

Pura Belpre Award: Latino cultural experience: Narrative, Illustration. Biannual.
1996. www.ala.org/alsc/belpre.html

Scott O'Dell Award: Historical fiction for children and young adults. Annual.
1984. www.scottodell.com/sosoaward.html

Sibert Informational Book Award: Informational book for children. Annual.
2000. www.ala.org/alsc/sibert.html

Spur Awards: American West: Juvenile Fiction, Nonfiction. Annual. 1954. www.sl
co.lib.ut.us/spur.htm

Sydney Taylor Book Award: Jewish children's literature. Young readers, older
readers. Annual. 1968. www.jewishlibraries.org/

Tomás Rivera Mexican American Children's Book Award: Mexican American children's and young adult literature. Annual. 1995. www.education.swt.edu/ Rivera/mainpage.html

Washington Post/Children's Book Guild Nonfiction Award: Contribution to nonfiction for children. Annual. 1977. www.childrensbookguild.org/award.html

International Awards

Hans Christian Andersen Awards: Lasting contribution to children's literature. Biannual. Author's Award, 1956. Illustrator's Award, 1966. www.ibby.org/Sei ten/04_andersen.htm

International Reading Association Children's Book Awards: Fiction and nonfiction for ages 4–10 and 10–17. Annual. 1975. www.reading.org/awards/children. html

Society of School Librarians International Book Awards: Language Arts: Picture Books, Novels; Social Studies and Science, Elementary, Secondary. Annual. 1995. http://falcon.jmu.edu/~ramseyil/ssli.htm

Appendix D

A Sampling of Best Book Lists

At the end of each year, literary groups, magazines, and newspapers compile a list of "Best Books of the Year." Many of these groups keep listings from years past on their Web sites.

Bank Street College Best Children's Books of the Year: Fiction and nonfiction. March. Annual. www.bankstreet.edu/bookcom/submission.html

Best Books for Young Adults: American Library Association. Fiction and nonfiction. January. Annual. www.ala.org/yalsa/booklists/bbya/

Child Magazine: Choosing the Best Children's Books. December/January issue. Annual. www.child.com/your_child/child_development/child_books.jsp

IBBY Honour List: International Board on Books for Young People. Children's literature selected from each IBBY member country. Biannual. www.ibby.org/Seiten/04_honour.htm

New York Times Best Illustrated Books: Children's book illustration. Annual. www.nytimes.com/pages/books/index.html

Notable Children's Books: American Library Association. Fiction, nonfiction, and poetry. January. Annual. www.ala.org/alsc/nbook02.html

Notable Social Studies Books for Young People: National Council for the Social Studies. Annual. www.ncss.org/resources/notable/home.html

Outstanding Science Trade Books for Students K–12: National Science Teachers Association. Annual. www.nsta.org/ostbc

Publishers Weekly: Best Children's Books. Picture books, fiction, nonfiction. November issue. Annual. http://publishersweekly.reviewsnews.com/

Quick Picks for Reluctant Young Adult Readers: American Library Association. Fiction, Informational Books. January. Annual. www.ala.org/yalsa/booklists/qui ckpicks/

School Library Journal: SLJ's Best Books. All genres. December issue. Annual. http://slj.reviewsnews.com/

Smithsonian Magazine: Notable Books for Children. November issue. Annual. www.smithsonianmag.com/

Appendix E

Book Contract Contests

Some publishers use contests to encourage new writers. The prize is a book contract!

New Zealand
Tom Fitzgibbon Award
Scholastic New Zealand. First novel for ages 7–13. Annual.
www.vuw.ac.nz/nzbookcouncil/awards/fitzgibbon.htm
Children's Literature Foundation, P.O. Box 96 094, Auckland 1030
Entries close on October 31.

South Africa
Sanlam Prize for Youth Literature
Tafelberg Publishers. Theme changes yearly. Annual.
www.unisa.ac.za/dept/clru/sanlamaward.html
www.tafelberg.com
Tafelberg Publishers:
Children's Books, P.O. Box 879, Cape Town, 8000

United Kingdom
Fidler Award
Hodder Children's Books. First novel for ages 8–12. Annual.
www.booktrusted.com/handbook/prizes/fidler.html
www.scottishbooktrust.com/awards/
Scottish Book Trust
The Scottish Book Centre, 137 Dundee Street, Edinburgh EH11 1BG
Received by November 30.

United States

Ann Durell Fiction Contest

Dutton Children's Books. First novel for ages 8–14. New in 2002.
www.penguinputnam.com
The Ann Durell Fiction Contest Coordinator, Dutton Children's Books
345 Hudson Street, 14th Floor, New York, NY 10014
August 31 postmark deadline.

Delacorte Prize

Delacorte Press. First Young Adult novel. Annual.
www.randomhouse.com/kids/games/delacorte.html
Delacorte Press Contest
Random House, Inc., 1540 Broadway, New York, NY 10036
December 31 postmark deadline.

Little Simon Pop-Up Contest

Little Simon. First pop-up book (author-illustrator). Annual.
www.simonsays.com/subs/txtobj.cfm?areaid=183&pagename=popup_new
Simon & Schuster
Little Simon Editorial Department/Little Simon Pop-Up Contest
1230 Avenue of the Americas, 4th Floor, New York, NY 10020
Entries received by December 31.

Marguerite de Angeli Contest

Delacorte Press Books for Young Readers. First novel for ages 7–10. Annual.
www.randomhouse.com/kids/games/marguerite.html
Marguerite de Angeli Contest
Delacorte Press/Random House, Inc., 1540 Broadway, New York, NY 10036
June 30 postmark deadline.

McElderry Picture Book Prize

Margaret K. McElderry Books. First picture book (author-illustrator).
www.simonsays.com/subs/txtobj.cfm?areaid=183&pagename=mkm_rules
The McElderry Picture Book Prize
Margaret K. McElderry Books, Simon & Schuster Children's Publishing
1230 Avenue of the Americas, New York, NY 10020
December 31 postmark deadline.

Milkweed Prize for Children's Literature

Milkweed Editions. Novels for children ages 8–13. Annual.
www.milkweed.org/2_1_2_a.html
Milkweed Editions

Open Book Building, Suite 300, 1011 Washington Avenue South,
Minneapolis, MN 55415-1246

No deadline. All manuscripts automatically considered.

New Voices Award

Lee & Low Books. First picture book (cultural heritage). Annual.

http://leeandlow.com/editorial/voices.html

Lee & Low Books, 95 Madison Avenue, New York, NY 10016

ATTN: New Voices Award

September 30 postmark deadline.

New Voices, New Worlds

Hyperion Books for Children. First novel (cultural heritage) for ages 8–12.
Annual.

http://disney.go.com/disneybooks/hyperionbooks/rules.html

New Voices, New Worlds First Novel Award

Hyperion Books for Children, P.O. Box 6000, Manhasset, NY 11030-6000

April 30 postmark deadline.

Appendix F

Market Resources

Keep up-to-date with the children's book market.

Children's Book Council
The membership list at www.cbcbooks.org is updated monthly.

Children's Book Insider
A monthly newsletter, includes *CWIM* updates.
902 Columbia Rd., Fort Collins, CO 80525-1838
(800) 807-1916 www.write4kids.com

Children's Writer
A monthly newsletter from The Institute of Children's Literature.
93 Long Ridge Rd., West Redding, CT 06896-1124
(800) 443-6078 www.childrenswriter.com

Children's Writer's and Illustrator's Market
A yearly comprehensive directory from Writer's Digest that lists book and
    magazine publishers, contests, and more.
4700 E. Galbraith Rd., Cincinnati, OH 45236
www.writersdigest.com

Society of Children's Book Writers & Illustrators Bulletin
Bimonthly. Market listings also sent via e-mail to *SCBWI* members.
8271 Beverly Blvd., Los Angeles, CA 90048
(323) 782-1010 www.scbwi.org

WritersMarket.com
Daily market updates from *Writer's Market*.

Appendix G

Children's Book Review Magazines

Another way to keep up-to-date with the latest books is to read review magazines. You will find many of these periodicals at your local library or newsstand.

Appraisal: Science Books for Young People
  Northeastern University, 5 Holmes Hall, Boston, MA 02115
  www.appraisal.neu.edu/
  Positive and negative reviews. Quarterly.

Booklist
  American Library Assoc., 50 E. Huron, Chicago, IL 60611
  www.ala.org/booklist
  Positive reviews. Biweekly.

The Bulletin of the Center for Children's Books
  501 East Daniel St., Champaign, IL 61820
  http://alexia.lis.uiuc.edu/puboff.bccb
  Positive and negative reviews. Monthly (except August).

The Five Owls
  2000 Aldrich Ave. South, Suite 100, Minneapolis, MN 55405
  www.fiveowls.com
  Positive reviews. Quarterly.

The Horn Book Guide
  56 Roland St., Suite 200, Boston, MA 02129
  www.hbook.com
  Positive and negative reviews. Semiannual (Spring, Fall).

The Horn Book Magazine

56 Roland St., Suite 200, Boston, MA 02129

www.hbook.com

Positive reviews. Bimonthly.

Kirkus Reviews

770 Broadway, New York, NY 10003

www.kirkusreviews.com

Positive and negative reviews. Biweekly.

KLIATT

33 Bay State Rd., Wellesley, MA 02481

www.hometown.aol.com/kliatt/index.html

YA only. Positive reviews. Bimonthly.

Publishers Weekly

245 W. 17th St., New York, NY 10011

www.publishersweekly.com

Positive and negative reviews. Weekly.

Riverbank Review

University of St. Thomas, 1000 LaSalle Ave., MOH-217

Minneapolis, MN 55403-2009

www.riverbankreview.com

Positive and negative reviews. Quarterly.

School Library Journal

245 W. 17th St., New York, NY 10011

www.schoollibraryjournal.com/

Positive and negative reviews. Biweekly.

VOYA: Voices of Youth Advocates

4720 Boston Way, Lanham, MD 20706

www.voya.com

YA only. Positive and negative reviews. Bimonthly.

Appendix H

Preparing Your Manuscript for Mailing

Before you put your manuscript in the mail, check these resources:

Children's Writer's & Illustrator's Market
  Edited by Alice Pope
  Published yearly by Writer's Digest Books
  Check the publisher listings for requested word counts.
Formatting and Submitting Your Manuscript
  Edited by Jack and Glenda Neff and Don Prues
  Writer's Digest Books
Society of Children's Book Writers and Illustrators
  8271 Beverly Blvd., Los Angeles, CA 90048
  323-782-1010 www.scbwi.org
  Publications include market listings, manuscript formatting, and more.

🐦 Index